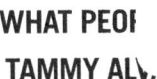

"*Escaping the Career Trap* is equal parts inspiration and a loving but firm kick-in-the-pants. If you really want a career and a life you love, Tammy is the perfect guide."

Jeff Baietto
Co-Founder & COO, InJoy Global

"*Escaping the Career Trap* is a game-changer for anyone feeling stuck in their job, providing actionable strategies and insightful guidance to break free and pursue a fulfilling career path. Highly recommended!"

Bryce Batts
Partner, Career Collective

"The stories, anecdotes, and real-life experiences of successful people in this book combine perfectly with Tammy's straight-talking direct style, making it an intense learning and mentor experience like no other."

Simon Bocko
Founder and CEO, Evolve

"You've put in the effort, you've given all of yourself, and you're just not feeling it anymore. Your career does *not* have to be a grind! *Escaping the Career Trap* is a practical guide to help you get *unstuck*. You're not alone—escape today and feel energized about work again!"

Nicole Butcaris
Customer-Obsessed Director of CX

"We all have the power to break free from the grind and chart our own course. It takes courage, vision, and self-leadership. This book and the many inspiring stories within will give you the spark and inspiration you need to build that courage and paint your vision."

Justin Clapp
Reinvention Coach

"If you're looking for ethereal, pie-in-the-sky ideas, Tammy isn't for you. But if you're looking to face challenges head-on, dig deep within yourself to find the answers, and chart a winnable path forward, do yourself a favor and spend some time with this book."

Daniel Cohn
Executive Vice President, Chief Strategy Officer,
Mt. Sinai Health Foundation

"Prepare for the heat—this book sizzles! The principles and tools that Alvarez offers are flexible, pragmatic, and most importantly *honest* for one to manage the bumpy and imperfect road to career satisfaction and success."

Lori Crever
Work Culture Evangelist and Author of
Protégé Power: A Roadmap to Mentorship

"Over the years, one meets many personalities, and many are forgotten; just as quickly, however, there are some who leave a lasting memory and have an immediate impact. Tammy has that special touch, and she found a way to parlay it into her new book written in her own voice and supported by experts in the field. Tammy's style is engaging and funny with a little sarcasm on top. The key is to take action on the suggestions outlined to receive maximum benefit from Tammy's guidance to finding your dream job and getting up on Monday morning with positive energy."

Walter Dusseldorp, FACHE
CEO, The Dutch Mentor and Author of
Pure Leadership Power: Climbing the Proverbial Career Ladder

"Not just fabulous brain candy but full of practical advice and exercises to transform your daily grind into a career that energizes and excites you!"

Miriam Gilbert
Founder & CEO, Coincidencity

"Tammy is a true force of nature. Not only will you see yourself in many parts of the book, but the aha! moments you will have will surprise and inspire you. Be prepared to laugh as she tells her stories and to be amazed at her way of thinking and her approach to coaching. She is pragmatic, insightful, knowledgeable, and very real. Everyone needs a Tammy Alvarez in their lives."

Susan Hollister
Founder of Hollister Unlimited

"Dismantles the cookie-cutter advice given by so-called gurus and embraces real-life experiences from real people."

Thomas Johnson
Founder & CEO, GetUpNGetFit Wellness Concierge

"Thank you, Tammy Alvarez, for writing a book that puts into perspective how easy it is to get trapped into thinking we are stuck in a career we don't like, and how easy it is to break free and find work that feeds our souls. *Escaping the Career Trap* is the perfect book for anyone seeking a career change, whether you're a CEO or an entry level worker. This book will change the trajectory of your work life, making you the CEO of your career."

Tyler R. Tichelaar, PhD
Award-Winning Author of *Narrow Lives* and *The Best Place*

"A must-read handbook for anyone who is an executive or wants to become one."

George B. Limbert
CAO Feazel Roofing
Adjunct Professor, Ohio State University, Moritz College of Law

"In *Escaping the Career Trap*, Tammy Alvarez serves as a much-needed career coach for the modern professional, offering actionable advice that feels as energizing as it is enlightening. With this book, readers are empowered to turn their career aspirations into reality, making it an invaluable tool for anyone looking to thrive rather than just survive in their job."

Maureen Metcalf
CEO, Innovative Leadership Institute and
Author of *Innovative Leadership & Followership in the Age of AI*

"This book is a game-changer for anyone stuck in a soul-crushing job—a must-read for those ready to take control and thrive."

Kate Milne
Healthy Aging Specialist

"There is nobody better at coaching you on how to escape the career trap than Tammy and her team of world-class coaches."

Brian Montes
Founder of Scalelocity Works

"*Escaping the Career Trap* by Tammy Alvarez is a powerful and insightful guide to breaking free from the mundane and rediscovering your career's passion and purpose. Tammy's wisdom and personal journey are truly inspiring."

Stephen J. Morris
Founder of Renowned Leadership

"Life is short. We hear this all the time, and then very often we wait too long to do something meaningful and fulfilling. *Escaping the Career Trap* takes you on that journey with countless examples of individuals who broke through the noise to find their perfect song so that you can find yours too."

Teresa Quinlan
Executive and Emotional Intelligence Coach,
Author of *You Belong Here: HumansFirst Stories*

"In *Escaping the Career Trap*, Tammy Alvarez exposes the lies we tell ourselves that keep us trapped and then the truths about how we can get back to finding work that fulfills us. With practical tips, inspiring stories, and refreshing humor, Tammy will make you believe you really can love Mondays again!"

Nicole Gabriel
Author of *Finding Your Inner Truth*
and *Stepping Into Your Becoming*

"If you want to get up in the morning excited to say, 'I get to' and begin to author your career so you can live out your purpose and passion, this book is for you."

Julie Riga
Leadership Coach, Speaker, and Author of *Stay on Course: The Life and Legacy of Ennio Riga, "Chef to the Stars"*

"A fantastic journey into the ins and outs and practical tools for supercharging your career—Tammy has lived through and overcome the challenges many of us face in finding our best selves and success at work, and she's teased out the lessons that make the difference between surviving and thriving in our careers."

John Schoew
Founder of Storied Future Ventures

"If you know you are meant for more but cannot see a clear path to get from where you are now to where you want to be, this is the book that will provide you with the clarity you have been seeking. Investing your time in this book will pay off more than you ever could imagine."

Autumn Shields
Transformational Coach for A New Angle Coaching, Inc, and Author of *Living Your Life Alive*

"This book, like its expert author, is thorough, comprehensive, and able to open pathways to new career dynamics for those who want to choose their own journey."

Shilpa Joshi
CEO and Founder of Impower, and Author of
Impower Code: 7 Personal Powers for Your Next Level

"When navigating challenging times, executives should definitely reach for this book. It gives proven techniques to improve your decision-making abilities under pressure and pragmatic advice on maintaining your leadership edge."

Lenore Vassil
Founder, Dagny Ventures, LLC

"*Escaping the Career Trap* is a groundbreaking book that challenges conventional wisdom and offers a fresh perspective on navigating the ever-changing landscape of careers. The author's insightful guidance and practical strategies provide readers with the tools they need to break free from the constraints of traditional career paths and forge their own fulfilling and successful journeys. This book is a must-read for anyone seeking to unlock their true potential and find true career satisfaction."

Jonathan H. Westover, PhD
Managing Partner and Principal of Human Capital Innovations, Author of *Leading for Transformation: Navigating the Shifting Landscape of Work*

"If you read one book this year, it needs to be *Escaping the Career Trap*. Tammy provides actionable advice on developing a unique career blueprint—one that allows you to do what you love with people you love."

Kristine Gross
World Tree Productions, Creator of the
+1 Eco Odyssey Reality TV Series

"Network or die! Ignore your network and the skills to grow your network at your own peril. Tammy has it right! Relying on sending resumes to job postings on LinkedIn is death by a thousand cuts and a waste of time. Networking is how you will find your next gig."

Jeff Kaplan
Managing Member, Signat Capital LLC

"*Escaping the Career Trap* is written by someone who has successfully broken free from the chains that bind our minds into thinking change isn't possible. Tammy Alvarez will walk you through all the ways you can stand up and get noticed in your field and be appreciated for what you have to contribute so you soar rather than stagnate and create your own career destiny rather than let your boss keep you enslaved."

Patrick Snow
Publishing Coach and International Bestselling Author of
Creating Your Own Destiny and *The Affluent Entrepreneur*

A SELF-LEADERSHIP BLUEPRINT FOR HIGH ACHIEVERS WHO WANT MORE

ESCAPING THE CAREER TRAP

TRANSFORM YOUR APATHY INTO AMBITION AND NEVER HATE MONDAYS AGAIN

TAMMY ALVAREZ

AVIVA
PUBLISHING
New York

ESCAPING THE CAREER TRAP

Transform Your Apathy into Ambition and Never Hate Mondays Again

Published by:

Aviva Publishing
Lake Placid, NY
(518) 523-1320
www.AvivaPubs.com

Address all inquiries to:
Tammy Alvarez
680 E. Main Street, Ste A #865
Stamford, CT 06901
+1 646-868-0567
Support@CareerWinnersCirlcle.com
www.CareerWinnersCircle.com

ISBN: 978-1-63618-300-8 – Hard Cover
ISBN: 978-1-63618-301-5 – Soft Cover
ISBN: 978-1-63618-302-2 – eBook

Library of Congress Control Number: 2023918306

Editing: Superior Book Productions
Cover Design: Angel Dog Productions
Interior Book Layout: Angel Dog Productions
Author Photo: Anastasia Kurokhtina

Every attempt has been made to properly source all quotes.

First Edition

2 4 6 8 10 12

DEDICATION

To Steve

Cheers to always saying "Yes" to shenanigans and "Hell no" to the status quo. Laughing through each day with you is one of life's greatest gifts (along with our vintage wine collection). Having magnums of inspiration just waiting for us to uncork our next adventure is pretty cool too. I love you and the life we've built together.

ACKNOWLEDGMENTS

This book would not have been possible without the encouragement and support of the team at the Career Winners Circle. Your dedication to our mission and serving our clients is unparalleled in the industry. It is an honor and privilege to work with all of you. Christina Bolden, Keli Brace, Susan Hollister, Stephen Morris, Patricia Ortega, Julie Riga, Mark Robinson, and Autumn Shields, keep sharing your brilliance with the world.

I am beyond grateful for my clients and colleagues who generously shared their stories and insights in this book so others may benefit and step into a thriving career that serves them. The ambition and courage you have and continue to demonstrate are inspiring and set an example for others to follow. Jeff Baietto, Bryce Batts, Simon Bocko, Nicole Butcaris, Pooja Chandrasekaran, Justin Clapp, Dan Cohn, Lori Crever, Walter Dusseldorp, Miriam Gilbert, Kristine Gross, Tameeka Henry, Thomas Johnson, Shilpa Joshi, Jeff Kaplan, George Limbert, Maureen Metcalf, Kate Milne, Brian Montes, Andy Pires, Teresa Quinlan, Emily Soloby, Lenore Vassil, John Westover, Zachary White, and Tori Zahn, your commitment to success is inspiring. Never stop following our passion.

To the miracle workers who helped me get all these ideas out of my head and into a format people can read and enjoy, I can't thank you enough. Susan Friedmann at Aviva Publishing, thank you for your support in turning a lifelong ambition into reality. Nicole Gabriel, your creative flair was exactly what I needed and your enthusiasm is contagious. Thank you for an eye-catching cover and beautifully designed book. Patrick Snow, your inspirational coaching and guidance took the feelings of being overwhelmed out of the entire process and kept me on track. Now the real work begins. Thank you for your wisdom and guidance. Tyler Tichelaar and Larry Alexander, your editing is superb and your clever wit kept me smiling. Thank you for helping me *level up* my writing and turn this manuscript into a book I can be proud of.

To my small but mighty family, Steve Collins, Emily Alvarez, and Yvonne Steveson, you are a constant source of support and encouragement. I can dream bigger knowing I've got you in my corner. I love you all more than words can express. And in loving memory of my parents, Louise Savio and Ray Steveson, you left us too soon and I miss you both. I know you'd be proud and utterly confused after reading this.

CONTENTS

NO ONE PREPARED YOU FOR THIS

Do you wake up energized on Monday mornings, ready to take on the world, or are your weekends ruined because you start to stress about work on Sundays?

Which of these situations is familiar?

- Feeling stuck in a job you don't like and you feel like there's no way out.
- Having a front-row seat on the struggle bus when you try to think about doing work you'd enjoy.
- Sitting through meetings so pointless you want to gouge your eyes out.
- Barely surviving the last round of layoffs and secretly wishing you hadn't.
- Worrying it's too late to change careers.

If you find yourself thinking, *What's the point*? then the zombie apocalypse is here, and the undead have invaded corporate life and your career.

My research shows that most knowledge workers over forty feel stuck in a soul-crushing job. Perhaps you are one of them, and your job also sucks. You're surrounded by managers who couldn't lead their way out of a paper bag. You and your team are disengaged. Everyone is stressed. Sometimes it feels like the crappy decisions your company makes are made just to screw with you.

No college classes teach you about the mid-career funk and how to avoid it. Being in this situation is one of the most challenging problems you'll face in your career. It feels completely overwhelming, and it hit me too.

It's sneaky. You don't see it coming. Then one day, you look around and wonder, *How the hell did this happen?* You dread Mondays; work seems pointless because you're no longer doing work that matters.

You start to panic because you've been sidelined. You worry no one will want you, that you're too old, and you'll never make this much money again. You are inadvertently pulling away from the family and friends you love and hobbies you enjoy because you're consumed with trying to survive the daily grind of corporate life.

There is a way out. You don't have to struggle alone. You can reinvent a vibrant career where you thrive again. It doesn't require super-human resolve. You don't have to be the smartest person in the room or be able to motivate and inspire like the top influencers on social media. Ordinary people like you and me say no to the status quo daily. They take the small steps needed to control their careers and love every Monday again. I've done it, I've helped my clients do it, and I'll show you how.

This book is a story about career and leadership renewal. You'll learn why almost everyone eventually becomes dissatisfied with their career and you will learn how to put an end to the soul-crushing grind. I'll reveal to you the five lies holding you back and how to break free of those misperceptions and thrive. I'll show you the power of playing to your strengths and how to crush the inner voice that keeps you stuck. You'll learn how to treat your career like a business, leverage your unique edge, take on the right projects, and strengthen your power base to move forward faster.

You will create your ultimate advantage, learn how to thrive during times of chaos, and discover how to pave the way for others. And finally, you'll learn how to transform your apathy into ambition and see what it feels like to love Mondays again.

The stories are from clients and successful entrepreneurs who have been in your shoes, and each story teaches us something we can apply to our lives. I hope you find them inspirational. Each person deserves an entire chapter about their epic journey and the struggles they faced along the way, but (rightfully so) my editor had different plans. Some of the names were changed to maintain client confidentiality.

When you absorb the lessons from each story and master the proven strategies I share with you, you'll escape the career trap, get off the hamster wheel, and build a thriving career.

A fair share of epic wins and losses have occurred along my journey. Each outcome brought experiences and perspectives you can draw upon. For most of my twenty-five-year corporate career, I worked in and around Wall Street and became a C-level executive who thrived during the chaos of three economic crises. There was ample opportunity to fuel the adrenaline rush being on the front line of tech during Y2K and the dot-com bust, and to understand and handle the pressure of being on Wall Street during 9/11 and the 2008 financial crisis.

Ambitiously fumbling through my career resulted in me typically being the youngest person and only female at the leadership table. Oh, and all without a college degree, which finally came at the tender young age of forty. (It's a long story, and you'll read the short version later in this book.)

I've had the honor of leading more than 2,000 people in thirty-five countries, working with world-class teams to solve some of the biggest financial services problems, and holding two patents on regulatory compliance solutions, the details of which would bore you to tears.

Success is not linear, and my career weathered thirteen promotions, two firings, one job elimination, and a job change that doubled my income. (I can't wait to show you how to do that.) These experiences spanned five different industries, and eleven different positions leading teams from sales to auditors and everything in between.

Today, I lead a thriving executive and career strategy coaching business called the Career Winners Circle (CWC). Our team of exceptional coaches and I help mid- to senior-level leaders navigate difficult situations and achieve levels of success they never thought possible in their careers and businesses.

We've helped hundreds of successful leaders who were embarrassed because they felt they should have had it all figured out but didn't. Trust me—there's no judgment here. If you're like most business professionals, your career just happens.

You've spent your career becoming excellent at what you do. That's where your talents lie. You haven't spent your career learning how to get out of a career or leadership funk. If you haven't built that muscle, it's only natural that you are struggling. Everyone does. And instead of stressing about how you ended up where you are, I hope you feel excited about what's to come.

Let me be your secret weapon. I know what happens behind closed doors and will tell you everything so you can make well-informed decisions that serve you.

Each chapter has some *Brain Candy* for you to chew on. These are thought-provoking questions intended for you to dig deeper as you explore each topic in the book. Keep a journal as you answer these questions so you can steadily move forward instead of feeling like your great ideas are bouncing around in your brain like a five-year-old on a sugar high.

If you want to move even faster as you take control over your career, I strongly recommend you check out the *Escaping the Career Trap Transformation Guide* at EscapingTheCareerTrap.com/Guide. You'll gain access to dozens of exercises and activities to help you transform your ideas into action.

Are you ready to make a change for the better? Is this your moment to take control over your career and thrive? Is it time to say "Yes" to you and "No" to all the BS that's held you back? If so, let's begin

PART I:

REVEAL

THE DYNAMICS BEHIND THE DYSFUNCTION

Everyone deserves to love Mondays.

Chapter 1

NAVIGATING A MASSIVELY BROKEN SYSTEM

"Work takes on new meaning when you feel you are pointed in the right direction. Otherwise, it's just a job, and life is too short for that."

— *Tim Cook*

It's Never Too Late to Have a Thriving Career

Do you worry it might be too late for you? As you transform your apathy into ambition, it is vital to thoroughly understand the landscape you're operating in. Today, the relationship between employee and employer is about as messed up as I've ever seen it, and there are no signs of it getting any better.

Does that mean you should give up and tolerate a subpar career? Absolutely not! Should the people who can influence this process boldly advocate for meaningful change? Yes, please! Whether you make the rules or follow them, you have an opportunity to change how the game is played to effect meaningful change.

Everyone who has a thriving career has two things in common—they break the rules, and they have an experimental mindset. When you understand the dynamics of your playing field, align with what motivates you, and don't let fear get in the way, you can make better decisions and have a deeply fulfilling career. Let's start putting the fun back into the dysfunction so you can rise above it all and thrive.

If you feel stuck in your job and insist on playing by the rules, here's what you're up against. Somewhere between 60 and 80 percent of employees are disengaged, contributing to worsening mental health in the United States, and very few people are making the connection.

Layoffs are happening everywhere. Artificial Intelligence (AI) is encroaching on knowledge workers' jobs, automation is taking the humanity out of hiring, top talent turnover is high, the remote work battle rages on, and quiet quitting is still a thing.

Social instability, macroeconomic worries, geopolitical volatility, looming recession, more bank failures, and the breakneck pace of change continue to cloud our judgment.

Despite companies' ongoing efforts, empowerment and accountability remain elusive. Most organizations' ability to develop talent, create winning cultures, align with purpose, and define a vision for success falls short of everyone's expectations.

Employers want highly engaged, passionate workers and strong talent. Employees want a job that leverages their skills and makes a difference. They want to feel connected to the organization and their coworkers and customers.

How can two interdependent groups want the same thing so badly yet still be miles apart? The gap is widening; the issues are getting increasingly complex. The solutions needed to fix the imbalance are unclear and we must put humanity back into our businesses.

Competing priorities are at the heart of this divide. When two groups want the same thing for different reasons, all hell breaks loose. It might feel like the only option is to throw in the towel and give up the dream of loving your job.

Hope is not lost. People are making the changes needed to reinvent a vibrant career that lights them up. People just like you are thriving. The first step to being one of these people is to understand how to navigate the insanity we've created for ourselves.

Once you understand the dynamics and how to make them work for you, you can rise above the morass of career apathy that has taken over corporate life. You'll be shocked at how easy it is to change course and reignite your thriving career.

*"When the grass looks greener on the other side of the fence,
it may be that they take better care of it there."*

— *Cecil Selig*

The Day Everything Changed

I remember it as clearly as if it happened yesterday. I was a member of an executive leadership team, and my peers and I were sitting in the boardroom after the quarterly earnings call. The stress hung so heavily in the air we could barely breathe.

The company had missed earnings (again), and the analysts were brutal and unrelenting in their loaded questions. Despite all the preparation, we got our asses kicked, and it was a train wreck; there was no way we were getting out gracefully.

You could almost hear the resounding thud of the stock price falling. There was blood in the water, and the sharks were circling. I'd like to say we were all surprised, but we had known this was coming. The call ended, and no one moved.

The door opened, and a terrible day was about to get much worse.

The flogging began, and the blame game ignited. Someone started the endless barrage of excuses, deflections, and counterarguments.

"The operations team sucks, and we're losing customers. The sales team can't bring in enough new deals. Our prices are too high. The economy is bad. The interest rates are low. Our best talent is leaving us in droves. I never remember agreeing to those numbers."

On and on it went, with each leader firmly convinced their department was not at fault and more than happy to toss the hand grenade across the room to one of their peers. While this happened almost every quarter and had become a matter of sport over the years, this time was different, at least for me.

I felt like I was having an out-of-body experience. You know—the ones you see in the movies where you're floating on top of the room watching what is happening, aware of every moment, yet bizarrely disassociated from the current reality.

I was typically more than happy to get into the fray. Not today. I could only passively observe, even when the grenade was launched my way.

I felt consumed by a massive case of "I-don't-give-a-shit-itis."

The executive career I had worked so hard for, the high-stakes environment where I thrived, and the work I had loved for decades received their death sentences.

It wasn't instantaneous. I didn't even recognize it at the time. But the shadow of apathy slowly deepened. I had seen this happen to others, but I never thought it would happen to me. I tried to make the job more exciting and focus on new challenges. Nothing worked. I was bored, didn't care about what happened, wasn't fully present for my team, and our business results suffered.

It took a while, but eventually, I made a very bold move. I cashed out of Wall Street, moved to a tropical island in Belize, and started my new business, Career Winners Circle. People thought I was out of my mind and accused me of giving up. Others thought I was brave and wished they could follow in my footsteps. All I felt was relief.

Six years later, the business is thriving and Mexico City is my newly adopted home. Helping clients achieve epic results and traveling the world are no longer competing priorities, and I don't hate Mondays anymore.

Now it's your turn.

Getting in the Door

Would you rather jump out of a moving car than start looking for a new job? "I love job hunting!" said no one ever. Running the gauntlet of changing companies is stressful and depressing.

In a *Harvard Business Review* article, "Your Approach to Hiring Is All Wrong," human resources and management academic and author Peter Cappelli wrote, "Businesses have never done as much hiring as they do today. They've never spent as much money doing it. And they've never done a worse job of it."

I agree with Cappelli. You would be hard-pressed to find another business process that has gone through such a pervasive automation overhaul and only gotten worse. Hiring methods today are ridiculous. Yet companies continue to throw more and more automation at the problem, hoping it's the pixie dust they need to bring in the right candidates.

Researchers estimate that hiring executives takes three to six months, and it takes two to four months to hire mid-level leaders. If a company can go that long without hiring, it makes you wonder how badly they need that position filled in the first place.

The system is broken at every step, starting from the ridiculous job requirements designed by HR departments and attorneys that are so far removed from reality no one could qualify for the role as written.

Today, applicants must run the gauntlet of applicant-tracking software (ATS) that sifts through your resume and does a keyword count. These algorithms will disqualify you as fast as possible. If you pass the

ATS hurdle, you have the honor of participating in a fully automated video interview.

During this dehumanizing process, you sit in front of your computer and answer three to five questions in less than two minutes each. These video interviews typically send my clients into panic mode.

The tech companies selling this process have convinced HR departments their software can identify the likelihood of your success based on body language, voice inflections, and eye movements. They'll thoroughly scan your social media accounts, and all the cookie crumbs you've left on the internet.

Ready for the cherry on top? They fire up their machine to analyze you with algorithms, AI, and predictive analysis tools, and voilà! You are deemed worthy or unworthy at the press of a button—all without anyone wasting their precious time speaking to you. It's a modern miracle.

One of my clients was testing a leading hiring technology solution. She submitted ten versions of her resume for a position she had open on her leadership team. She used fake names and flooded her resume with keywords. Nine of the ten resumes she submitted were rejected. For the one that made it through, my client had someone else do the video interview, and get this, she gave them the answers! The person was rejected in under two hours. My client didn't buy the snake oil that particular software company was selling and abandoned the strategy completely.

The number of people who interview you throughout the hiring process is mind-numbing. On average, you will go through seven to ten interviews and talk to fifteen to twenty people. In addition to traditional interviews, today group interviews, presentation style, and case study interviews are all the rage. Unfortunately, the team typically doesn't agree on the criteria for picking a candidate, and the time you spend waiting for feedback is insufferable.

About half of companies outsource hiring to Recruitment Process Outsourcers (RPOs). The RPOs, in turn, subcontract to other companies, most of them offshore. These companies are often paid more if they can convince you to accept lower compensation. The hiring process is so obviously broken.

Here's a pro tip that may sound insane, but I doubled my income in one career move by doing this. When asked about your salary requirements, your response should be, "As much as you can possibly afford. What's your budget?"

I know this sounds arrogant, and you should say it nicely. Using this approach puts the conversation back on them, and because they don't hear it very often, it puts you in the driver's seat. I've had many CWC clients successfully use this approach.

The hiring process directly reflects what it will be like to work with a company. If you have to face flying monkeys, burning scarecrows, and wicked witches as you follow the Yellow Brick Road to your next job, chances are good the beautiful land of Oz won't be waiting for you once you get hired.

If the process is bureaucratic, inconsistent, and riddled with missed deadlines and false promises, your job will be too. My advice is to run—don't walk—and get far away as fast as possible. If the process is streamlined, promises are kept, and the team is aligned, you've found your unicorn. Hop on and begin your next adventure.

"The best way to predict the future is to create it."

— Abraham Lincoln

Amy was miserable in her role. Her boss was insane, her peers were toxic, and her team had lost the will to live. She quickly went down the rabbit hole of the job boards and found herself in a dark, scary place.

Amy was usually confident, optimistic, and high energy. Lately, she'd had difficulty getting out of bed. She began procrastinating and second-guessing every decision. Her husband started getting worried about her and suggested she get help. She needed to get out of her workplace hell hole and get her career back on track.

Amy had a long history of success, but she had lost her mojo. She lost track of her value and no longer knew what she wanted to do.

When she hired me as her coach, getting a fresh perspective on old wins was the first step. We then used that to figure out what her best next move should be. Once we determined that, she faced the gauntlet of resume black holes, vacuous interview processes, and dead-end job searches. She just didn't have the energy.

So, Amy took a different approach. She reached out to the ten people who made her the happiest throughout her career. Amy had one rule when talking to this group—she was not allowed to talk about her current job or mention wanting to leave. These were not job-hunting discussions but fun opportunities to reconnect and recharge.

Amy met everyone in person; they went to lunch or happy hour and reminisced about the good ol' days. Before too long, Amy had a little more pep in her step and started feeling like she was getting some of her mojo back.

About two months later, one of her lunch dates called. He needed someone on his leadership team and thought she would be perfect. He wasn't sure if she was looking, but he figured asking couldn't hurt. Amy said she would love the opportunity to work for him again (not to mention she was looking to hop on the first train out of crazy town) and agreed to meet.

The new role was a perfect fit, and she was offered the job on the spot. One interview and boom! Done and dusted. She even managed to arrange for two months off between jobs to detox from her old job.

Need to get your mojo back? Mindset is critical if you're looking to make a change. Reconnect with people who remember you in your rockstar days and get your swagger back.

Growing Within Your Company

Do you feel you are being held back from growing as fast as you'd like to? It's not your imagination. It's ridiculous to be forced to stay in your current position for two years before you can apply for a promotion or to have your compensation increase capped at 20 percent if they promote you, even when the market rate for that role is significantly higher.

How does that inspire ambition, creativity, and drive? Surely, companies should realize this is the fastest way to lose their best people. These ridiculous rules give you no choice but to leave if you want to grow in your career.

If you don't want to change jobs, I've found three things to short-circuit the system holding you back.

- Embrace the mindset that the rules only apply to others.
- Do great work and align with your companies' top priorities.
- Become the poster child for optimism.

Most of my clients weren't doing any of these regularly. Once they started, they got unstuck and grew their careers quickly.

Exceptions are made every day when you have the proper business case and sponsorship. Step into the expectation and belief that you are not limited by the growth confines of a structure built for the masses.

Do great work and align with what matters. Everyone is super-busy. It's like your colleagues have morphed into the White Rabbit from *Alice in Wonderland*. This frantic pace is the perfect breeding ground for accomplishing nothing. How many times have you ended your day and realized you accomplished nothing?

Know what success looks like for you, your boss, your business partners, and the company. Use it as your North Star. When looking at your day full of meetings, ask yourself, "Does this help achieve the most important goals for the company?" If the answer is yes, you need to go all in. If the answer is no, deprioritize it or assign it to a rule follower you don't like very much.

Be the optimist. It's contagious and scarce these days. How many people do you come across who genuinely make you smile or laugh? Everyone is so serious. Most of us aren't saving lives or curing cancer and just need to relax.

I'm not suggesting you bring your pom-poms or be fake happy. But people need a break from the intensity. They need to smile, laugh, and feel human again. If you make people feel better, they will gravitate toward you. When more people gravitate toward you, you have more opportunities. When opportunity knocks, you know you're going to open the door.

> *"Most people work just hard enough not to get fired and get paid just enough money not to quit."*
>
> — George Carlin

I have learned to never underestimate the power of optimism. Once I was leading a massive transformation project. The project was a fast-paced, year-long, exhausting process. If you've ever tried one of those couch-to-5K training apps, this was like putting 100 people on a couch-to-Ironman program with two weeks to train.

The more significant the change we wanted to make, the more contentious things became politically. The days were grueling, and it usually felt like we were trying to nail Jell-O to a tree.

Despite the pressure, people were having fun. My optimism carried the team when things got hard. When people felt exhausted, I'd make them laugh. When the stress was super-high in a meeting, I'd make a snarky comment to lighten the mood. When people felt overwhelmed, I made a safe place for them to do so. It was hard work, and everyone was stressed, yet we all had fun through every win and most of our setbacks.

Running the Gauntlet of Being Stack-Ranked

Stack-ranking your team and being stack-ranked by your boss during your company's annual talent planning process is the worst, and everyone does it. Instead of hiring good leaders who can manage performance in real time all year long, companies opt for the painstaking process of conducting a bottoms-up talent review over a six-week period in an effort to thin the herd.

You have to put your entire team on a list ranked from most important to least, and there are imposed limits on how many people can receive the top ranking. There are also requirements to give a certain percentage of people the bottom ranking (even if they don't deserve to be there).

Once you finish your ranking, it's time to check the rules. Are your DEI (diversity, equity, and inclusion) metrics within guidelines? Have you excluded everyone from the top rating who hasn't been in their role for at least a year? Do you have documentation for the people you're forced to put on the bottom?

Once you go through the painstaking process of stack-ranking your team, you sit in a two-day talent planning meeting to stack-rank the entire department. This equates to a cage match pitting your team against your peers' teams, battling to keep your people in the top ranking and prevent your people from being pushed into the bottom ranking.

Stack-ranking people at the same level who perform different functions doesn't work. How can you calibrate the value of someone who brings in revenue with someone who works in the audit department? They're both important, but the salesperson will win every time. Their job is way sexier, and no one *really* likes audits, right?

And while you're fighting like hell for your team, you know that the same thing is happening to you. Your boss has stack-ranked you, you are being aggregated with your peers, and your livelihood depends on the outcome.

The winners get the lion's share of the promotions and bonuses; the losers are the first to go, and those in the middle get mediocre compensation adjustments and feel like they've dodged a bullet for another year.

How do you survive and thrive during this annual process of thinning the herd? If you're like most people, you just work hard and expect your efforts will be rewarded. You refuse to sell your soul by participating in dirty office politics and end up disappointed year after year.

Someone has to lose for you to win. No wonder this is so hard. How will you get a manager to love you more than their people and agree to give you the big fat bonus they've promised their top manager all year? You do what Jack did.

"Keep away from people who try to belittle your ambitions. Small people always do that, but the really great make you feel that you too can become great."

— Mark Twain

Jack leads a multi-discipline team of engineers, salespeople, business relationship managers, and customer service professionals. He is two levels down from the CEO, and the competition among his peers for the top ranking each year is fierce. The leadership team is strong and they work incredibly well together. Despite their best efforts, they had a tough year. Revenue and profits were down, and bonuses were going to be slim.

Jack has been through five performance reviews and knows how things work. He has typically landed in the top-middle of the pack in the stack-ranking exercises. His relationship with his boss is solid. Jack regularly interacts with his boss' peers and has even worked on a special project with the CEO.

About four months before performance management season kicked off, Jack met with each member of senior leadership and solicited feedback on his team's performance. His team improved where needed and delivered a few new game-changing innovations.

During talent planning, everyone was singing Jack's praises. He made the top box, received the maximum bonus when most only got 70 percent, and was promoted the following year. His team also did well, and Jack gained some street cred with his team.

Jack took the time to do what he could to help others succeed. His motives weren't selfish. He genuinely cared about the value he and his team delivered. No one forced Jack to conduct the feedback sessions, and he didn't make promises he couldn't keep. Jack's efforts paid big dividends for his career growth.

Following Jack's example is probably a good idea. Craft your plan to build advocacy without feeling like you need to shower to remove the stink of office politics.

Create a power base heat map to gain the right sponsors. Here's how you do it:

1. On a spreadsheet, list your boss, their boss, peers, and the stakeholders you work with (other business units, HR, legal, compliance, etc.). Put one name in each row.

2. In the cell next to their name, color code each person with red, yellow, or green. Red is the person who couldn't pick you out of a crowd of one, yellow is when you know each other a little, and green is when you've worked together for a while.

3. Prioritize your list starting with the stakeholders who have the biggest impact on your career.

4. Gain insights into what each person needs so they can succeed.

5. Create your plan to engage on meaningful projects and get to work strengthening your relationships.

Discovering Your Good Work Isn't Good Enough

Have you ever seen a blindingly inept leader and wondered, *How did they get promoted*? Alternatively, I'm sure you've seen someone who is incredibly talented but never got on the radar for promotion. Are you one of them?

If you are ambitious and want to increase your ability to make a difference, waiting for your excellent work to get recognized won't work. You've watched others kiss ass incredibly well, and you don't want to be that jerk. Where's the balance?

You do not have to play politics to get promoted, but you do need to build strong relationships, engender trust, and link your work to creating success for others.

Being seen as a leader is less about politicking and more about demonstrating your influential leadership capabilities at all levels of the organization, regardless of title and organizational lines.

Nadine is a financial services leader and had to learn the importance of leading through influence to grow her career the hard way. She had been passed up for a managing director role two years in a row. Her company had another stupid rule. They only allowed three managing director nominations per person. If you didn't make the cut by your third attempt, you were officially out of the running.

Nadine hated office politics, preferring to allow her excellent work to stand on its merit. This strategy got her nominated but couldn't get her over the finish line.

"Our greatest weakness lies in giving up. The most certain way to succeed is always to try just one more time."

— Thomas A. Edison

As we worked together, Nadine identified the leadership attributes and talents she had that were valued within the firm. She started treating her peers and other departments as if they were hers. She didn't take over any of the work. She just led through influence and focused on their success.

To the executive team, it looked like Nadine had made a massive transformation and stepped up her leadership abilities. In reality, she simply extended her behavior and leadership style.

When promotion season came up again, her performance numbers weren't as strong as before. She had medical issues and had spent the last half of the year distracted. She was sure it was going to be her final defeat.

But Nadine did get the managing director title she had worked for. She didn't just squeak by either; she was the top-ranked candidate across the firm. Nadine's loathing of office politics slowed her career, but it didn't stop it. She did what came naturally and extended her influential leadership skills to finally get the recognition she deserved.

Great leaders build deep relationships with their teams. Consider the entire organization as your extended team and treat them similarly. Strong leaders engender trust by being relatable and approachable.

Don't hide in your department. Get out there and work your magic. When you use your work as the catalyst to help your stakeholders succeed, you'll have a lot of new best friends who are happy to advocate for you.

Summary

The system needs to be overhauled from start to finish. Hiring, career development, talent planning, and promotion cycles are a disaster. While some companies are getting it right, there is little hope the vast majority will ever see their way out of the nonsense and put humanity back into hiring and employee development. Despite the circumstances, you can still have a thriving career. The journey and opportunities are yours for the taking.

Keep your eye on the market and always be looking. Even if you're happy today, you know how fast things change.

Realize people make exceptions every single day. Embrace the mindset that rules apply to others, and don't let them slow you down.

Align with what matters. Get clear on what success looks like for you, your boss, your business partners, and the company, and use these goals as your North Star.

Do not underestimate the power of optimism. It's contagious and scarce these days. If people feel happy around you, you will have more opportunities. If you help others be successful, you will have many sponsors singing your praises around the leadership table.

Good work isn't good enough; and you don't have to play politics to get ahead. Don't let hierarchy or organizational structures keep you from shining. Leverage your natural leadership style outside your organization; then more people will recognize your talents and contributions.

Brain Candy – Important Questions for You to Chew On

Grab your journal and get started on your ABCs for growth.

Assess:

- Do you still think it's too late to have a thriving career or are you ready to say, "Oh hell, no! I deserve better!"?

- What dysfunctional elements have been holding you back the most?

- How long has your career been held back from reaching its fullest potential?

Baseline:

- Have you been leveraging the talent planning process to grow your career?

- How can your most significant projects benefit people outside your department?

- Which wins can you credit your team with that will elevate your visibility and reputation?

Conquer:

- How can you meaningfully reconnect with the top ten people who can make things happen for you?

- What matters most to the success of your company, your boss, and you?

- What is your path forward regardless of the barriers put in place by your organization?

- What five things can you do differently to build trust as you create your strategy for building stronger relationships?

Everyone deserves to love Mondays.

Chapter 2

BREAKING FREE FROM THE SOUL-CRUSHING GRIND

"It is never too late to be what you might have been."

— George Eliot

The system is broken, but you can navigate crazy town to succeed. It's exhausting when you feel trapped in the soul-crushing grind, slogging to work, going through the motions, and stuck in a mind-numbing routine like in *Groundhog Day*.

What's even worse is that it hasn't always been like this. Things used to be good, maybe even great for you. You know what it feels like to succeed, to have confidence, and to enjoy all life has to offer.

You're not sure what exactly, but something changed. If you think, *This is just how things are*, and hope just maybe if you wait long enough, things will turn around, you are doomed, my friend. This situation will not fix itself. Hope is not a strategy. Summon all your courage to break the cycle.

Being in a career coma is catastrophic for your happiness. Gallup research pegged employee disengagement at more than 70 percent for the last decade. We spend an average of 90,000 hours at work over our lifetime. If work sucks, it stands to reason it naturally spills over into every other aspect of our lives.

Being unhappy at work doesn't mean you're at a dead-end. You can wake up and recreate your career. You can focus on making the last fifteen-plus years of your professional life an epic journey by rebounding and finishing strong. You can put the pieces together and get out of the grind once and for all.

It's time to reignite your career.

Suffering from the Sunday Blues

Where did Sunday-Funday go? You bust your tail all week and, finally, the weekend! Even if you love your job, the few precious days of downtime are a welcome break. Doesn't it seem incredibly unfair to have nearly half of your precious recharge time stolen right out from under you?

It's like clockwork. Around three o'clock on Sunday afternoon, my inbox fills with messages from CWC clients who are online working, trying to get a head start on a week that's already in prime position to steamroll their will to live before lunchtime on Monday.

The sacrifices you make in the name of your career introduce anxiety, stress, and time away from your family and the things you love doing.

You start to get that feeling in the pit of your stomach thinking about the barrage of meetings and deadlines. You lose focus on what's important: joy, those you love, and having fun. You created this monster, and you have the power to destroy it.

When you master these mindset shifts, the urge to work on Sundays will fade. You can embrace the magic of Sunday-Fundays for the rest of your life.

Work can wait. You're backed into this always-on, response culture, and it's largely unnecessary. Rarely is something so urgent you need to drop everything and abandon your recharge time. I get that everyone else is doing it, but it's wrong. Overworking is diminishing your executive presence and hurting your career.

You can't do your best work when you're not at your best. If you are tired, cranky, and stressed because you haven't taken enough downtime, it will take you longer to do your work, you'll make more mistakes, and you'll be less effective as a leader. When you properly recharge, you can do twice the work in half the time, and you're way more fun to be around.

Time is unrecoverable. You've heard (and ignored) that when you die no one will care how hard you worked and it's not the number of years in your life, it's the life in your years that count. Think back on all the emergencies you've had at work that caused you to miss out on life. Was it worth it? Put yourself first—every time. When you do that, everything around you will get better.

*"Your career is like a garden. It can hold an
assortment of life's energy that yields a bounty for you.
You do not need to grow just one thing in your garden.
You do not need to do just one thing in your career."*

— Jennifer Ritchie Payette

Justin Clapp knew the cost of being stuck in the rat race. He had built a thriving design agency specializing in higher education branding.

Justin had all the markers of success. He had a thriving business, drove a fancy car, lived in the right neighborhood, and hung the right art on his walls. He built a business that consumed his life.

Justin recalls when he reached his breaking point, "I was so miserable. I would wake up every day with this feeling of dread. I would have paid anyone any amount of money to deal with it. I was exhausted, and all I wanted to do was sit on the couch. I remember thinking, *God, is this all there is? What's the point?*"

When the student is ready, the teacher appears, and Justin's coach arrived at the right time. A lot of work went into unpacking the mess Justin had created. His entire identity was his business, and it was killing him.

Despite these realizations, Justin kept going for a few more years because he couldn't see a way out. His breakthrough finally came. After more work and digging deeper into his self, he finally saw his path forward. "I learned that our journey, challenges, and obstacles are our lessons."

Within a few months, Justin had wound down his business and started fresh. He felt the calling to coach, teach, and guide people on the journey he had traveled. He wasn't sure how this would work out, but he knew it was his next big thing.

Justin returned to his core values, reignited his creative spirit, and found his truth. Breaking free from his old beliefs and the mindset holding him back opened up a new world for him.

"There is the moment when you wake up, and life presents you with a choice. You can embark on a self-discovery journey or continue with how things have always been. This is one of the biggest choices everyone faces."

Justin had been visiting Dubai for years and loved it. He moved there permanently. "There is an abundance mindset. Everyone chooses to be here, and it's a different dynamic."

He built his business from the inside out and believes we all have a gift meant to be shared, which is our true calling. Today, helping burnt-out business owners and leaders get back on track gives Justin a sense of fulfillment and alignment that energizes him.

Justin advises his clients, "We all have the power to create what we want. There are always barriers, the timing is never perfect, and it may not align with others' expectations of you. There is always a path forward. What will you regret later if you don't make the bold moves?"

Getting Out of the "I Should Be Happier Where I Am" Trap

Are you expecting too much? "I love my boss, make great money, and have great life balance. I should be happy. So many people have it worse. I should be grateful, but something is missing." Sound familiar?

Being content doesn't quell your ambition, and getting too comfortable in your role is dangerous for your career.

Finding the motivation to make the change before you need to is hard. It's like getting out of your warm, cozy bed to stand in the middle of a blizzard. You won't run out in your footie pajamas to stand in the snow unless your house is on fire.

When your house is on fire, you are in crisis mode. You are looking for a hose. If you'd planned better, you would have installed a sprinkler system and avoided the problem.

Gratitude and ambition are not mutually exclusive. You can (and should) have both. Growing your career requires a proactive approach, and making a good situation even better is what many leaders strive to do.

Feeling you should be happy with what you have is also a defense mechanism. A job search, career change, or promotion comes with risks. You have no guarantee things will be better, so you hunker down, do what feels comfortable and safe, and ignore the warning signs.

When have you been happy about ignoring your gut instinct? Every time I ignore mine, I regret it. You make decisions based on data, facts, and observable trends, not because you have a hunch.

You feel ridiculous saying, "I know life seems perfect right now, but I feel like something is wrong. I'm not sure what it is, but I will take a massive risk and hope things work out." That argument is hard to sell to yourself, let alone those who love and depend on you. What should you do? Learn from past mistakes, and don't be like Rudy.

"The reasonable man adapts himself to the world; the unreasonable one persists in trying to adapt the world to himself. Therefore, all progress depends on the unreasonable man."

— George Bernard Shaw

Rudy led a high-performing global sales team for six years. Each year the team exceeded their goals by a wide margin. Rudy's boss was cool, Rudy's work was good, and he liked his coworkers—but he had fallen into a rut and had thought about leaving a time or two. He rationalized that he could balance his time with his growing family and things weren't *that* bad.

When his boss left the company, Rudy and a peer, Alexandra, applied for a promotion. Alexandra got the top spot. She then did everything possible to make Rudy's life a living hell. She micro-managed his every move, refused to let him work remotely (although others could), screamed at him in staff meetings, and moved his best salespeople to other teams without his buy-in.

Rudy was struggling with his confidence, and his marriage felt strained. He was at his wit's end and knew he had to get out of this situation pronto, but he was worried he would have to make significant financial and lifestyle changes if he made a career change. Rudy couldn't believe this was happening. He always had high-performing teams, good working relationships, and enjoyed his job.

Within months of her promotion, Alexandra laid on the final straw, putting Rudy on a performance plan that attacked his leadership credibility. When Rudy came to CWC, he had just been fired and was in a terrible head space.

After a lot of work, Rudy's mojo was back where it belonged. He identified industries, roles, and company cultures he was excited about. With his powerful brand, he marketed himself as the best candidate for those roles. He put all the new skills he learned into action and landed his dream job.

Rudy switched industries and landed a job he was passionate about. His new boss respects his capabilities and treats him as a valued team member. Rudy cut his commute in half, increased his income by 30 percent, and now has a renewed commitment to continuous growth. Rudy said, "I let myself stay comfortable and ignored the warning signs. I put my career, my family, and my financial security at risk. I'll never do that again."

Rudy heard Alexandra was fired nine months after she got promoted. Is that karma I hear knocking?

As you read the stories in each chapter, you'll see a pattern of other leaders feeling dissatisfied and unfulfilled on their journeys. They found themselves stuck in the "I'll be happy later" trap. Learn from their insights and choose happiness today.

Recovering After the Boss from Hell

Do you have shitty boss PTSD? With the abundance of bad bosses out there, you would be hard-pressed to find anyone who doesn't have a horror story (or ten). It may feel like you have a better chance of finding a unicorn than working for a good leader you can trust and learn from. I have my share of horror stories too, and once you have that experience, it's tough not to paint everyone with the same toxic brush.

You can't always avoid having a crappy boss, but you can control how it affects you and your career. Too many of my clients have allowed these bad leaders to bring thriving careers to a grinding halt. Why would you give them that power? I'm not victim-blaming here. I'm just saying you genuinely have more control over your situation than you may realize. And when you exert your power and start calling your own shots, the cycle of toxicity ends.

If you've never had the experience of going from hero to zero in the blink of an eye, I'm sure you've seen it happen to others. You're on top of the world, doing your thing, and crushing it. Everything is aligned—everyone loves you, you're doing great work, and you're having a blast doing it.

Then, suddenly, an organizational change happens. Your boss quits or your company gets bought out, and everything goes down the tubes. You feel like you can't do anything right. Your biggest fans walk away when they see you coming, and your boss is more than happy to point out the 700 ways you have failed in the last hour.

It's impossible to stop this from getting to you. You start to wonder if your detractors might be right, and your confidence takes a nosedive. You start second-guessing everything and everyone around you. Before you know it, you're a shell of the person you used to be. But the only thing that changed was your boss. Coincidence? I don't think so.

> *"When everything seems to be going against you, remember that the airplane takes off against the wind, not with it."*
>
> — Henry Ford

I was in this exact situation. I was doing work I loved for a boss I adored. She was brilliant and could cut through BS faster than anyone I knew. I learned a lot from her while we worked together.

I was leading a massive global transformation effort. It was high-stakes, complex, politically charged, and doomed to fail, according to those who had tried to do it before me. Despite the odds, things were going well. My team was crushing it. We were recognized and respected. Life was good.

I had just boarded a flight to Singapore when my boss called. She had just resigned to take a job at a different company. I was her chief of staff and we were close (or so I thought), so this came out of nowhere for me. I was shocked and a bit pissed about getting blindsided. The only thing I liked about my job had just vanished.

The weeks following an unexpected organizational change are critical. Jockeying for position, protecting your team, and vying for power happen in the blink of an eye. You need to be on the ground, have closed door conversations, and catch the vibe near the water cooler to thrive. I was stuck in Asia for three weeks and completely cut off from what happened back in New York.

Three weeks later, I returned to New York and met my new boss. Nothing could have prepared me for the nightmare that was about to unfold. When I entered her office, she shot me eye daggers and said, "You are no longer leading this project. I'm giving it to Amber, effective immediately. I have no idea what we'll do with you or your team yet (insert eye roll here), so sit tight, and I'll let you know when we've figured something out."

I was shocked.

She took great pleasure in torturing me and my leaders in the following weeks and months. We got all the shitty projects, she publicly berated us during large meetings for no reason, and she screwed with our annual bonuses.

Things kept getting worse until I got rescued by a friend who put me on a great team. It took me a year to regain trust in the organization and get my mojo back. It was a long road back to being the confident leader I was before this experience.

In this kind of situation, your priority is to get out. Things will not get better, and the bad boss will not have a change of heart. You are now (for whatever reason) public enemy number one, and it's time to bounce before they send you packing. Fire up your organizational and external network, and find a new role where your talent will be appreciated again.

These situations are unfortunate, but they do provide learning opportunities. Once the situation settles down, take some time to reflect on what you could have done differently. Doing something differently may not change the outcome, but it could reduce your pain and suffering if you reencounter the situation.

Get back into your rockstar status as quickly as possible. Surround yourself with your biggest fans as you weather the storm. If you don't believe you're fantastic, how will you get anyone else to? Resilience is vital in recovering from horrible managers.

And finally, try not to punish your future leaders for the sins of your previous ones. Reach out to former managers who inspired you. Time spent in their energy and vitality will remind you that not all leaders are toxic.

More bad bosses may be in your future. Limit the damage they inflict and shorten the time it takes to recover.

Realizing You're Hurting Others

Are you trying to hide your career unhappiness from those you love? It may feel like you're being brave in persevering with a career that drains you. You feel obligated to do the right thing, pressured to keep up with your colleagues, and forced to hide the exhaustion of being in perpetual survival mode.

No big deal…you're the only one who's suffering. You're strong. You can handle it. The sacrifices are worth the upside of a solid future, good money, and all the toys and holidays you could want. You walk in the door after a shitty day at work and it's showtime. "Hi, honey, I'm home!" You feel like Mr. Roark on *Fantasy Island*. "Smiles everyone…smiles."

You never suffer alone. The value you place on your career makes it virtually impossible to prevent dissatisfaction from spilling into other aspects of your life.

You don't live in a bubble, and when you start to feel insignificant, unfocused, mentally and physically exhausted, distant, and insecure, everyone around you feels it too. You can't be your best for others when you're not your best self.

When I hit my career slumps, I pulled back from friends, family, coworkers, and activities I loved. It didn't make any sense. I needed these things to bring me joy when my career couldn't. Yet I pushed everything away, making my suffering even worse. It turns out everyone I loved was suffering too.

My clients tell me that their marriages have improved, their children have stopped misbehaving, they've started exercising again, and/or they've returned to the hobbies they love. One client confessed, "My friends told me they like me better now that they don't have to listen to me talk about work constantly. When I'm with them, it's just fun time." These are the upsides of problems they never connected to unhappiness with their jobs.

No one knows this better than Alison, who found herself in a toxic environment and couldn't escape.

"Never continue in a job you don't enjoy. If you're happy in what you're doing, you'll like yourself, you'll have inner peace. And if you have that, along with physical health, you will have had more success than you could have imagined."

— Johnny Carson

Alison had a promising start to her financial services career, which began in a woman-led organization. The culture was collaborative and high energy; everyone was focused on achieving goals. She felt valued and mentored.

As Alison grew and gained more responsibility, she mentored others. "I felt for the first time that feeling of wow, I'm really helping others grow too." She had found her sense of purpose and loved the feeling of success.

Alison was offered a tremendous growth opportunity at another firm. This was her first time in a large corporate setting, and she was excited to expand her horizons. Unknowingly, she landed in the middle of a horrible culture with a very toxic leader.

Looking back, Alison said, "I knew six months in that the environment was pretty bad, and I should have left then. I needed the job and decided to stay because the hostilities weren't directed at me."

Things were bearable until she became the scapegoat about a year later. Her boss would demean her in front of other team members, send her hostile text messages and voicemails at all hours of the night, and gaslight her at every opportunity.

By this point, Alison's personal situation had changed, and she couldn't leave. She was a single mother and the only breadwinner. She tried everything she could to cope, but things became increasingly uncontrollable. The more her boss knew she had to stay, the worse things got.

Alison felt beaten down, and her self-esteem was shot. "I was a wreck. I started having major anxiety attacks, and the stress also undermined my physical health." During this time, Alison's son was having behavioral issues in school. She knew the stress she was under was affecting him.

Unfortunately, Alison had to hit rock bottom before finding the strength to take action. She knew she had to escape the situation for her and her son's welfare.

Alison took drastic action by going to senior leaders in the organization about the situation. Instead of being supported, she was pegged as a whistle-blower, and things got worse. Retaliation escalated, and her boss removed her from the team, causing her to lose a significant amount of her income. Staying in that toxic environment and waiting for people to do the right thing was no longer an option.

It's been a few months since Alison left her job, and she is still looking for work. Despite being out in the cold, Alison said, "When I was under that stress, I couldn't make the best decisions for my family because I was so caught up in work anxiety. Now, I feel like I can breathe again. My son's behavior is already starting to improve."

So many people are struggling in a toxic environment. Alison's advice to others who are in a similar situation is to get out as soon as you can. It will never get better. Your mental health will only worsen, and you won't be in the best position to make good decisions. No job, no amount of money, is worth the personal sacrifice you and your family will make.

Summary

If you're feeling that pang of anxiety on Sunday afternoons, dreading the week ahead, it's time to make a change.

Three mindset shifts are necessary to start to break the cycle.

- Realize work can wait and, unless you save lives, the always-on mentality disrupts your recharge time and diminishes your leadership reputation. Time is irreplaceable. You can never return the lost moments with friends and loved ones.
- The "I should be grateful and I should be happier" trap is a defense mechanism. If you feel like something isn't right, trust your gut instincts and take action.
- Working for a toxic boss raises the soul-crushing grind to a new level. Remember, you can't control the horrible things your boss does, but you can control what you do about it. Don't languish a moment longer than necessary before you move on to a new role. Things will not get better.

If you aren't motivated to get out of the soul-crushing grind for yourself, do it for those you love. The connection between your well-being, career satisfaction, and happiness are indelibly linked. Even if you think you've got a handle on it, you don't, and everyone around you can feel it.

When you recognize the warning signs and understand you deserve better, you'll find the energy and motivation to create a better future for yourself and those around you.

Brain Candy – Important Questions for You to Chew On

Grab your journal and get started on your ABCs for growth.

Assess:

- Do you feel guilty for wanting more?
- Are you too comfortable?
- Have you been ignoring the warning signs?

Baseline:

- Which moments have been disrupted by work, and could work have waited?
- What thoughts are keeping you from making a change?
- Who suffers when you're not at your best?

- How different is your energy, mindset, presence, fitness, optimism, social life, and downtime when you're at your best versus when you're at your worst?

Conquer:

- What can you do to set boundaries that work for you?
- How will you be able to see the warning signs?
- What mindset shifts can you make now to prepare for the future?

Chapter 3

REJECTING THE FIVE LIES

"I am not a product of my circumstances.
I am a product of my decisions."

— Stephen Covey

Being stuck in a draining job isn't just a slight inconvenience; it is devastating for you and those you love. Let's dig into why you and millions of successful and talented people tolerate staying stuck in a job that doesn't serve them.

Five Big Fat Lies Revealed

These five lies are deeply embedded in our beliefs. We work under these woefully flawed assumptions and never question them.

Once you realize how much these lies hurt your career and what to do about them, you'll never tolerate being stuck in a crappy job again. You will begin to see a light at the end of the tunnel, and I promise you, it's not a freight train coming your way.

Here's what *they* want you to believe (whoever "they" are):

1. No one loves what they do.
2. You don't have the experience to do something else.
3. Companies won't hire outside of their industry.
4. You'll have to take a step back if you want to change careers.
5. Be patient and the company will take care of you.

How many of these lies are holding you back?

Loving Your Job Is a Pipedream

Do you think it is impossible to love your job? This is the first systemic belief holding people back from having a perpetually fulfilling career. We've been led to believe no one *really* loves their job, and doing what we're passionate about won't pay the bills.

We also worry about what others will think if we "give up" on the job we're supposed to have according to our education, social standing, and career trajectory. We purposefully make ourselves play within these self-imposed limitations and then wonder why we're so unfulfilled.

Career moments in which you loved what you were doing are special. Maybe it was working for a specific company or on a particular project, or perhaps you've had the luxury of having long stretches of loving what you do. It feels great, right?

If you can experience these moments sporadically, why is it so hard to believe you can love what you do all the time? Why does it feel so hard to say, "Um, thanks but no" to the sucky job and move into an environment where you thrive?

Ambitious people stay stuck longer than they need to because it's hard to find viable career options they can feel excited about. If you're over forty, a bit of self-shaming comes with being unsure about your next career move even though you are in excellent company.

The right fit, the best new direction, eludes even the brightest minds. It's hard to figure out what you want to be when you grow up. (Pro tip: Don't grow up…. It's a trap!)

Being on the struggle bus sucks, but we need to break through the haze of apathy and embrace a career that energizes. Research shows people who love what they do for a living are more optimistic. They learn faster, make better decisions, have more influence, leave lasting legacies, and make significantly more money.

If it were easy, everyone would be doing it. Right? Wrong. Cracking the code is easier when you plan your next move, zone in on what lights you up, figure out where you're in high demand, and find your ideal environment.

> *"The future belongs to those who believe*
> *in the beauty of their dreams."*
>
> — Eleanor Roosevelt

Andrew is an excellent example of making a career correction. He was a senior-level technology executive in the healthcare industry and had been with the same company for a long time. He wasn't feeling challenged or growing as much as he had in the past and his career was on cruise control.

He was comfortable, made good money, had a good boss, and had a strong leadership team. The longer he spent on cruise control, the harder it was to turn it off. He was bored out of his ever-loving mind for years.

Eventually, Andrew's bonuses started shrinking, and internal sponsors distanced themselves from him. Leadership changed, and he got layered under a new leader who was unqualified and intolerant. Andrew had no choice but to start paying attention. His easy street was about to hit a dead end, and he felt like a squirrel who couldn't decide which side of the road to run to.

Feeling burnt out from tech and healthcare, he had no idea what he wanted. He had fifteen years left before he could retire and needed to keep his income up. Andrew wanted to make these remaining years count.

As he went through the discovery process with CWC, he focused in on something completely unexpected. Andrew loves lighting. He's one of those people who goes nuts decorating their house for Christmas, synchronizing the lights and music. Cars line up for miles to see his creations.

A tech exec can't pivot into the lighting business. Can he? I wouldn't be telling this story if he hadn't. Andrew made a massive change in the name of career and whole-life fulfillment.

Andrew was afraid people would think he was crazy (which they did). But he realized he was the only one he had to please. He also knew he had not been his best self with those he loved because his job made him super-cranky. Knowing career happiness would flow into his relationships was a big motivator.

Armed with a new sense of purpose and direction, Andrew started figuring out the elements of the lighting industry where he could earn enough money. Being the head of a lighting crew for a band sounded super-fun, but he was about twenty years too late to that party. He started networking, attending trade shows, learning the industry, and figuring out where he might fit.

Once he identified roles he would be awesome at, he got to work and started the dreaded job search, which was fun for him because he was around people who were just like him and geeked out about the same stuff.

Today, Andrew is rocking his new career and living his best life. He's making more money, helping drive the company's growth, and expanding its products and customer base.

Andrew was a regular corporate leader who fell out of love with his job and was willing to do what it took to get back on track. If Andrew can do it, I know you can too.

Loving what you do for a living isn't a pipedream. It's a requirement. When you step into what you love, your whole life gets better. It's normal to be unsure of what to do next. But you can find a clear path forward, and it doesn't take superhuman abilities to decide what and where your next move should be.

Transferring Your Skills Is a Longshot

"Do I have what it takes?" If I had a dime for every time a successful, seasoned professional believed they didn't have the skills they needed to move into a new field, I wouldn't have to work anymore.

You work your tail off building your career, becoming an expert in your field, and learning to solve bigger and bigger problems.

Then when it comes time to think about doing something different, you feel like you're starting from scratch. Most of the things you've done, the problems you've solved, and the difference you made no longer count.

And at this stage in your career, you don't want to prove yourself all over again. When you make the change correctly, you won't have to.

Your skills are transferable, and everything you've done up to this point hasn't been a complete waste of time. You know that on an intellectual level, but believing it on an emotional level is an entirely different story.

Hiring managers only care about one thing. Once you understand what it is and how to leverage it, the rest will fall into place quite nicely.

Even if you've hired people before, the game changes when you're on the other side of the table. You lose sight of what was important to you when you were hiring.

Despite ridiculous job descriptions that have 700 skill requirements and require seventeen post-graduate degrees, when it comes down to it, the only thing your future boss is trying to figure out is: Can I count on you to help me succeed?

That's it. Ten interviews and three months later, that's all they care about: "What's in it for me? Are you going to help me get promoted, stand out from my peers, eat dinner with my family, and cover my ass when I need it?" You win if you're the one they feel most confident about trusting their success to.

"A mind that is stretched by new experiences can never go back to its old dimensions."

— Oliver Wendell Holmes, Jr.

I once had to hire someone for a mid-level management position. No internal candidates fit the bill, so we had to broaden our search. I read a resume that piqued my interest. Julie didn't have a banking background, hadn't held this specific role before, and wasn't a referral. I brought her in for an interview and fell in love. It was like the skies opened up and a beam from heaven shone on her head.

We spent two hours connecting on all the things I cared about. I felt like Julie was reading my mind. She understood what I was passionate about, asked what kept me up at night, and showed me she knew the path forward. It was almost a little creepy.

Despite her *inexperience* on paper, she had all the *skills and perspectives* I needed. I wanted her to report to me instead of working for one of my leaders as initially planned.

Hiring Julie was messy. She was too high-level and expensive for the open role. I caught a lot of flak, and people thought I was out of my mind. I didn't care. I eliminated two open positions to get the funding I needed for Julie and created a new role for her.

Julie was a rockstar. My job got significantly easier, and I was promoted a year later. Julie became my successor. Everyone won.

If Julie had thought her skills didn't count or she hadn't done her homework and discovered how to bridge the gap between where I was and where I wanted to be, we would have never had our magical moment.

Your experience is only a small part of the equation. Your ability to make a difference is your biggest asset. Hiring is the most significant buying decision someone will make without using their own money.

People buy on emotion first and then back it up with data. Position yourself as the strongest person to help your boss get what they want, and your lack of experience will be dwarfed by the awesomeness of your ability to help them succeed.

No One Wants an Outsider

Are you feeling stuck in a soulless industry? Do you ever wonder what it would feel like to work for an industry or company that is actually having fun?

If your industry is getting its clock cleaned by geopolitical, economic, or market conditions, the job you enjoyed can lose its luster really fast.

In every economy, there are winners and losers. You want to play for a winning team in an industry that's thriving instead of suffering through fruitless cycles of cutting your way to prosperity.

Do you have golden handcuffs because you make too much money to consider a career change, or are you stuck in a specialty you don't think is relevant or valued? You may feel tethered to the sinking ship you chose twenty years ago and fail to see the value you can bring to other sectors.

Why would someone want to hire you instead of another job candidate who has been in their industry for a long time? How do you compete for senior-level roles when coming from the outside?

You can change careers and have fun sitting at the cool kids' table if you know where to look and how to position yourself properly. Did you know being different can be a competitive advantage? I learned this later in my career, and I wish I had known earlier.

A large corporate client was in hyper-growth mode for a decade. It was the land of milk and honey with seemingly unlimited investments from multiple venture capital firms. Whenever a challenge or opportunity arose, the answer was to hire more people and throw money at it. Easy peasy—until they went public, and a major competitor got their shazizzle together and started gaining market share.

The company was facing real pressure and had to start to unwind the lavish spending and customized operating models. Here's the problem: The entire senior leadership team grew up at the company. They had no one who understood the complexities of growing while spending less or how to move an intensely siloed culture to a cohesive organization.

They were doing their best to lead through the headwinds, but having never done it before, they were burning money like crazy, their investors were pissed, and they were kind of screwed.

They had to look outside the organization to acquire the expertise they lacked. Leaders from outside the organization who possessed these skills were like gold. They immediately had the authority to get the hard stuff done and had a blast showing the founding team members a new way of leading.

When you apply your skills and talents to an organization that desperately needs them, magic happens. You get to do the work you love most and have massive influence. You start getting your mojo back, have the ideal balance of contributing and learning, and your career thrives.

"Be so good they can't ignore you."

— Steve Martin

Leverage your unique perspective as the catalyst to move your organization forward faster. When you come from the outside, you have views no one else has, you don't have the biases and assumptions people get from being in the same environment for years, and you bring different skills to the table.

With a fresh perspective, you can challenge the status quo and develop brilliant ideas. Being different is good, and you should use that to your advantage at every opportunity.

You'll Lose Too Much If You Start Over

How much are you willing to give up to be happy? Your answer should be not a damn thing. Why would you? The fear of giving up everything you've worked so hard for is legitimate. And it's the biggest reason people stay stuck where they are despite being at risk, unhappy, and unfulfilled.

You busted your tail to get where you are and crafted a lifestyle to go along with it. You can't become a barista, sell everything, and live in a yurt. You have houses, spouses, kids in college, and fancy toys. These things shouldn't be on the chopping block because your job no longer serves you.

You're afraid you'll have to take a step back if you make a change because it happens to people all the time—particularly those in high-paying industries or positions. You hear stories about people finally getting so fed up they jump ship and take a massive hit in influence and compensation.

This situation is preventable. Hundreds of CWC career strategy clients have pivoted careers and are doing something they've never done before and earn an average of 20 percent more. Fast forward two years after working with us, and their compensation has jumped another 15 percent. There is money in doing what you love.

You've worked hard to build a reputation and professional brand. You trade on your credibility, influence, and ability to make a difference. Starting over and reestablishing yourself is a daunting task.

Senior leaders regularly say, "I'm willing to take a step back if I have to." Wait. What? Seriously? After twenty-plus years of battle-tested experience, why do you give up before you start? It happens when you start to feel desperate.

How do you break away from the inertia, find your new happy place, and continue growing and moving forward? Find your niche as precisely as possible and then do your homework.

One of the biggest mistakes you can make is going too broad. You can do many things well and think if you cast a wide net, you'll have a better chance of success. That may feel like a good strategy, but it's the completely wrong thing to do.

People are busy and have the attention span of a five-year-old. No one has time to read between the lines or consult tea leaves to see your potential. They will pass you by if you don't smack them in the face with exactly what they're looking for and that will leave you on a long, sad train to Nowheresville.

Don't let the fear of giving up everything you've worked so hard for slow you down or stop you from pivoting into a career that serves you. When you lack experience, you cannot lack expertise, so find your niche and do your homework so you don't appear like a rookie.

"Chase the vision, not the money; the money will end up following you."

— Tony Heisch

Before joining CWC, Susan Hollister, stayed in a career she didn't love for far too long. Now she's coaching her clients so they avoid making the same mistakes she did.

Susan had a twenty-five-year career in human resources. She started as a recruiter, found it wasn't her jam, and moved into an HR management role working with businesses, helping them make better decisions for the company and their employees. Susan rose to leadership quickly and leveraged her foundation in HR to work in more than ten industries and five countries.

But Susan's career in human resources didn't energize her. "I was tired of beating my head against the wall with bad leadership. Everyone hates HR, and no matter what I did to show them HR could be different, and I was different, nothing worked."

As an expert in transformational leadership, her sweet spot is helping startups grow quickly and creating the proper structure and culture from the beginning. She wasn't the typical "Dr. No" you usually see in human resources.

She enjoyed creating strategy, collaborating, and balancing employees' needs with the needs of the company in a way that was fair for everyone. She found her passion in mentoring young HR professionals. But the work no longer challenged her, and she was tired of the constant barriers she faced.

Susan tried to leave HR three times. Each time she reached the end of her rope, she would start a job search and get headhunted for HR positions offering more money and more responsibilities than the role before. "You don't get out because the money is there, and people want you because you're an expert. It's a real ego boost."

Not knowing how to repurpose her skills to pivot and advance by doing something completely different, Susan reached out to CWC for coaching to learn how. Once she started leveraging her decades of global leadership experience, she landed a job neither of us expected.

Susan became the Chief Administrative Officer of a Canadian First Nations community and made significantly more money than she had in HR. This non-indigenous woman became the most senior employee/executive of a small First Nations municipality in which every department reported to her. Senior council members were typically male and members of the community. Her appointment was virtually unheard of.

Susan had to set up the tribal police force and rebuild the majority of departments to run the community. This required working with various government entities and other First Nations communities. She advised the Chief and Council and helped drive the adoption of new policies, worked with the CEO of their development corporation to manage funding from their business interests, and introduced a new way of thinking so they could better serve their community.

Feeling she had taken on the biggest challenge in her career, Susan was invigorated. "I could apply all those transferable skills in this role. I used everything I've learned over the years, developed knowledge in areas I had no previous experience in, and did it on a bigger scale, which was exciting."

Even an HR expert can get stuck in the misconception that you have to take a step back if you want to change careers. Susan is among many senior leaders who learned to pivot while moving forward and feel energized once again.

Having Patience Is the Key to Career Success

Have you fallen for the "be patient" shtick? Patience is a virtue (said no one with high ambitions for a skyrocketing career). If you are stuck in the trap of waiting for your employer to do the right thing and hoping your good work will be rewarded, it's a crappy strategy.

Companies want you to be successful, and they want to maintain high profitability margins. In almost every case, the demand for profitability will take priority. So, you have to advocate for your career.

When you become impatient and start to take control, you'll be less frustrated and start doing work that lights you up more often. Instead of patiently waiting and playing by the rules, it's time to get more strategic with your career and take bold action.

The following are the five steps to being successfully impatient. Each will quicken the pace of your professional growth.

1. Set big goals that scare you a little bit.
2. Create a winning strategy.
3. Embrace agility and strategic timing.
4. Execute like a pro.
5. Build a repeatable success formula.

Set big goals: Nothing can wake you from the apathetic haze you've fallen into better than a big scary goal. But it's not good enough to set your goal. You need to write it down, start behaving as you will once you've achieved success, and tell people about it. The more you talk about it, the more you step into your future self and it becomes real.

Create a winning strategy: Knowing what you want is half the battle; creating your path forward to reach your goals is equally important. Focus on a strategy that puts you in control of your career and start taking action to make it a reality. Take smaller steps if your plan is too big for one move. As long as you're moving forward, you're winning.

Embrace agility and strategic timing: You can be sure nothing will go according to plan. Life has a way of screwing with you to test your resolve and determination. When things start to go sideways, all is not lost. Treat each surprise as a gift.

What can you learn from it? How can you use the new situation to move faster by taking a different path? How can you adjust and still stay on course? Think of these moments like a warning from your GPS telling you there is construction ahead and asking if you want to take a different route. It may not be the way you planned, but you'll still get to your destination.

Execute like a pro: Nothing speaks more highly of you in your career than being a card-carrying member of the GSD (get shit done) team. You will always be in high demand when you are known for executing. Your career should benefit from your tenacity as much as your current employer does.

Build a repeatable success formula: It's tough to recreate the wheel every time. When you find tactics that work, use them repeatedly. The more repeatable successful processes you have, the more you can achieve.

It's okay to be impatient. Get control over your career, and you'll still be one step closer to breaking away from a career that doesn't serve you.

> *"The most common way people give up their power is by thinking they don't have any."*
>
> — Alice Walker

Veronique used all these ideas, so I love sharing her story. She's an engineer in the automotive industry and a damn good one. Her skills go far beyond the technical elements. She has excellent leadership skills, she is creative and ambitious, and driven to collaborate and unite people.

Everyone knew Veronique was a rockstar, including her boss. Sadly, she intimidated the crap out of her boss, and instead of leveraging her strengths to help improve the whole team, he chose to keep Baby in the corner (and you know how that turned out in *Dirty Dancing*).

Veronique loved the company and the mission. She loved her coworkers, and despite her frustrations, she was patient and felt confident her outstanding work would soon be rewarded.

After three years of empty promises, Veronique had had enough. It was time to act. She tried to push her boss to do the right thing and hit a brick wall. She tried to follow the rules with HR and asked her internal sponsors to advocate for her. Nothing was working. As her frustration mounted, her work started to suffer. She had too much integrity to allow that to carry on for long, so she began to look elsewhere to find the growth she was looking for.

Veronique landed a significant role at a company she had worked for previously. While many senior leaders knew her, they only knew the old Veronique. No one knew the new and improved leader she had become. It was a pleasant surprise, and they put her talents to work immediately.

Veronique can now grow and use her leadership talents every day. She's traveling the world, driving strategy and innovation and fully stepping into her ability to mentor emerging leaders. Her incredible leadership style and ability to "speak geek" bridges the gap between engineering and business. The results have been excellent.

It's true…no one puts Baby in the corner.

Patience is not a virtue and will ultimately stifle career growth. Corporate career track programs are well intentioned but focus on the company's interests and, unfortunately, fall short. Color outside the lines and promote your abilities by focusing on the five steps to success.

Summary

Here are the big fat lies holding you back from a thriving career:

- No one really loves what they do.
- You don't have the experience to do something different.
- Companies won't hire out of their industry.
- You'll have to take a step back if you want to change careers.
- Be patient and the company will take care of you.

When you step into what you love, your whole life gets better. It's completely normal to lack clarity, but there is a path to figuring out how to move forward, and it doesn't take superhuman skills to figure out your next move.

Your experience is only part of the equation. Your ability to make a difference is by far your biggest asset. Position yourself as the bridge to success and your lack of experience will be dwarfed by the awesomeness of your ability to change your team, peers, and company for the better.

Don't stay on a losing team. You can quickly pivot, changing industries and roles when your unique perspectives are needed by companies where those skills are not readily available.

You don't have to give up everything you've worked so hard for if you do your homework and find your niche. But remember, when you speak to everyone, you talk to no one; when you lack experience, you cannot lack expertise.

Patience is not a virtue and will slow your career growth. Corporate career track programs prioritize the company's interests over yours. When you stop letting these five lies slow you down, you'll find success.

Brain Candy – Important Questions for You to Chew On

Grab your journal and get started on your ABCs for growth.

Assess:

- How has your belief in the five lies prevented you from achieving your career goals?

- What worries you most about trying to achieve greater job satisfaction?

- Do you believe your experience can help you do something completely different?

Baseline:

- Where do you think your skills are in the highest demand and shortest supply right now?

- What changes would you make if you were guaranteed the same or better compensation and influence?

- How different would things be if you felt energized by your career and those you work with?

Conquer:

- How can you reframe your belief in the five lies to achieve your career goals?

- What should you do differently to advocate for yourself and get more of what you want?

- How can these new insights help you reach your career goals faster?

Everyone deserves to love Mondays.

Chapter 4

EMBRACING A CHANGE MINDSET THAT DOESN'T HURT

"The secret of change is to focus all of your energy not on fighting the old, but on building the new."

— Socrates

Never let the five lies hold you back again. I hope you feel inspired to act. Change can seem hard; the mountain may look insurmountable. After years of playing it safe and settling for second best, feeling out of your depth is normal.

Why is change so hard? We think if we ignore it, it won't happen. We know that's not true, but ignoring change and hoping everything works out is much easier. Everything around us is changing, and at a pace faster than we've ever experienced before.

When you embrace change and have an abundance mindset, you will preempt forced change and make moves that set you up for success.

I don't believe you fear change; you fear loss. If you won seventy-million dollars in the lottery, I don't think you'd fear or resist the change, yet it would alter your life significantly.

The prospect of winning the lottery brings a sense of abundance, not a sense of scarcity. But we normally default to a scarcity mindset whenever we face change, which holds us back.

Our thoughts go to, *What if I fail? What if it doesn't work? What if I do all this work and it's no better? What if I look foolish or make less money? What if I'm less happy?* These worries kick in when we consider making a significant change.

What if you replaced your scarcity mindset with an abundance mindset? Instead of thinking about everything going wrong, what if you thought about everything going right? *What if I succeed? What if this works? What if things get better? What if I look brilliant? What if I make more money? What if I thrive?* Imagine how much easier and less stressful change would feel.

Defaulting to failure instead of success doesn't make any sense. You've got a track record of more wins than losses. You start projects, and they work out. You've built your career on a consistent record of success, so it stands to reason that any change you make will work to your advantage.

If you apply the same principles of change to your career as your work, you'll take risks and embrace change with confidence. Create a vision that excites you, plan your strategy, execute, mitigate risks, and measure success just like you do in the office.

Like it or not, your life and career are constantly in flux. Who's going to drive how you change, you or someone else?

Looking for the Monsters Under Your Bed

What's under your bed? Are they monsters or dust bunnies? How many times have you avoided something to the point where you're procrastinating, stressed, and starting to lose sleep? I do it occasionally, and it's usually connected to my finances. Because I grew up poor, I've got some deep-rooted money issues. No matter how much or how little I have in the bank, I'm a hot mess when it comes to money, and I prefer to ignore it because it gives me so much anxiety.

When I can't take it another minute, I'll look to see what's going on. Once I finally look, everything is fine. There are no monsters under my bed; they're just dust bunnies. I get so aggravated, having wasted days, weeks, and months losing sleep, being stressed, and being preoccupied. Over this? It makes no sense.

If you aren't happy in your career, now is an excellent time to look under the bed. What is holding you back? Why are you letting it prevent you from moving forward and being happy? Whenever you want something, and you know it will be good for you, yet you're not taking steps to move forward, it's a fear-based response.

When I was working with a business coach a few years ago, I avoided taking a hard look at my business finances. I lacked the rigor and discipline needed to run a business effectively. After I had made the hundredth excuse, she asked me, "What are you afraid of?" I bristled at her comment. "I'm not afraid," I insisted. She'd hit a nerve, so we moved on to a different topic.

"The truth is that our finest moments are most likely to occur when we feel deeply uncomfortable, unhappy, or unfulfilled. For it is only in such moments, propelled by our discomfort, that we are likely to step out of our ruts and start searching for different ways or truer answers."

— M. Scott Peck

I sat with her question and unpacked what was holding me back. Much to my surprise, I was afraid of success. I loved scuba diving each morning and refused to feel chained to my business like I had in my corporate career.

I brought this discovery to our next session. We worked through the mindset and behavior changes I needed to make. I went from believing formalized business practices were a barrier to the freedom I wanted, to seeing how these routines could give me even more freedom. We crafted a plan so the business could grow and I could still maintain the lifestyle that was important to me.

Think about moments when you've avoided doing something you wanted to do. Maybe you're in one of those moments right now. Unpack some of your fear and figure out what is holding you back. Once you know what you fear, start planning to move forward.

As you plan, let your fears play out in the worst-case scenario. What happens if everything goes wrong? Assess your comfort level and build your risk-mitigation plan.

Which risks can you detect? Which can you prevent? How will you adapt when things go wrong? The worst-case scenario won't happen because you've already thought about your risks and made a plan. That puts you on track for a successful outcome.

Starting my business meant leaving everything I knew behind. My biggest concern was that the business might fail. I had never been an entrepreneur and was moving to another country. Everything was more complicated than if I had stayed in the States.

I went through every worst-case scenario. If nothing went right, I would sleep on my mom's couch for a few months until I figured out my plan B. I was okay with taking the risk at that stage of my life. Fortunately for Mom and me, I never had to worry about plan B.

Embracing Uncertainty as an Opportunity for Fun

Does uncertainty scare the crap out of you? The sense of certainty and predictability in your life is misplaced. You've seen how fast things can change in your personal life, the economy, and the job market. You can only control how you respond during extreme uncertainty.

No one knows what will happen next—everyone is on a level playing field in that respect. Why not use these moments for a bit of fun instead of feeding the doomsday vibe you're often surrounded by?

When people are stressed, they crave leadership. This is your moment. Step up and say, "Hey, I hate this uncertainty too, but there are things we can control. Let's rally and do what we can." When you show the human side of working in the gray, you provide something positive to focus on and introduce control into others' lives.

Be the leader who helps people get out of their heads and act. Thrive in the chaos and inspire others to smile, laugh, and find joy despite uncertainty. Enrich your life and others' and grow your career while having more fun. Focus on what you can control and bring others along.

"The most difficult thing is the decision to act, the rest is merely tenacity. The fears are paper tigers. You can do anything you decide to do. You can act to change and control your life; and the procedure, the process is its own reward."

— Amelia Earhart

I'm not sure if Brian Montes considers himself an adventurer, but when you look at his career path, it sure looks that way. Brian has thrust himself into the unknown, enjoying a thriving career that has been anything but linear.

Brian didn't want to get sucked into the corporate grind. He watched his father dutifully go to the same job for decades. His dad liked his job, but there was always that grind.

In school, Brian met his would-be boss, who was finishing his degree. After graduation, Brian dove into the less-than-exciting world of selling manufactured components for office seating. He had no idea what he was doing, but he was ready for a challenge and a steady paycheck.

A few years later, Brian's boss asked him to take over their supply chain in Asia. Brian rarely traveled and was up for the adventure. He thought, *What could possibly go wrong? I work for a Fortune 500 company. They'll set me up for success, and it will be great!*

That's not how things turned out. "I got a plane ticket to Taipei, a hotel room at the Hyatt, and a phone number to call when I arrived," Brian explained. He was alone in a completely new environment with zero supply chain experience and even less leadership experience. However, he figured out how to make it work for him.

"I learned the importance of putting time and energy into your team to make sure they have the tools they need to succeed." He spent the next ten years working for the company, traveling throughout Asia, and figuring things out along the way.

Brian was offered his boss' position, which entailed running a seventy-five-million-dollar division. Despite knowing the culture was up or out, he turned it down. He knew what was important to him. The next step up the ladder didn't fit the bill.

Next stop: working for a stock market education startup. Brian didn't know the markets or education and wasn't an entrepreneur. He was excited about the founder's vision and loved the pivot. He helped grow the company's revenue to more than a hundred million and hired fifty-plus employees.

Life was good, except the boss Brian had considered his mentor needed some serious adult supervision. Without a board of directors to guide him, the company acquired a jet, helicopter, and all kinds of fancy things they didn't need. They burned through millions in development without having anything to show for it. It looked like the fall would be as fast as the rise, and with SEC investigations into his boss looming, it was time for Brian to get out.

Brian was done traveling. And with this last experience, he didn't want to be an employee anymore. He told his wife, "We made him a lot of money, and he didn't do good with it. I need to go out on my own. I don't know what that looks like, but we'll figure it out."

Once again, Brian headed into the great unknown, starting Scaleocity Works. "I combined my business background with HR and my law degree to help business owners and founders run their businesses better by understanding their profit and loss, leveling up their operations, structuring their hiring, and doing it legally."

Uncertainty was the catalyst for the breakthrough moments in Brian's career. He's learned a lot and continues to have fun embracing all the uncertainty life has to offer.

Deciding Who Controls How You Change

How much control do you have over the changes in your career? You can drive the change or let someone else do it. Who would you trust? And why would you give away that power?

You can look after your career 100 percent better than anyone else will. Yet you often feel helpless, which makes you a victim of your environment instead of a master of it. It doesn't have to be that way.

With clear goals, values, and beliefs, you have much of what you need to keep your career on the right track. Watch the changing tides within your company, industry, and the marketplace. Pay attention to organizational shifts, changes in leadership, and internal political fluctuations.

Look for opportunities to drive more visible business results in the areas that matter most to your boss and the organization. Have open and frank conversations with your manager on your growth objectives, concerns, and the places you feel you can make the biggest difference.

You are more likely to benefit from being part of the change than ignoring it. I grew when I saw the organization was in trouble and led the effort to help us through the bad times. These efforts typically led to reorganizations and opportunities to get promoted.

"It's our choices that show what we truly are,
far more than our abilities."

— J.K. Rowling

Autumn Shields found her career inspiration through tragedy at a very young age. When she was in eighth grade, her friend committed suicide. The school hired a psychologist to help students deal with the tragedy and process death for the first time. As Autumn watched the psychologist on stage, she knew on some level it was the kind of work she wanted to do someday. She spoke with the presenter and learned more about her work. They kept in touch. After college, Autumn became a victim advocate in a neighboring town.

Autumn worked tirelessly with law enforcement, legal aid, and other advocacy groups to help victims get support. She gave everything she had to her career, which started taking an emotional toll. "I was giving everyone I loved my leftovers. When you're young and don't have a lot of responsibilities, that's okay. But when I started a family, I realized I couldn't keep going at that pace."

Autumn was skeptical when she was introduced to a network marketing opportunity. Amway and similar companies were making headlines for unethical business practices. She had every reason to pass on the opportunity.

But Autumn decided to take the plunge and do it part-time as an experiment. Before she knew it, her business had skyrocketed. She was a natural and eventually gave up her career as an advocate.

It wasn't easy for Autumn emotionally. "I was really worried about what people would think. And then I finally concluded that no one else was paying my bills and providing me this level of time and freedom. I need to take care of myself. No one else is going to come along and save me. I have to become my own hero."

Today, Autumn has a thriving network marketing business, is the author of the book *Living Your Life Alive*, and is a CWC coach helping leaders move into careers that serve them, no matter what everyone thinks.

You get to make the rules and decide how your career will change. The decisions about what serves you, what is in your best interest, and how to put yourself first belong to you.

You put the best team members on the most challenging projects at work. Use the same strategy by putting the best person in charge of your future. You.

Accepting Responsibility

Do you think *they* have lost touch with what's happening, *they* don't care about you, and *they* are making terrible decisions? Are you worried that *they* might fire you someday? You need to fire *them*. *They* are not responsible for you, your career, or your well-being.

Isn't it much easier to blame the system, your boss, the economy, your parents, and anyone else you can think of? The blame game is alive and well. Maybe you've fallen into that trap too.

Even if the system is rigged, your boss is a jerk, the economy sucks, and your parents messed you up, what you do from now on is on you. When you take responsibility for your actions and outcomes, you become empowered to do what's right for you. It's a little scary because there's no one else to blame when things go wrong. But when things go right, you revel in the joy of your victories.

Don't wait for good things to happen; make good things happen. Can you look at yourself in the mirror and be proud knowing you are taking ownership of everything in your career and life?

If you let obstacles and difficulties define you, slow you down, or stop you, you allow the circumstances to prevent you from living your best life. You're missing the opportunity to step into abundance and achieve everything you want and deserve.

If you've been playing the blame game for too long and need a reminder of how to take personal responsibility and regain focus, here are a few pro tips:

- Don't get stuck in the past. What's done is done. Focus on the future and take an active part in it.
- Pay attention to what you want and worry less about how to get it. Things change quickly; be flexible on how you can work to achieve the desired results. Accept that you will make mistakes, and use them as a learning opportunity.
- Win or lose, it's on you. Embrace the power of accountability.

Instead of believing "I can't," ask yourself, "How can I?" It is such a powerful question because there is always a way forward. Acknowledge that your future is in your capable hands and then take the necessary steps to build a vibrant career and live your best life.

"Nothing will work unless you do."

— Maya Angelou

Thomas Johnson uses his superpowers in problem-solving to guide his career. He inherently avoids the blame game and accepts responsibility for his outcomes. His drive for personal responsibility goes well beyond his personal needs.

Thomas gained a sense of purpose and direction after his grandmother died from diabetes complications. It inspired him to help people be more aware and care for themselves. He pivoted from the business management track he was on and changed to nutrition and personal training.

Thomas became a personal trainer and nutritionist. He was earning high six figures, hanging out with the who's who on jets and yachts, living the high life, and doing what he loved.

One day when Thomas reviewed a client's nutritional intake, he noticed she was hitting the booze hard; all her meetings were at bars and restaurants. He was worried. The next time they met, he sat her down, asked her what was happening, and called her out on the heavy drinking.

Her bottom lip quivered, and she burst out in tears. Thomas' words broke the camel's back, and she revealed how extremely stressed she was. As a young female executive for a huge company, she didn't know anyone who understood what it felt like to be in her position. She was becoming an alcoholic.

"I did not have any answers," Thomas said of their meeting. "All I could do was listen as she poured her heart out. This was the first time I was at a loss for words." Thomas realized the fitness industry was not serving this type of client well. They were not providing the support these clients need to deal with these high-pressure situations, and Thomas set out to change that. "I had to take responsibility. I needed to do better," and that's how he became obsessed with holistically serving his corporate clients.

Thomas created his company, GetUpNGetFit Wellness Concierge. He wanted to serve executives and support their wellness needs. Getting started wasn't easy. His sales team would finally get an executive to talk to him, and when they asked, "Who are you again?"

Thomas didn't have a good answer. "I was not well positioned to work with this type of client, so I had to go back and figure it out."

Thomas took responsibility to change whatever was needed to grow his business. "If you study success, you will find the clues you need to win." Thomas is now well-positioned to serve his community.

We can all learn great lessons from Thomas' journey. Are you looking for clues, or are you looking for excuses?

Summary

The amount of change we've experienced over the past decade has been extraordinary. The belief you have certainty and consistency is an illusion, and it doesn't serve you. Taking advantage of the opportunities inherent in our volatile professional world can be fun when you adjust your mindset and focus on the things you can control.

It's natural to focus on all the things that could go wrong, and there is a way to break the cycle and get unstuck.

- Move from a scarcity to an abundance mindset.
- Leverage the successes from your past.
- Shift from thinking *I can't* to *How can I?*
- Remember, you don't fear change; you fear losing things that are important to you.

Applying the principles and rigor you use for change and transformation in your business to your career increases your likelihood of success. Whenever you are not moving toward something you want, the pressures holding you back are usually fear-based. Spend time thinking about why you aren't acting. What are you afraid of? Then build your strategy to mitigate your risk and move forward.

Uncertainty provides a unique opportunity to level the playing field. It also offers the opportunity to lead. Without certainty, people seek leaders who can help them navigate the gray. Organizational alignment goes out the window. If you step up, they will follow, and everyone will be better for it.

It's time to end the blame game when you don't achieve the outcomes you want. Step up, take full responsibility for your actions, and stop hoping things magically work out. You are the only one who can make the changes you need to have a fulfilling career and life.

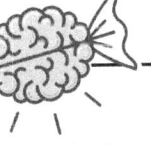

Brain Candy – Important Questions for You to Chew On

Grab your journal and get started on your ABCs for growth.

Assess:

- Have you been living in the past, or are you looking ahead?
- What has been holding you back?

- How much responsibility have you been giving away regarding your career development?

Baseline:

- When can you leverage the uncertainty to create opportunity?
- How well can you read the room and understand what's happening beneath the surface?
- Are you skilled at adapting and adjusting your tactics?

Conquer:

- How would showing up differently change your career and leadership brand?
- Where can you change your *I can't* mindset to a *How can I?* perspective?
- How should you show up when you need to work in the gray?

Chapter 5

SHIFTING YOUR LOYALTY TO WHERE IT BELONGS

"Know where you want to go and make sure the right people know about it."

— Meredith Mahoney

Let's talk about the loyalty trap you may have fallen into. It's great to be loyal. The question is, what and who are you loyal to?

You associate much of your identity with your career. That connection isn't reciprocated. It's like you're in a one-sided relationship where you're the clingy girlfriend whose boyfriend barely realizes you're in the room. It's tough to swallow knowing you've attached so much of who you are to a situation where the commitment isn't mutual.

Company loyalties are a weird thing. You're supposed to be loyal, yet when is that loyalty reciprocated? When times get tough, you're put on the chopping block without a second thought.

The boss you've been loyal to schedules a random meeting. You see them sitting with the HR rep and immediately know your time is up.

Your boss reads a canned script and barely makes eye contact. The HR rep then tells your boss to leave the room so they can mechanically walk you through the details of your severance package as your desk is packed. Seriously? This is what you're loyal to? Everyone knows this is how they play the game. Why do we have this misplaced sense of loyalty?

What we do is a big part of who we are. If our core foundational identity is a one-way street, that diminishes how we value ourselves. Too often we manufacture this unhealthy commitment to our company to make us feel better and more valued. It's hard to admit that one of the most critical relationships in our life doesn't love us back.

What if what you did for a living had no bearing on your identity? What if you had a healthy relationship with work and could have a meaningful commercial arrangement without all the destructive emotional connections that sabotage your career? Shifting your loyalty to where it belongs while maintaining your commitment to your career gives you a powerful balance.

Are you ready to reconsider your loyalties?

Decoupling Who You Are from What You Do

Here's a new cocktail party trick. Next time you're in a room full of strangers, make a point to avoid talking about work, your job, or anything to do with your or the other people's livelihood. Think you can do it? I bet you'll find it much more challenging than it sounds.

I always love my job, and when I don't, I make the changes needed to love what I'm doing again. I get fired up and excited to talk about what I do to anyone curious enough to ask. I had no idea how damaging this was until I met my partner, Steve, about eight years ago.

Steve loves what he does, but he doesn't associate his career with who he is. Most of his friends have a vague idea about what he does for a living but no details. What they do love about him is his passion for life, wine, travel, food, and science, and the well-informed discussions they have with him.

This concept was utterly foreign to me. On Wall Street and with many friends, your career is the first thing someone wants to know about. You size people up by understanding their title, job, and company. Wanting to know what someone does for a living is so commonplace, especially in America, that I didn't even realize there were better options.

"Wanting to be someone else is a waste of the person you are."

— Kurt Cobain

When Steve and I moved to Belize, I found a lot of expats, and the question, "What do you do?" never came up. I was itching to talk about CWC, but what I did wasn't important.

It's a weird feeling when who you are, not what you do, defines your identity. It's also the most freeing mindset shift I've made in years. It takes a lot of pressure off—no measuring up and wondering what people think. It can also be a rude awakening when you look at your non-work life and don't have much to talk about.

At the time, I had spent my life consumed by work. Outside of business and financial market conversations, I had little to say. Eventually, I found hobbies I loved, and travel became my passion. My inspiration came from nature. I became more present. Today my life is more balanced. My relationships are stronger, and while I love my business and our team, they don't define me.

If you are in the same boat, here are a few things to try:

- Get current on things you're passionate about. It doesn't matter what they are. If you're passionate, it will resonate with anyone you speak to.
- Set fun goals outside of work.
- Leave work at work by giving yourself ten minutes to decompress; then fully embrace personal time mode.

Setting Boundaries

Does your team drive you bonkers? Most find joy and fulfillment in the people they work with. These people could also be your downfall and drain your tank if you let them. Setting boundaries for the coworkers you love isn't being mean or unsupportive. It's the best thing you can do for everyone.

It feels good to be needed. It fills you with a sense of purpose and makes you feel important, plus you like to help others. If you are in the middle of everything, you need a divorce from your love affair with being needed.

It's hard to pull away because you fear you won't be viewed as a team player. Or maybe the culture is always on, and you feel that if you don't work 24/7 like everyone else, you'll fall behind somehow.

Your inability to set and stick to your boundaries slowly kills your career. You end up feeling stressed and overwhelmed. Your team gets frustrated, work slows down, and results suffer. Before you know it, you are sending email until eleven o'clock every night, checking in on weekends, and becoming a significant bottleneck.

What would happen if fewer people needed you? Would you feel less important? Do you worry that your job will be at risk? Will your team make mistakes you can't recover from?

Most of the time, if you run at breakneck speed, feeling crushed by the demands of your day-to-day, it's your own doing. If you created the mess, you can uncreate it.

Leaders need to find the balance between being supportive and being a crutch. Be a resource for knowledge instead of doing the work for them. Trust them to do their jobs well. Instead of micro-managing, guide their career development and let them take responsibility for their forward momentum.

Get comfortable with being needed less. Surround yourself with independent, intelligent people who can think, solve problems, and adapt without you. When you are needed less, you can focus on the high-value things that move you and the business forward. You improve your executive presence, your team feels empowered, and you get more peace. Everyone wins.

Setting boundaries requires more than adjusting your physical availability. It's equally as important to be aware of your mental presence.

Do you find yourself constantly preoccupied? When you're at home, are you thinking about work? And when at work, are you thinking about home? Being present is the key to success. How do you break the distraction cycle?

Tell your team and your boss you are unreachable when you're finished for the day. Ask your team to do the same. When one person starts firing off email or instant messages, it creates a firestorm of largely unnecessary activity. If you think about work, write it down and save it for the next day.

Ruthlessly rank the meetings you attend and only go to the ones where you can contribute. Meet with stakeholders and business partners as a group. It'll keep you from having to repeat yourself and encourage collaboration.

Make time to do things that energize you. If it's morning yoga and meditation, don't look at your phone or check in until you've finished— put yourself first. If it's a relaxing walk after work, leave your phone at home and enjoy nature.

"Don't confuse having a career with having a life."

— Hillary Rodham Clinton

I used to be terrible at setting boundaries, and even after years of practice, I still struggle. Once I was leading a large team at a company where senior leadership seemed to be running around with their hair on fire. There was always a crisis, shifting priorities, and fire drills.

As a result, my days were largely out of my control and meetings were constantly shifting. I usually had to reschedule my one-on-ones with my managers, move my leadership team meeting at the last minute, and live at the beck and call of my boss and his peers.

One day, one of my leaders approached me and walked me through the effect all the rescheduling had on my team. In one week, I had rescheduled ten meetings with less than twenty-four hours' notice. The downstream disruption was staggering.

He did the math. My meetings had about five people each, which meant fifty people had to move their meetings because of my change. When they did, it disrupted at least 300 people. The productivity costs and morale issues were significant.

I had never thought of things in those terms before. Accommodating your boss is something everyone does without question. I brought these insights to my boss, and we talked about the pace, the lack of discipline, and the unnecessary rescheduling.

As expected, he was accommodating his boss, and together, we brought this to the attention of the head of the division. When you extrapolated the disruption over a 10,000-person team, the numbers were mind-blowing, and when you monetized it, the financial drain was in the millions.

The leadership team's frantic pace gradually normalized. Everyone stepped into a rhythm they could count on. We were able to manage our days instead of our days managing us. Team morale improved, more work got done, and all it took was raising awareness and setting boundaries.

Setting boundaries isn't just about you—it's about leading by example and creating the right team environment. Your teams will do what you do, not what you say. If you tell them to unplug on the weekends, don't work while on vacation, and stay off email, but you aren't doing the same, nothing you say matters.

Separating the Mission You Love from the Job You Hate

What happens when you love your company and hate your job? You are finally working for a company you can believe in. The mission is clear and exciting, and you can see yourself helping to make a big difference in the world.

There's only one problem. The job, boss, or corporate culture crushes your will to live. Every day feels like a slog. It wasn't always this way. These changes happened slowly, and it was hard to recognize the warning signs at first. Then suddenly, you look around and wonder when it all started going sideways. Panic sets in and you feel stuck. You know you need a change, yet you are deeply committed to the mission. Something has to give—but what?

When Michelle came to me a few years ago, she was burnt out and stressed.

She was short-staffed and the company was in trouble, so she was at a breaking point. She had been there for many years and was in a senior position. Michelle's professional background was stellar. It would have taken her two seconds to land a new job. I asked Michelle, "Why are you staying?" Her answer surprised me.

"I learned that working for a company whose mission I believe in was inspiring. Along the way, work will get hard. But if you really believe in the mission, it is much easier to get through those hard moments. And so, I truly believe in the mission, I believe in the product, and I love the people attracted to the product. The four years building the company were epic, and I loved it. And then, when it crashed, I was heartbroken. But I loved it so much I stayed because I wanted to help restructure everything we built to save the company."

Michelle stuck it out a bit longer. There was a shakeup at the top. While the new leadership team didn't fix everything, it fixed enough that she could stay dedicated to the mission and lead with strength and confidence. Were it not for the leadership change, Michelle would have abandoned ship and fueled her passion elsewhere.

"In a chronically leaking boat, energy devoted to changing vessels is more productive than energy devoted to patching leaks."

— Warren Buffett

Finding a company you believe in is essential, but it's only one part of the equation. If your ideal company changes the world in whatever way matters to you, yet it's sucking the life out of you, it is time to make a change. You need the whole enchilada. You first. Mission second. The organization must fit your values, your vibe, and your culture.

Company dynamics change over time. The company culture Michelle was in was different from when she started. As companies grow and shrink and leaders come and go, things shift. A good fit doesn't always remain a good fit.

Don't sacrifice your career or emotional well-being for a mission-based company that's fallen out of alignment with your values. Many others have a healthier culture that will let you thrive in spirit and contribution.

You still need to survive the daily grind as you wind your way out of your environment and find a new place to apply your time and talents. When it's time to make a change, you'll need to be at your best. Toxic environments deplete your energy, enthusiasm, and confidence.

If you suspect that might be happening to you, set firm boundaries, get lots of rest, and spend extra time doing things you love with the people you love during your off hours. Your primary focus should be keeping your battery fully charged and your mindset where it needs to be.

Summary

Shift your loyalty to you first, and embrace the idea that your job is simply a commercial arrangement between you and your company. You provide your services in exchange for your salary, bonus, and benefits. Putting yourself first doesn't preclude you from having meaningful relationships with your colleagues. And you can still be excited and energized about delivering fantastic results and growing within the organization. It simply brings balance to the relationship.

Two of the most important things to do as you make this shift is to decouple your sense of identity from what you do for a living and break up with your addiction to being needed. Adding value, making a difference, and helping others progress in their careers are all very important. However, aligning your identity with your job causes an imbalance in your whole-life happiness.

Running from meeting to meeting for nine hours straight before getting any work done is unsustainable. Set boundaries for your team, stakeholders, and business partners so you can be your best self more often. Don't be afraid to say no, limit your availability, and ruthlessly prioritize where you spend your time.

Remember, you first, mission second. When you are working for an organization where you align with their mission and are committed to helping them achieve their goals, it cannot be at the expense of career satisfaction and mental well-being. If the mission you love is tainted with a toxic culture you hate, it's time to make a change.

Brain Candy – Important Questions for You to Chew On

Grab your journal and get started on your ABCs for growth.

Assess:

- Are you emotionally overcommitted to work?

- What other interests do you have?

- Are you spending enough time nurturing your interests?

- Do you leave work back at the office (even if it is in the spare bedroom)?

- How long has the culture been draining you?

Baseline:

- How would you introduce yourself if we met and you could not discuss your career?

- How comfortable are you with not being needed?

- Do you have the right people on your team?

- Are you empowering them as much as you should be?

- Are you conflicted between your organization's mission and your well-being?

Conquer:

- How can you streamline your routines?

- What boundaries can you set at work right away?

- Where else can you help make the world better?

Part I: Reveal—The Dynamics Behind the Dysfunction

I hope you acquired new perspectives in Part I of this book as we revealed the dynamics behind the dysfunction, and that you are inspired by the small steps you can take to thrive despite the current environment.

If you have been journaling your ABCs as you thought about all that brain candy, I'm sure you've had a flood of realizations come to light. As American futurist Joel A. Barker said, "Vision without action is merely a dream."

It's time to transform your insights into action. Head over to the *Escaping the Career Trap Transformation Guide* and continue your journey toward creating a thriving career. Visit our website at: EscapingTheCareerTrap.com/Guide.

When you get there, you will find tools and a roadmap to:

- Build your strategy to thrive in a broken system.
- Break free from the soul-crushing grind.
- Hone your rule-breaking skills.
- Become a master at leading through change and uncertainty.
- Navigate your path forward when you love the mission and hate your job.

PART II:
ALIGN

PRIORITIZING YOUR VISION

Everyone deserves to love Mondays.

Chapter 6

CREATING YOUR CAREER SUCCESS BLUEPRINT

"A goal properly set is halfway reached."

— Zig Ziglar

With a fresh perspective on the remarkably broken system and new skills to navigate and thrive, now is a great time to align with what's most important: You! Among the most significant feedback I get from CWC career strategy clients is despite twenty-some years of experience, they have rarely taken the time to reflect on what they truly want and why they want it.

Do you have an accidental career?

Your career just kind of happens. You go along, do a good job, opportunities come, and you take them (or not), and before you know it, you're looking around feeling a bit disenfranchised and start wondering, *How did I get here?*

An accidental career will only work for so long. At some point, the big wake-up call comes, and despite appearing successful on the outside, something feels off on the inside. You have ten to fifteen years left to work, a lifestyle representative of your success, and you haven't laid the groundwork to know what to do next.

It's the moment of truth. Are you going to pretend everything is fine and hope for the best? Or will you realize you need to start focusing on what you really want and make some intentional changes?

Paying attention to these warning signs, figuring out what you want and why, and refusing to settle for being sidelined will lead you to a thriving second-act career. You'll feel vibrant, make a huge difference, have fun every day, and, believe it or not, you'll earn more money. Who doesn't want that?

Let's dig into how to create your career success blueprint.

Unleashing Your Ambition

Has your ambition taken an extended vacation? Earlier in your career, you were full of ambition and drive. You were ready to take on the world. As time passed, your ambition kicked into cruise control, and complacency became your silent companion.

The ups and downs of your corporate career can slowly drain the fire from within, and you may find yourself in an apathetic haze. You are good at what you do, so it's easy to put everything on autopilot and pretend all is well. Until all is not well; then it's time to release the Kraken! It's had a very long nap, but once you wake it up and dust off the cobwebs, you'll find your ambition is thrilled to be called back into action.

Do you ever set big goals, but as time passes, nothing happens? Do you get busy or lose focus, or do things get too complicated? I have a four-step process that will help you reignite your ambition and maintain the momentum you need to succeed and thrive.

1. Set a goal that scares you a little.
2. Write it down and keep it visible.
3. Tell everyone about your crazy dreams.
4. Create a detailed plan that allows you to flex.

Start by setting an ambitious goal. I'm talking about a scary, everyone will think you're crazy, making you throw up in your mouth a little goal.

Once you have your goal, write it down and put it in several places where you can see it. Move it around occasionally if you find yourself looking past it due to familiarity. I have my big scary goal as a daily task on my phone so the reminder appears every day, and it's the first thing I see.

Next (here comes the scary part), tell everyone who will listen about your goal. If you do this right, they should be sick and tired of hearing about it. Keeping your goal a secret significantly decreases your chances of success. When you tell others about your ambition, you're reinforcing it for yourself and giving people an opportunity to help.

It's incredibly difficult to get from where you are to that big, lofty goal in one step, so the last and most crucial step is mastering the ancient art of elephant eating. One bite at a time. Taking small steps to achieve a massive goal is the only way to succeed.

Setting big goals is exciting and motivating, but it can be overwhelming and cause a sense of failure. Create your path forward with detailed actions and milestone dates. Find an accountability partner who will help you stay motivated, celebrate your wins, and recover from the setbacks you encounter along your journey.

The plan you make will be different from the path you take. Obstacles and opportunities will pop up along the way, and you need the agility to adjust. The journey is half the fun, so enjoy it and all the learning opportunities that come along with it.

In 1979, Harvard did a ten-year study on their MBA class. Of the students, 84 percent set a goal, 13 percent set their goals but didn't have a plan, and 3 percent set goals and created a plan. Ten years later, the 3 percent with goals and a plan earned ten times as much as the other 97 percent of their classmates.

As you set goals, address the seasonality of your career. You can take different risks at different stages of your life, and that, in addition to your natural risk tolerance, should always be considered when mapping your path forward.

For example, I'm a high-energy girl with no issues taking big risks and putting it all out there. Even with a high risk tolerance, I was comfortable with different levels of risk during my career. I took big risks earlier because I had nothing to lose. As I moved into the middle of my career, I was more conservative—I had a family to support.

And now that I'm at the end of my career, my risk tolerance is back to high again.

> *"A man can succeed at almost anything for which he has unlimited enthusiasm."*
>
> — Charles Schwab

Right now is the ideal time to give yourself the luxury of introspection. If your accidental career no longer serves you, it's time to align with your core values.

Consider these two primary elements as you chart your future—your primary values and your beliefs. Assess your core beliefs and values and get reacquainted with them.

We all are motivated by six primary values. One or two will stand out as you consider them.

The six primary values we all share are:

- Certainty
- Variability
- Significance
- Connection
- Growth
- Contribution

As you look at these words, which one or two resonate the most? The value you identify with the most will guide your journey and be the source of your fulfillment.

Suppose you're moving from point A to point B and certainty is your primary value; then you will take a different path from someone whose primary value is significance, and that journey will be different from that of the person who values variability. There are no right or wrong answers. Your primary core value will inform your next bold move and how you get there.

If you're feeling disconnected at work, which core value is missing from your environment?

Two beliefs direct how you react to the world—global beliefs and rules you believe in.

Global beliefs are our perspectives on how life and things should be. These are things that guide us and the bigger world around us. Thinking about your beliefs could start with phrases like "life is," "people are," or "I am."

Your beliefs can hold you back or help propel you forward. Understand what your current beliefs are so you can assess how they are guiding the decisions you make every day.

My global beliefs are very different now from what they were earlier in my career—the old ones held me back. I didn't get my college degree until I was forty, which was a constant source of anxiety. I lived with imposter syndrome before it was even a thing.

I believed you could only be an executive if you had a degree. Full stop. No matter what, you could not do it. And that was slowing me down. As long as I held that belief, I never tried to advance because I thought it was a waste of time. Thankfully, I managed to disprove my global belief and grow my career.

Many CWC clients put off getting the coaching they need because they have a global belief that it's too late to make a major change. They imagine this invisible line, and once they cross it, they are too old, too expensive, and too unmarketable to shift out of a dead-end career into something that energizes them. Fortunately, these people are disproving that belief too.

What are your global beliefs? Are they serving you, or are they keeping you stuck? If they are keeping you stuck, it's time to challenge them and reengineer your beliefs so you can continue to grow.

Rules are the if/then statements we use to judge ourselves and others. You frame rule statements like this: "If you love me, you'd never do that." "I need X to get Y." Much like your global beliefs, they can help you or hurt you.

Early in my career, one of my rules was if I were valuable to an organization, they would invest in my leadership development. I attached my value to this and took it very personally. Now my rule is if I'm independently growing, I will achieve my goals because I'm increasing my value.

Beliefs and rules are so ingrained you don't even realize you're following them. Here's how to figure out yours.

Think about a time when you were stuck. It could be now or a time when you felt like you were standing in quicksand and no matter what you did, you couldn't make progress. Write down all the reasons you were stuck. Then go back and critically evaluate each statement. Are your beliefs and rules true, or must they be reframed? The beliefs and rules that held you back before will slow you down repeatedly until you reframe your core beliefs and assumptions.

Next, go back to your rockstar moments. Why were you crushing your goals at the time? These insights will allow you to uncover the beliefs that work well for you.

Is thinking about your values, beliefs, and rules when making a career decision a new concept for you? Most of us look at opportunities through the lens of compensation, influence, people, and the company's reputation without running the opportunity through our values, beliefs, and rules test. And then we wonder why after the honeymoon is over, we're right back where we started.

Aligning with your core beliefs is one of the fundamental differences between people with thriving careers and those without. Don't worry about the probability of finding a job that fits you to a tee and has the title, influence, and compensation you need. For now, put yourself first and align with the essential things. The rest will come.

Clarifying What You Want and Why

Why do you want the things you want? Do you want them for yourself or for someone else? So often, when I ask my clients to identify why they want the things they want, the answer is hollow.

Keeping up with the Joneses, doing what others expect, and following the "normal" path all feed into goal setting. And then there's money. (Warning—rant coming.) How much is really enough? I have clients killing themselves in miserable careers taking happy pills to cope, with spouses who are ready to call it quits, and kids who are acting out. These clients are miserable, fatter, disconnected, and a shell of whom they used to be. They own their homes, have virtually no debt, and make mid to high six figure salaries. Why do you do this to yourself?

If you make loads of money, live your best life, and love every Monday, then fantastic. If you have backed yourself into a financial situation and need to make a few concessions to get back on track, even that is understandable as long as it's temporary. Most business leaders do not fall into either of these categories, yet they continue to chase the all-mighty dollar at the expense of everything else.

It is time to break out of this Stepford life and define what you want, why you want it, and how to get it on your terms. Feeling shackled to a soul-crushing job because of the constructs you created in your life is unnecessary. So how do you start to break the cycle and recreate your path?

You hear a lot about purpose these days. More people recognize its importance. How do you find your purpose? How do you break out of the esoteric nonsense and make practical changes?

Inspirational author and speaker Simon Sinek and other thought leaders espouse the merits of understanding your "why." I have found what works best for me and my clients is taking the time to get to your *Level 7 Why*.

Here's how it works. Write down the biggest goal you have right now. Then simply ask yourself, "Why do I want that?" Reflecting on your answer, ask yourself why that answer is important. You'll have your true purpose once you've asked yourself *why* seven times.

Give it a try right now. I'll wait.

Did you tear up a little? Do you feel in your gut your *Level 7 Why* is raw, ugly, and maybe something you've never told anyone? If you answered yes, you're there. Suppose you didn't—go back and keep trying. Dig deep because when you find your true purpose, you become unstoppable.

I did this for the first time when I started my business. I was making loads of mistakes, business was progressing slowly, and I felt like giving up. So, with my coach's advice, I did the *Level 7 Why* exercise. What I found was hard, raw, and scared the hell out of me.

I'll share some of my backstory to give some context on my "why." Growing up in a small country town in New Jersey, I always felt wealthy. We had a great house, a pool, and went to private schools. We went on long vacations in the winter, and my mom didn't have to work.

We had everything we needed. When I was fifteen, my parents split up. No big deal—my dad was a total control freak, and I enjoyed the freedom until one day, he just vanished. Within a few weeks, we were kicked out of our house; the IRS was after my mom for a decade of unpaid taxes, and we were homeless and destitute. We spent months staying with friends and couch surfing with relatives until we could finally get a tiny apartment in a shitty part of town. As it turned out, Dad was living in New Orleans under an alias. I found him several years later.

My poor mom was a wreck. She got pregnant with me in high school and never graduated. She supported my dad's business and cared for me and my sister. She was ill-equipped to handle this new reality. The only job she could get was waiting tables at a local diner. My teenage years instantly went from bright and breezy to dark and hard. I saw how much my mother struggled. I know how shitty it felt for me and my sister.

My *Level 7 Why* was that I did not want to end up like my mother. I would never depend on anyone for my financial security. I was not going to go through life uninformed or ill-equipped. Losing everything we had was an incredible motivator.

When you reach your *Level 7 Why*, you'll realize the trappings of the box you've put yourself into are unimportant. You'll experience the freedom to break out and do things because they fulfill your purpose.

You'll know that failure is not an option, and that career success is no longer a luxury. Your vision becomes clear. And you bravely do the hard work because you've got that strong anchor.

"There are many things in life that will catch your eye, but only a few will catch your heart. Pursue these."

— Michael Nolan

For Florence, getting to her big *why* was a game changer. She was leading one of the largest business units in her company. She stacked her team with rockstars and was at the top of her game. She was up for a promotion to executive vice president, which was a huge deal in her company. There were very few of them, they were all men, and the Board of Directors ultimately made these decisions. She did all the right things to prepare for the promotion process, aligned with the right people, took on all the challenging projects, and worked seventy-hour weeks.

When Florence did not get the promotion, she was devastated. She had busted her tail all year only to get turned down. After she dusted herself off, she returned to the groove, and another year passed. She didn't get the promotion this time, either. Florence was ready to quit.

We started working together so Florence could figure out what she was doing wrong and think through her options. She couldn't bear to go through the process and rejection one more time. When I asked her why the promotion was so important, she gave me the same answer almost everyone else does—money, prestige, recognition, etc.

The problem was Florence didn't connect her desire to get promoted with her *Level 7 Why*. She didn't have the drive that comes when you are genuinely connected to what's most important. Despite doing all the right things, she fell a little short.

Shortly after we began working together, Florence needed to put her mother into long-term care. They couldn't afford the type of facility she wanted her mom to be in. Getting that promotion was a make or break for her because if she didn't get it, her mother would have to be in a care facility neither was happy with. Florence was horrified by the guilt of not being able to care for her parents.

Because of her mother's situation, Florence started working fewer hours, took on fewer projects, and spent less time networking and politicking. She did her work with much more conviction; Florence was less patient and pushed her agenda harder, and she built deeper relationships with the senior leaders through her excellent work.

In the third year, Florence got her promotion. When she asked her manager why, he said the leadership team and board finally saw the edge they expected from their senior leadership team.

Florence changed by connecting to her *Level 7 Why*. She knew failure was not an option, and she found the resolve to do what it took to accomplish her goal.

Doing What You Love with People You Love

When you end work each day, do you feel like you just survived ten hours in the spin cycle, or are you energized and ready for more? Each day can be a slog if you're not doing work that energizes you and doing it with people who energize you.

How do you figure out what would energize you? You get your brag on. Write down the seven proudest moments in your career. They don't have to be the swoon-worthy stories you use on your resume and during interviews. Most of our proudest moments go unnoticed. Your top seven of all time are the ones that matter most to you.

After your stories are written down, write down why you're so proud of these moments. Go into as much detail as possible. You'll find themes threading through all of them. These themes are the moments and environments you thrive in. You'll have a clear picture of your foundation when you see the common elements.

You are flexible and have mastered the ability to be successful in various areas. Just because you can do it doesn't mean you love doing it, nor does it mean it energizes you. When you reframe your thinking and start to identify the things you can do for twelve hours straight and never get tired, you've found the vibe you are looking for.

Close your eyes and imagine yourself in your ideal role at work every day. What time do you wake up? What time does your head hit the pillow? What does your work life look and feel like? What projects are you working on, and what are you doing daily? Who's around you? What kind of schedule do you have? What's the cultural energy? Do you want the vibe and power of a shared space, or do you enjoy a quiet area where you can think? What's the cadence of your meetings? Do you have time between them, or do you love it when things are crazy all the time? Are you traveling, and if so, to where? Are you working at home, in the office, or both? What things naturally give you the most energy?

Paint that picture for yourself. Don't worry about where it is, precisely what you're doing, who you're working for, your title, or what the industry is. Just create that vision of your ideal life.

"Whatever you decide to do, make sure it makes you happy."

— Paulo Coelho

What do advertising, event planning, telecommunications, race car driver training, a ventilator manufacturing startup, and fintech to support the underserved have in common? My client Kristine Gross. She's the CEO of World Tree Productions, and the creator of a Gen Z reality TV series to save the planet.

Kristine has become a pro at prioritizing doing work she loves and surrounding herself with great people who energize her. It took her a few crazy bosses and companies she wasn't thrilled about to realize how important this was to her.

Kristine started her marketing career supporting a cigarette manufacturer. It was such an anti-feminist culture, which went against everything she stood for. It was her first job out of college, and she needed to quickly learn as much as she could so she could get out and start using her powers for good and not evil.

Things started to change for Kristine when she ended up on a startup team that recruited and trained race car drivers. Race car driving is in her DNA. Her great-aunt Greta was a famous race car driver in the 1950s and the first woman to win the Monaco Grand Prix. Here is where Kristine learned the power of doing what you're passionate about and working with a team you love.

Kristine's career took a variety of turns. She has this incredible knack for getting to the root cause of a problem or opportunity and getting the right people around the table to take action. Her superpowers are equal parts marketing savvy and the executive presence to inspire others and get stuff done.

Through trial and error, Kristine realized large corporate environments didn't suit her. She felt compelled to do work in areas where she could have a more significant influence in society and for the company. That drive and ambition fueled her newest environmental protection startup and reality TV series.

"I pivoted a lot. I've always had an entrepreneurial mindset, and I knew what I didn't like, and I knew what I liked. Later in my career, I realized you need to be around good people, and sometimes you really have to search for them."

Debunking the Confidence, Passion, and Purpose Myth

Are confidence, passion, and purpose overrated? If you have these things, they seem highly valuable. They get dismissed if you don't. What camp are you in?

If the confidence, passion, and purpose fairy ran out of pixie dust before getting to you, you are probably making one classic mistake— waiting for confidence, passion, and purpose to arrive.

These feel like illusive emotions that come and go without your control. You have one project that lights you up; the following ten projects bore you to tears. Occasionally, you feel deeply connected to what you're doing, but you're usually lulled into a numb haze.

You only achieve confidence, passion, and purpose by taking action, and you can only keep them by staying aligned with your true self.

Confidence is tricky. The majority of my clients are successful mid- to senior-level leaders. They have had more than their fair share of wins and are confident. However, 100 percent of the time, their confidence is a blocker. When you have a long track record of success and suddenly things start falling apart, you're ill-equipped to deal with the moments of low self-confidence. (We'll talk more about this in Chapter 9: Crushing the Fearsome Four.)

Depending on how long you've been in this funk, it may be severe enough to make you feel stuck. I find many of my clients are waiting for their confidence to return. They think one day they will wake up and feel like a million bucks again. That never happens. Inaction has eroded your confidence, and inertia keeps you there. Your confidence will only come back once you take small steps to regain it.

Is anyone genuinely passionate about their job? It seems like a bit of a stretch, doesn't it? I've only had two jobs I felt passionate about, where the entire situation was in my wheelhouse. The work, the people, my ability to grow and learn, my influence, and the recognition were all aligned, and I was on fire. It's a small number, given how long I've been working and how many different jobs I've had.

But in every position I've held, I found something to be passionate about. I chose to lean into the elements of the role that energized me and focus my time and abilities on that part of the job. In some cases, it was the work itself. In others, I loved the people. Sometimes I had a tremendous opportunity to grow. When nothing was left to be passionate about, I was out of there.

Passion is a choice, and you can choose to find aspects of your role today that fuel you. Understanding your passion and aligning with what energizes you is crucial to escaping the career trap.

Some people have a deep sense of purpose. They want to save the planet, end hunger, stop genocide, and prevent wars. We need these people desperately. In my experience, these people are few and far between. So, what do you do if you don't feel a burning need to save the world? You bring things closer to home and connect with your *Level 7 Why*. Remember, Florence, in her quest to get the EVP promotion, didn't have that extra "something" she needed until she found purpose. Find your purpose, and let that be your guide.

"I was always looking outside myself for strength and confidence, but it comes from within. It is there all the time."

— Anna Freud

In his teens, Jeff Baietto had a bad attitude. He was butting heads with his father at every opportunity, and to his dad's credit, he didn't just dismiss Jeff as a surly teenager and wait for it to pass. Jeff was handed a cassette tape from Earl Nightingale titled *The Strangest Secret*.

That twenty-minute message gave Jeff an entirely new perspective. It was the first time he heard anyone discuss goals or your ability to create your future.

Jeff was hooked and became a total self-leadership junkie before it was even a thing. This grumpy teenager morphed into the most optimistic kid in his small hometown, which put him on a path of self-awareness.

After college, Jeff wanted to travel, so he picked up whatever work he could in Mexico and Europe. Jeff wanted to be an entrepreneur and started a video game company with one of his best friends. They grew the business, but Jeff didn't love video games.

"I would wake up every six months and have this horrible feeling in my stomach. I remember thinking if I were to die soon, this is not what I came here to do." Jeff was grateful for the success, but the lack of fulfillment weighed heavily.

Jeff sold his part of the business and started investing in real estate. California was booming, and Jeff was in his thirties, wealthy, and flipping houses. He was on easy street until 2008, when the housing crisis hit. Jeff was overextended. "I remember telling everyone I lost everything. I was devastated."

Jeff had to swallow his pride and reach out to his dad for help. He dreaded making that call. But his father did not judge. He offered only love and concern for his son's wellbeing. Jeff lost it and began to bawl. That was when he started to shift toward his purpose and passion instead of identifying his self-worth with his bank account.

Jeff realized no one cared about his business or outward success. They cared about who he was as a person. "I started to think about all the things I could do now that others' expectations were no longer in the equation." Jeff got a master's degree in spiritual psychology and found coaching.

Until life forced Jeff to recalibrate how he viewed success, he kept delaying happiness and fulfillment and fell into the "I'll be happy when" trap.

"I kept telling myself I'll be happy when I'm successful, and my happiness kept being pushed farther down my path. If there were one thing I'd love everyone to sit with, it is this—focus on the happiness, contentment, fulfillment, feelings, and the quality of experience you want now. That is the lens I'm evaluating my experiences through. Outcomes are just one part of the equation."

Jeff waited for his passion and purpose to appear as he chased all the wrong things. Finding his true calling took a lot of inner work and perseverance. Aligning his passion and purpose has enriched his life beyond anything he could have expected. Today, he is coaching and has a thriving software company, InJoy Global, which is helping coaches significantly improve their clients' lives and businesses.

Summary

Reignite your ambition and set huge goals—ones that scare you a little bit. As you do this, consider your core values, global beliefs, and the rules you judge yourself and others by. Use the themes found in the rockstar moments in your career as the foundation to ensure every new project, promotion, or job has a heavy dose of these elements; then you will be well on your way to career fulfillment.

Doing the *Level 7 Why* exercise will provide new insights and clarity into what motivates you. Anchoring to your why will allow you to persevere when things go sideways. If you are on the treadmill because you're *supposed* to be, because it's what people expect, or because you think it's the only thing that will support your current lifestyle, think again.

Challenge and test your current path to see if it aligns with your ambition, core values, beliefs, and rules, and if it helps you achieve your *Level 7 Why*. Write down your perfect work week and how it fits into your idea of success—then leverage your newfound alignment to write your next chapter.

Find your courage, passion, and purpose by taking small steps to regain your mojo. It won't magically reappear. You *are* the boss of you, and when you're in complete alignment with who you really are, you become unstoppable.

Brain Candy – Important Questions for You to Chew On

Grab your journal and get started on your ABCs for growth.

Assess:

- What big goal are you ready to take off the sidelines?
- Are you your own worst enemy in creating lifestyle requirements that don't align with what's truly important to you?
- Have you been living to please everyone else?

Baseline:

- How closely does your job align with the vibe and work culture that energize you?

- How will your core values help you achieve more and find work that fits you?

- What global beliefs and rules have been holding you back, and how can you reframe or replace them?

Conquer:

- How can your career support your *Level 7 Why* today?

- How can you break free from the status quo and feel more fulfilled?

- Where can you find passion in your work today even if the situation doesn't serve you?

Chapter 7

SETTING YOUR VISION AND STRATEGY

"The harder I work, the luckier I get."

— Samuel Goldwyn

When thinking about your vision, strategy, and execution, imagine planning a trip to the mountains or the beach for a long weekend. You look around and choose a destination that's a five-hour drive away. That destination is your vision; it's where you want to go.

Next, plan your route. Do you want to take the fastest route, avoid toll roads, only take back roads, or stop at a few points of interest along the way? You decide how you will get there, and that is your strategy.

It's time for your long weekend getaway. You follow your navigation system and hit traffic or construction. The navigation system asks you if you'd like to change your route, and you decide. The process of adjusting to things as they happen is your execution.

When you keep things as simple as a five-hour road trip, setting your vision and strategy and making it all happen will be a piece of cake.

Are you ready to chart a new path forward?

Aligning Your Vision, Strategy, and Execution

Do you have a formal career strategy? You spend much more time crafting business strategies than career strategies. Apply the same principles to increase your chances of success.

When you develop a vision at work, you focus on the future, innovation, and aligning with purpose. Add in a splash of inspiration and a pound of motivation, and you're good to go.

Developing a vision for your career is no different. You'll want to take a future-focused view instead of taking things day by day. Your vision should align with your *Level 7 Why*. Your inspiration and motivation come from breaking the cycle and building a career that serves you.

As you apply your strategy, use the same tools you use in business. Think about when you launch a new product or business unit. You want to determine your market position, build your roadmap, execute, monitor performance, and adjust as things change. These are things you probably do without even thinking about them.

Yet when charting your career strategy, staring at a blank screen can feel daunting. And yes, you do need to write out your plan in detail. You're not getting any younger, and your life is too busy to count on your memory to retain all the essential information. Here's how you apply it.

Determine your current market position and identify where you'll be in the highest demand. (We'll get into skill stacking, your "*IT Factor,*" and your three levels of value later, which will help you enormously.) Identify what goals you want to achieve in the short-, mid-, and long-term. Be sure to align your values, vision, edge, *Level 7 Why*, and big goals as you build your overall strategy. I recommend creating your plan up to three years out. Things are changing too fast to plan any farther into the future than that.

Build your plan using the tried and tested SWOT (strengths, weaknesses, opportunities, and threats) process, create a project plan to execute, and develop key performance indicators (KPIs) to track your progress. You inspect what you expect at work; the same goes for your career. Embrace the same level of agility you show in the office as you respond to changing market conditions or consumer demands.

You'll need to find your balance when it comes to agility. Awareness of what's working and what's not and keeping your finger on the pulse of what's happening is essential. Move too fast and you won't have given your strategy enough time to prove itself. Move too slowly and you'll miss golden opportunities. You'll need to decide when and how to adjust. This is a blend of data (KPIs) and gut feeling based on experience.

"Luck is what happens when preparation meets opportunity."

— Seneca

Following your strategy and adjusting as you execute is easier when you are clear on what's most important. Jonathan Westover found his *Level 7 Why* early in his career. His "family first" purpose allowed him to follow a clear (yet indirect) path forward.

After switching majors four times, Jonathan fell in love with training and development. One summer interning for LG Electronics in Korea had him abandoning his aspirations to be an accountant and excited about his new direction.

Jonathan was passionate about working with multiple organizations and helping them maximize their people's potential, so he started working in consulting. Once he started doing the work, he quickly realized it was not for him.

The lifestyle went against everything Jonathan wanted for himself and his family. The travel, the long hours, and the on-demand culture did not align with his vision of having a well-balanced life.

Jonathan considered internal opportunities at large companies. It was no better—working seventy to eighty hours a week, with frequent relocations. It was even worse than the consulting work he was trying to escape.

Jonathan's vision was clear, but most of the roads he tried were full of potholes and detours he wasn't willing to endure. Jonathan needed to find a different path forward. "I love consulting work. I love the research components, and the training, and the teaching. Then it clicked. Why don't I become a professor?"

Jonathan shared this new idea with his wife and went on to get his PhD. He landed his first faculty job and continued consulting through his company Human Capital Innovations. Now he only works on projects that energize him and only when his schedule allows it.

"It wasn't about having a ton of prestige or money. It was about doing something meaningful, fulfilling, and something I was good at and enjoyed. Making these moves was easy because my foundational motivations were clear. My family was my top priority. There are societal norms and pressures about what is valuable and that you should have a career just like everyone else. I had to navigate that and get comfortable with myself. I needed to be willing to set those things aside. I avoided making ego-driven decisions in favor of making priority-based decisions based on my values."

Jonathan knew his joy came from doing meaningful work without sacrificing quality time with his family. He had to pivot several times on his road to success, which was worth it. Because his vision was clear and he adapted his path to achieve it, he was happy with his career. His wife was able to earn her PhD while raising six children. That could not have happened if he had gone the consulting or corporate route.

Balancing Success and Failure

Do you have an unhealthy relationship with failure? Is it a binary relationship of pass/fail, win/lose, succeed/fail? Life isn't like that. Nothing is all good or all bad.

Take any situation right now. Are you failing or succeeding? What you choose, what you focus on, is your reality. It's about perspective and outlook.

With so much fear-mongering and negativity all around us, staying in a positive mindset is difficult. Instead of looking at failure as the opposite of success, look at failure as an essential part of success. We cannot succeed without failure. Treating failure like the enemy and relentlessly avoiding it will destroy opportunities to achieve success. No wonder people are stuck!

When you embrace failure as part of the process and plan for it, you will win. You will thrive when you take an experimental approach instead of a make-or-break approach to your career. I have learned much more from my failures than my wins. The lessons you learn and the battle scars last forever. They make you better, stronger, and more resilient.

It's normal to fear failure. You don't want to lose momentum, look bad, or feel like a schmuck. Think about what could go wrong, plan for failure, and decide what you will do when those bad things happen.

When you do that, you won't lose momentum. You'll accelerate by learning, adjusting, and moving forward. You won't look bad. You'll look smart because you anticipated those things a long time ago. And you won't feel like a schmuck. You'll feel empowered and resilient because setbacks didn't slow you down.

While you are rethinking failure, stop taking everything so seriously and have some fun. Relax and stop making you and everyone else miserable by making small things more significant than they should be.

Embrace humility. When you laugh at yourself and show others you are fallible, you become likable, trustworthy, and less stressed.

Learn how to fail fast and fail forward. Instead of seeing failure as defining moments, treat them as data points. Keep the things that worked, eliminate those that didn't, and replace them with new ideas. As you iterate, you'll work out the kinks and be much farther along than if you had stopped midstream.

> *"You don't learn to walk by following rules.*
> *You learn by doing and falling over."*
>
> — Sir Richard Branson

Sometimes life needs to kick you in the teeth to get your attention. Zach White, the founder of Oasis of Courage, learned this lesson the hard way. Zach is a seasoned overachiever with a mechanical engineering degree from Purdue University. Upon graduation, he was immediately hired into the top talent leadership development program at a Fortune 500 company.

"I was on top of the world, continuing the success streak I'd had throughout my academic career," said Zach. He approached his career the same way he'd approached his whole life: Get smarter and work harder. This approach provided some success, but Zach's career-first approach caused him to lose sight of his personal life. His marriage got rocky, he stopped doing the things he loved, and he started to isolate himself. When things got hard, Zach became a lone wolf, and six years later, he came home to an empty house and a note from his wife asking for a divorce.

Zach had hit rock bottom. Career success and promotions no longer mattered. He no longer cared about the paychecks and bonuses that used to drive his ambition. "I was so unhappy; I was depressed, discouraged, and embarrassed. No one knew my personal life was falling apart. I kept it to myself. This state of mind sent me into a season where I had to ask new questions."

Zach wanted success and recognition at work, but he knew he needed a different approach. He wanted whole-life fulfillment but didn't know where to begin, so he hired his first coach, who helped him align with his vision and purpose. "You can't have success without fulfillment."

A bit of introspection uncovered Zach's tendencies to become hyper-focused on success and achieve the next thing at all costs, ultimately driven by his fear of failure. It took a massive failure in his personal life for him to realize the true cost of fearing failure.

Zach's transformation was significant. He slowly returned to a life of fulfillment and joy. He chased growth, experimentation, and fulfillment, not the next promotion. He no longer had a fixed mindset built on performance and perfection.

Having the tools to create a healthy relationship with failure, Zach was now open to new opportunities and experiences. He was having fun; his positivity and curiosity drew people to him. Many came seeking advice and mentorship to get past their own struggles.

"We need to turn our mess into our message and be willing to be courageous." Zach knew his calling was not to be the world's best engineer. His calling was to help engineers avoid making the same mistakes he had made, find fulfillment and balance earlier in their careers, and achieve whole-life success.

Zach advises his clients to stop pretending they're not afraid. Everyone faces fear and the potential for failure. If you're honest, you can find your way forward and enjoy getting out of your comfort zone. If you want to make a difference and be happy, it takes courage.

Gaining Momentum by Saying No First

Okay, all you people pleasers out there, this one is for you. Did you know you can achieve more by saying no? It's a fascinating concept. You spend your days saying yes to everything. Yes, I'll attend that meeting. Yes, I'll take on that extra project, mentor you, accept a weekly touchpoint routine, and work the weekend. Your yes culture moves steadily forward, adding more to your plate until you are overworked, burnt out, and exhausted.

What if you started with no? My friend, who is a financial mindset coach, introduced me to a similar principle. When it comes to managing your company's finances, she says the first thing to do is scrutinize everything you spend money on. Is it critical to your success? If it's not, kill it. If it is, keep it. And if you're not sure, stop using it for sixty days and then decide.

You can follow the same principle in your work and personal life. Remove every meeting, every project, every committee, and every extra credit activity you are currently committed to. Then, using the work you did in Chapter 6: Creating Your Career Success Blueprint as your baseline, add only the meetings that align, cancel the ones that add no value, and delegate the rest.

There is incredible power in starting with no. When you say no to the things that don't matter, it makes room for saying yes to the things that do. Putting limits on your time elevates your brand and reputation as a strong leader. Freeing up wasted time allows you to focus and make fewer mistakes. No longer running from one useless meeting to the next will enable you to work more closely with your teams and get real work done.

> *"I cannot give you the formula for success, but I can give you the formula for failure, which is: Try to please everybody."*
>
> — Herbert Swope

My client Dierdre was a yes woman. It didn't matter who asked; she was always there to help. She took pride in being a team player and was very popular within the organization. Dierdre was devastated when she was turned down for a promotion she really wanted. It was in her department, she knew the work inside and out, and she thought she was a shoo-in.

Dierdre needed help understanding how someone who did half the work she did got promoted. "It doesn't make sense. I never say no. I'm a team player and excellent at my job."

Dierdre quickly dismissed this as the boys' club or being bad at playing politics. It's easy to blame the system when things don't go your way. But there's always a lesson to learn, so I encouraged her to dig deeper.

Together, we made a list comparing what Dierdre and her peer did. Then we aligned the work with the company priorities. Next, we assigned an effectiveness score based on revenue, productivity, and cost savings. Finally, we compared the two to gain some insights.

Dierdre's holy shit moment hit fast. She immediately saw why she got passed over. While she was busy, helpful, and took on extra work, most of her work didn't matter much. They were doormat projects. She did them because no one else wanted to do them or cared.

When Dierdre looked at her peer, she realized that while he did half the work, nearly everything he did aligned with what was essential for the company and delivered quantifiable results. She started to cry out of frustration. She felt like an idiot who had been taken advantage of.

Dierdre wasn't taken advantage of and wasn't an idiot. She just said yes too often, failed to focus on the critical things, and ran herself ragged. It was time for Dierdre to learn the power of saying no.

The first thing Dierdre needed to do was get clear on her vision, purpose, and goals. This clarity would serve as her foundation for decision-making. Next, we removed all her meetings, responsibilities, and extra credit work. Using her new filters, we added a few things back, delegated others, and built an exit strategy for the things not serving her.

Dierdre's final task was to have a conversation with her boss. She showed her the work we had done comparing her and her former peer. She explained her disappointment and career goals, and together they worked on a solution to get Dierdre out of the low-value business and use her energy and expertise in areas that mattered and would be recognized.

Dierdre is getting better at saying no and has also adopted these principles in her personal life. Having a thriving career and four children requires ruthless prioritization, and now this self-identified people pleaser has become an expert at saying no first so she can say yes to the right things.

Planning for Detours

Do your setbacks define you? They used to define me. Being young, ambitious, and having a high-risk tolerance meant nothing went as planned for me. But it's what you do when things go awry that counts.

Remember that five-hour road trip you were taking? When your navigation system warns you about construction slowdowns ahead, you don't turn around, go home, and scrap the entire adventure. You automatically decide on what you want to do next and keep on driving. Why don't you do that with your career? Or your life for that matter?

Too often, you hit a bump, immediately give up, and turn back. You may think you lack resilience. I disagree. I believe everyone has strength when they're connected to their purpose. What you lack is certainty. I bet if you knew you had to fail thirty-seven times before you reached your goal, you would do it because you knew for sure you'd get what you wanted on the thirty-eighth try.

But you don't know how many times it will take, so you give up. And too often, you give up right before your big win. When you're ready to quit, return to your *Level 7 Why* and regain the resilience you need to persevere.

Several times I have been ready to give up on a dream. Time after time, I would face brick walls, and after a while, I felt exhausted and defeated. It's hard to keep going when there are no guarantees about how many different ways you'll have to try before you get what you want. But there is always a way.

When you hit an obstacle, you only have two choices: Climb over it or go around it. Running through it is way too painful, and with the cost of healthcare these days, who can afford that?

The best way to stay resilient during setbacks is to assume an imperfect path. Think about all the things that can go wrong with each step, come up with alternatives when they happen, and set your success criteria ahead of time.

Set specific criteria so you know your approach is working and check in periodically. Clarity on the micro-goal will help you adjust faster instead of bumbling along to get to the finish line only to realize you've been running the wrong race.

When you plan for detours, anchor to your *Level 7 Why*, and stay out of the binary success/failure trap, you'll have what it takes to reach your loftiest goal.

> *"Discouragement and failure are two of the surest stepping stones to success."*
>
> — Dale Carnegie

One of the most significant detours I had in my career and life was the first time I got fired. I was in the staffing business and had recently relocated my family to New Jersey for a job. My daughter was less than a year old, and my husband was a stay-at-home dad. I had just pivoted to hop on the Y2K and dot-com boom that was gaining momentum.

We were young, in debt, and living from paycheck to paycheck. This job was a big jump in salary, and the bonuses well outpaced traditional staffing work. My new boss was terrific, and the team I was leading knew their shit, which was good because I was still learning. Life was good. I was getting the hang of things, the team was doing well, we were hitting our numbers, and I loved this new pivot.

Then my boss invited me to happy hour. Over a cocktail, he broke the news. He was leaving. He had received a better offer at a competing firm, and the opportunity was too good to pass up. I was happy for him and sad for me. I was six months into the job and felt I had a decent handle on things, so I wasn't too worried about my situation.

A few weeks after he left, my regional director came in. My Spidey senses were tingling from the minute I met him. The misogynistic jerk kept calling me "kiddo" (granted, I was young, but it was a total BS power play) and embodied the antithesis of everything a good leader should be.

I was on full-scale asshole alert. I spent the next two months playing whack-a-mole with every trivial request and rabbit hole he sent me down. He criticized my team and loved to embarrass them on the sales floor. It was miserable.

Then one Wednesday, I walked into the office and barely had the chance to put down my coffee before he fired me. My job was over immediately. No warning, no severance, no medical coverage. I was to get my shit, get out, and fuck off. I was shocked. I had a family to support, bills to pay, no money in the bank, and only two weeks of pay coming to me.

I packed up my shit, fired off a few expletives his way, and drove home. My husband met me at the door and said, "You're home early." I tried to make a joke about the gravy train being over, but I burst into tears instead. I lay on the couch and cried for three days.

The self-doubt (I should have stayed in staffing), inner critic (why would I think I could be successful in this industry—look at me?), panic (I don't have a college degree, and I've just been fired. No one will hire me), and disappointment (My daughter will have to go to daycare, I've failed my family) ran in a continuous loop in my head.

On day four, I decided I couldn't make a living crying on the couch and needed to get my act together. I still felt like a complete failure, a fraud, and I knew no one would hire me after what had happened.

I was doing it for my family and my *Level 7 Why*. I knew I had gotten us into this mess, and I needed to get us out. If I hadn't been so greedy (aka ambitious), and I didn't have this compulsion to grow and achieve more, I could have been in my previous job for decades, and we'd be safe living happily ever after. I would have been bored out of my mind, but we would have been safe.

Luckily for me, we were in the early days of a tech boom, and all our competitors knew my regional manager was a flaming asshole. The minute I started putting my resume out there, I felt like a professional athlete who just became a free agent. Interviews came fast, offers came faster, and I had my choice of excellent opportunities, paying more money, with great people to work with.

I hadn't been prepared for unexpected changes, but I had dodged a bullet. My quest to grow my career as quickly as possible didn't turn out as expected. But I found another way to achieve my goals, and I believe you can too.

Summary

Consider the road trip analogy when setting your career vision, your strategy, and how to execute it. When there are detours ahead, you don't turn around and go home. You change course and keep going. It's a great lesson to embrace for your career and your life.

As you create your vision and strategy, use the same principles you use at work. Consider the future and your uniqueness, use the SWOT process, create a project plan, establish your KPIs, and be sure to measure them regularly. Inspect what you expect at work and in your personal life.

You can't have success without failing. When you treat everything like an experiment, you can keep the things that are working, eliminate the things that aren't, and replace them with new ideas as you move forward.

Saying no first will set you up for extraordinary growth. Keep things that align with your goals and values. Get rid of everything that doesn't. And delegate the things you're not sure about. Saying no first leaves more room to say yes to strategic thinking and working closely with your team to get better work done.

Detours are inevitable. Whoever said it's not about the destination, it's about the journey never had a huge goal and a tight timeline. You don't lack resilience; you lack certainty. Assume imperfection and focus on your micro-goals to avoid running the wrong race.

Brain Candy – Important Questions for You to Chew On

Grab your journal and get started on your ABCs for growth.

Assess:

- Is failure the enemy?
- How comfortable are you with saying no?
- Have setbacks been slowing you down?

Baseline:

- How can you view your setbacks differently?

- What would it look like if you cleared every obligation from your work and personal calendars and only put back what aligned with your values and goals?

- What micro goals can you set to stay the course and adapt quickly?

Conquer:

- What can you do to start failing forward?

- What can you eliminate or delegate right now?

- How will you define success at each step so you can quickly assess what is and isn't working?

Chapter 8

PLAYING TO YOUR STRENGTHS

"Find out what you like doing best, and get someone to pay you for doing it."

— Katharine Whitehorn

You have the focus, alignment, and strategic plan to get some cool stuff done. It's time to concentrate on how you will achieve your goals. If you are like most, you spend too much time doing something you don't enjoy or aren't very good at.

If you could spend 80 percent of your day doing the things that come naturally to you, you would be a whirling dervish of productivity and joy.

Instead, you spend countless hours doing work that doesn't come naturally because it's part of your job. Most of your self-development time is spent trying to get mediocre at something you're bad at instead of becoming excellent at things you're good at. You should be playing to your strengths much more.

Fatou Darboe's blog post for CRM.org, "Why You Should Play to Your Strengths at Work," cites the results from a Gallup study on people who use their strengths every day and found that, "People using talents and strengths can lead to improved health and wellness; less worry, stress, anger, sadness, and physical pain; more positive emotions; and increased energy. The study showed that people who use their strengths and talents daily are six times more likely to be engaged at work."

I think Darboe's findings ring true—I have experienced this truth myself. You feel energized and get more done when you do work you love. When you slog through the day doing work you hate, your productivity takes a nosedive.

Whether you want to call it your superpower, zone of genius, *IT Factor*, sweet spot, or anything else fashionable, playing to your strengths is essential to a thriving career.

Let's explore how to double-down on your strengths and thrive.

Strengthening Your Natural Talents

If you had to list your top three superpowers, what would they be? You have some work to do if the answer doesn't come instantaneously. You can't strengthen your natural talents until you know what they are.

Julie Riga is an author, Ted-X speaker, podcaster, and executive coach for CWC. Her varied career path and a random encounter with a stranger at a wedding shaped her superpowers into an incredible career.

Julie loved all things radio, TV, film, and music. Her time as a DJ for her college radio station and as a personal assistant for well-known rap artists gave her a perspective she would have never had if she had gone straight into a corporate career.

When Julie's days as a personal assistant ended, she was trying to figure out her next move. She had no idea a random conversation with a stranger at a wedding would hand her the key to the next phase of her career in the pharmaceutical industry.

Julie was excited to work for a major pharmaceutical company, but once she got there, she hated every minute of it. She went from pursuing her dream of fame and fortune to counting the minutes until her lunch break as she managed stacks and stacks of regulatory compliance documents.

Once again, fate stepped in, and a mentor appeared. She showed Julie how to grow in a large company, network, and create jobs aligned with her passions from the opportunities presented to her.

Julie's superpowers were learning cutting-edge technology, simplifying processes, and telling a great story. She showcased her talents in each role. "In every job I took, I did something big. If it wasn't interesting, I made it interesting."

These superpowers and a heavy dose of ambition helped Julie quickly move up the ranks. Her days of counting pieces of paper were replaced by leading critical projects and managing teams.

Caught up in a big layoff, Julie struggled to find her next big opportunity. She attended a workshop for Stephen Covey's 7 Habits of Highly Effective People. Creating a life around her mission statement was a transformational mindset shift for Julie. She shared her knowledge and coached anyone who showed an interest. She enjoyed coaching so much she continued training in it.

Julie had finally found her passion. "I would go to class and think to myself, *There's nowhere I'd rather be than right here.* When I was in the class, it was freaking magical. I enjoyed every moment of it. I was fully present. I was in my element."

Excited and passionate about coaching and personal development, Julie reentered the pharmaceutical industry and became a director-level executive. "I would raise my hand to host panel discussions. We did a lot of live events, and I was the interviewer. I was passionate about leading the discussions and facilitating large meetings. I said yes to everything, which gave me the skills and experience to lead."

Julie oversaw leadership development training and onboarding for a department with about 11,000 people. Understanding how big organizations worked, the challenge the leaders faced, and how to manage stakeholders set her up with the personal experience she needed to start her own coaching company, Stay on Course.

As Julie grew from a paper pusher to a director supporting a huge team, she continued to strengthen her natural talents and customize her jobs to showcase her natural talents. "I was kind of a unicorn. I didn't fit in. I had a lot of passion and purpose and didn't navigate my career like everyone else."

Julie's advice to her clients is, "Be a unicorn. Have a passion for what you do, and get excited for Mondays. When you do, everything in your life comes into focus and gets better."

> *"Change the game to suit your strengths…use*
> *your strengths to change the game."*
>
> — Annette Lynch

Don't confuse what you're good at with what you enjoy. You are often good at many things, but only a few will energize you. Monitor your energy levels as you go through your day and identify the things that check all the boxes.

Once you know your strengths, do everything possible to make them even stronger. Find a mentor or a coach, learn from the gurus, create opportunities to use these skills as much as possible, take on new projects, and test different approaches as you go.

Every job will require you to do things you're not good at or don't like. While you can't avoid all of this, you can drastically shift the balance of where you spend your time. The more time you spend playing to your strengths, the more successful you will be. Your brand will be elevated, and people's perception of you as a leader will improve.

Breaking the Toxic Cycle of Self-Improvement

Are you always trying to fix something about yourself? According to Grand View Research, in 2022, the self-help industry was worth a staggering forty-three billion dollars, and Wordsrated estimates ten million self-help books were sold that same year. The industry has exploded, and forecasts continue to rise.

Self-improvement is all the rage these days. If you are unhappy, there are answers for you, which is probably why you're reading this book. Continuous improvement is essential, and working through challenges with others to guide you is the fastest way to become the best version of yourself. I fully support continuing to raise the bar and get better. It keeps life challenging and exciting. You are on a quest for growth, and that is fantastic.

When does the quest for self-improvement turn toxic? When it stops you from acting. When it makes you feel like you're not enough, and when it sucks you into the delayed happiness trap.

I have a friend and former client, Tracy, who is a self-help book junkie. With each book, she would read, journal, create her plan, and then move on to her next book. She missed the most crucial part. Tracy never took action. After some prodding, she finally put down the books and implemented some of what she'd learned. That's when things started to change.

Tracy went from feeling defeated and overwhelmed to taking baby steps toward making the mindset shifts she needed. She limited herself to one book per quarter so she could take the time to implement what she'd learned.

Continuous growth comes from strengthening your strengths and learning new approaches to improve your performance. Joy comes from doing what you love and are naturally good at. Confidence comes from taking action. Now you hold the keys to having all three.

"Not too many people could walk a mile in your shoes.
Only you know your struggles, challenges, and obstacles;
so be proud of how far you've come."

— Edmond Mbiaka

If you suck at something, you're never going to be excellent at it. You might become less sucky after spending time, effort, and resources, but you will never be great. That is no reason to feel inadequate.

The theory that you can be excellent at anything if you just work hard enough is complete crap. I disagree with the notion that everyone can be an eagle. No, they can't, and why would everyone want to be an eagle? What if you want to be a flamingo? Or a peacock? Can you imagine a world full of eagles and nothing else? How dull!

Feeling like you have to fix something about yourself is a terrible mindset. You don't need fixing. You may need some refining and a tune-up occasionally, but you are not broken. Spending your life thinking you need to be fixed prevents you from growing and puts you in a scarcity mindset.

Insecurity is a common motivator, but it's a toxic source. Any improvement efforts rooted in insecurity are bound to fail simply because they didn't start from a position of strength. When you accept yourself as you are, flaws and all, you can truly grow.

Beauty lies in imperfection. Grace and humility come with escaping the perfection trap. Lessons in teamwork can be learned by relying on others' talents, and empowerment comes from knowing how to think differently.

Compensating for Your Weaknesses

Do you know how to hide your weaknesses? I'll share a dirty little secret about how the most visionary leaders do it. They don't hide them at all. The best leaders have a keen self-awareness that many people lack. This perspective allows them to quickly identify the things they aren't good at and take action.

These leaders don't waste valuable time fixing their weaknesses. They spend their time finding exceptional people who possess the talents they lack. When you have a liability, chances are good you also hate whatever requires that skill.

When you have a strength, you can do something for twelve hours straight and never tire. Why wouldn't you want to surround yourself with people who are good at and love to do all the things you hate? It's a win-win for everyone.

Creating a stopgap for your skill gap is a logical approach to compensating for your weaknesses, yet only some people do it. Why? Because many people perceive others who are good at things as threats. Letting the competition in could jeopardize their position, make them look bad, and expose the soft underbelly of their leadership brand.

The perception of better is an interesting one. What if you changed your mindset and swapped out the word better for different? People who are different from you add value, help you gain new perspectives, and do the work better and faster than you can. When you embrace a "we win as a team" mindset, and have the confidence to surround yourself with excellence, you improve your leadership presence and accelerate your career.

> *"Never doubt that a small group of thoughtful, concerned citizens can change the world. Indeed it is the only thing that ever has."*
>
> — Margaret Mead

Throughout my career, I have always surrounded myself with people I felt were smarter than me. I had to have intelligent people around me because I lacked the skills to do everything myself. Every time I got promoted, I dealt with increasingly complex business problems and was farther away from knowing how to do the work myself. I knew I had finally mastered whatever I was leading when I could confidently ask a question instead of worrying about sounding stupid.

A great example of something outside my wheelhouse was math. I suck at it. Always have and always will. I can run a P&L better than most, but I struggled during metrics meetings, projecting trends, pouring over reams of data, and working with our actuaries and quants. My propeller doesn't spin that fast.

I initially felt like a failure and tried to hide that I couldn't keep up. Eventually, I realized there was power in admitting I was confused and didn't understand. Instead of hiding my weakness, I made sure everyone knew about it. That way, they took extra time to put things in terms I could understand.

As a result, I could make better business decisions. I empowered my teams to do their jobs. They had a strong voice at my leadership table because they had my trust and skills I lacked.

While I always thought they were smarter than me, they weren't. They were different from me. They lacked the skills to translate their geek speak into business terms, and I lacked the deep understanding of the data to make sound decisions. It was a match made in heaven.

I always hired leaders with a better grasp on the pulse of how the team felt so they could tell me when I needed to slow down or communicate better. I had leaders on my team who were more risk-averse, which protected the business from my rose-colored glasses when it came time to create a new strategy. I had creative thinkers who would devise unique solutions that never occurred to me.

None of these people threatened my career—quite the opposite. Because of them and our collective teamwork, I could grow faster than most, and so did they. If I had to rely exclusively on my own skills, you wouldn't be reading this book right now.

Revealing Your Blind Spots

How much honesty can you handle? Some people do not like to hear their baby is ugly. Call it what you want—feedback, constructive criticism, observations—you may say you want the gift of feedback, but research proves otherwise.

In a *Harvard Business Review* article titled "Negative Feedback Rarely Leads to Improvement," Scott Berinato interviewed doctoral candidate Paul Green who shared his findings on negative feedback. In summary, people who received criticism from peers or their business partners looked for new people to work with. Paul also spoke of the psychological threat negative feedback poses. Essentially, we don't like and we avoid people who give us negative feedback because it makes us feel bad.

You're stuck in this contentious battle. You're not perfect, and you push people away who will tell you the things you don't want to hear. Flying blind and unskilled is a dangerous way to lead and can lead to disaster.

Seek negative feedback proactively. Transparency becomes particularly important the higher up in an organization you go because the higher you are, the more three dynamics work against you. First, you move farther from work and lack first-hand knowledge of how work gets done. Second, people are less likely to be completely honest with you. Third, the decisions you make have far-reaching implications.

Surround yourself with people who will tell you what's happening and what you need to hear in clear, direct terms. Without this added information, you will make avoidable mistakes.

Knowing it's not your natural tendency to embrace negative feedback, how do you know if you send the right signals to your managers that it's safe to deliver bad news? When you solicit feedback, make it a requirement (not a request) to give you the unfiltered truth about what's happening.

Set up conversations in which your managers must poke holes in your ideas and share the problems the teams are facing. Have private feedback conversations with each of your leaders regularly to get a clearer picture of what is happening.

Don't reward your ass-kissers. Publicly acknowledge the brave leaders who do the right thing. Don't be defensive. Listen intently and take action when someone is brave enough to give you the feedback you need.

When you surround yourself with people who will tell you your baby is ugly and you give them a safe environment, you will develop stronger relationships, expose your blind spots, avoid mistakes, grow faster, and motivate your teams.

"Great leaders are not defined by the absence of weakness, but rather by the presence of clear strengths."

— John Zenger

Simon Bocko has the desirable combination of raw talent and endless ambition. He found his love for marketing early in his schooling and took a year off to work in the field. He received four pay raises and had a job offer after graduation.

Simon turned down that job offer in favor of working for one of the world's top five public relations firms. "I was hyper-ambitious to the point I didn't have a life. If you couldn't fit around my work life, you didn't stick around for long."

Simon got his first big break with the NHS account. The United Kingdom's National Healthcare Service had a tiny budget, and no one paid much attention to the account. To the surprise of the executive team, Simon took this opportunity to showcase his talents. He grew the account from two-hundred-fifty pounds to thousands of pounds per month. His bosses were thrilled and showered him with significant pay increases and more responsibilities.

His working style was direct and fast-paced. He'd limit meetings to ten minutes, wouldn't suffer fools, and would brazenly call out the elephants in the room everyone was tiptoeing around.

Simon's ambition outpaced every company he worked for. "I would work for a year in a job, and then I'd be out and on to the next one. I got promoted year after year for ten years by jumping from place to place. I'd get to the top, get fed up with that, and go on to the next thing."

Then Simon had an epiphany. "I hit a point where I realized I was hopping around all these jobs and nothing worked. The problem is me; it's not the work." It was a tough pill to swallow. Simon asked a mentor who was further ahead on his journey for advice.

Simon's mentor told him a story that stuck with him. His mentor used to work in a large management consultancy business and was the highest performer. He had started a new division and made the most money and the highest margins. He was a lone ranger, and everyone thought he was an idiot. Simon's mentor got fired. On paper, it made no sense. He was a high performer, had the highest profit, and had low overhead; he was a machine. But no one wanted to work with him. He told Simon, "People will forget what you do, but they will always remember how you made them feel."

Simon realized he was trying to be the cleverest person in the room. He wasn't bringing everyone along on a journey. He wasn't trying to galvanize everyone around an idea. "I was just that smartass in the corner who said, 'I know the answers; now go do it.' So I changed. I galvanized people and got everyone to work together. I helped everyone find common ground so we could all move forward together. That's when things started going better at work—when I stopped being a smartass lone ranger and became someone who united people and listened."

Simon's interests started to shift from working for the business to running the business. Branding was interesting, but business became more interesting. "I sometimes got frustrated with clients when I was more ambitious for their organization and business than they were. I felt like the person I was working for had put a handbrake on their success, and I didn't want to work for a business that wasn't ambitious. That's why I decided to start my own."

If Simon hadn't discovered his blind spot, he'd still be hopping from job to job, wondering why everyone else was so daft. Today, Simon's business, Evolve, is thriving, and he's no longer a lone ranger. He and his team help high-growth businesses rebrand and prepare for transformation.

Summary

You want to be known as a leader who can get things done. Playing to your strengths will advance your career faster than continuously trying to become adequate at the things you're not suited for naturally.

Discover that sweet spot between your talents and what you enjoy doing. Maximize the time you spend doing the things you're best at so you can showcase your strengths.

End your unhealthy relationship with self-improvement. Not everyone can be an eagle, nor should they want to be. Embrace your inner flamingo or peacock, accept your flaws, and do what you do best.

Find as many people as you can who love to do the things you suck at. They aren't your competition; they are your lifeline. Surround yourself with people who will tell you your baby is ugly. You're in dangerous territory when you start to buy your own BS. Create a safe environment and require your leaders to tell you everything you need to hear, especially if you aren't going to like it.

Brain Candy – Important Questions for You to Chew On

Grab your journal and get started on your ABCs for growth.

Assess:

- What are your superpowers?
- Are you ready to expose your weaknesses and surround yourself with people who have talents you don't have?
- Will your managers be candid with you?

Baseline:

- How often are you able to do work you enjoy?
- What gaps do you have that are holding you back?
- Do you create a safe environment for your managers to give you bad news?

Conquer:

- Where can your talents be showcased more broadly so you can reach your goals?
- What if instead of trying to fix something, you focused on improving your current awesomeness?

- Do you have the right people on your team to compensate for your weaknesses?

Everyone deserves to love Mondays.

Chapter 9

CRUSHING THE FEARSOME FOUR

"Doubt kills more dreams than failure ever will."

— Suzy Kassem

Your inner voice drives how you interact with the world. As you go through the journey of escaping the career trap, ensuring you have a healthy inner voice is essential. So, you'll need to crush the fearsome four.

What happens when you get a snarky email? If you're in a positive frame of mind, you're like, "Hey, I don't quite understand what you said. Would you mind explaining that to me?" If you're in a bad state of mind, you immediately think the person is a jerk and trying to sabotage you.

Have you seen that image where a perfect banana is in front of a mirror and the image reflected is a banana full of brown spots and bruising? The image resonates with many people. What do you see when you look in the mirror? Do you see the perfect banana or the damaged one?

You don't usually share what's going on in your head. When was the last time you told your boss, "Hey, I'm feeling a little insecure today. Let's talk about it over coffee."? Probably never. You don't say these things out loud. You keep them all in your head and assume they don't affect anyone else, but they do.

A negative inner voice will cause you to be more reluctant to take risks, slow down your decision-making process, make you a less effective communicator, and cause hesitation when you need to advocate for yourself.

It affects your team because they question their loyalty to you as their leader. They stop bringing ideas forward, get frustrated, become confused, and lose focus. Your company will see it through missed deliverable deadlines, loss of employee engagement, a stagnant operating environment, and weaker business results.

You think you can put on your game face as you start each day. No matter how good you think you are when your inner voice rages, it causes havoc for everyone around you.

When your inner voice starts going haywire, pay attention to your thoughts because words matter. Find the fact-fiction balance; only some things you tell yourself are true. Get an outsider's opinion to gain the clarity you can't find. Eliminate the haters because they suck and only make things worse. Find your center and stay true to who you are.

How do you lead through all the background buzz and get to a good head space? You conquer the fearsome four. When you think about your negative self-talk, you may lump all the negativity into one big category, but there are four: your inner critic, second-guessing, imposter syndrome, and low self-confidence.

The fearsome four are cyclical. Triggers bring these negative mindsets to the forefront. The chances of eliminating their guest appearances are low, but you can shorten how long they stay so you don't languish in the spin cycle of despair any longer than you have to.

When you break down the negativity of your inner voice into four categories, you can start to deal with them differently. Each member of the fearsome four is unique, shows up at different times, and requires different strategies to overcome.

Let's get to work and crush the fearsome four.

Ending the Cycle of Self-Sabotage

Are you your own worst enemy? If you have a hyperactive inner critic, you may be responsible for slowing down yourself and your team. Everyone has insecurities; most of the time, they are your deepest, darkest secrets. Have you listened to your inner critic lately?

Your inner critic is the voice within that expresses thoughts about your self-image. You'll think things like, *I'm different. There's something wrong with me. I'm* (fill in the blank).

Most of the time, your inner critic lurks in the background, and it's doing more damage than you realize. It's like drinking tainted water. You can't taste it, you feel fine, and then you gradually start showing symptoms of being poisoned years later.

Our clients get up close and personal with their inner critic, and here's how they do it. Carry a notebook and pen for a week. Every time your inner critic speaks up, write down precisely what it's saying word for word, even if you've written it down before. Don't ignore repetition, no matter how many times you've written it down. Writing by hand and not typing is essential here.

Take your week's worth of inner critic quotes and organize them according to what you say to yourself, from the most frequent to the least. Then (I know you'll feel ridiculous doing this) stand in front of the mirror and read every phrase out loud using a mean voice.

Break down your inner critic's statements into two categories— thoughts you know are total BS and thoughts you genuinely believe.

I recommend giving your inner critic a name, maybe someone you hated in high school. Then, with statements you know are complete BS, whenever those thoughts come up, say, "Shut up, Karen," or whichever name you choose, and move on with your day. Remember, you've already dismissed these as invalid.

When the thoughts you genuinely believe rear their ugly head, dig in, find evidence to the contrary, and reframe your thinking. Look for moments from your past when you've been in a similar situation and had a successful outcome. The next time you need to quiet your inner critic, be prepared to remind yourself of all the times you've conquered this demon.

> *"Make sure your own worst enemy doesn't live between your own two ears."*
>
> — Laird Hamilton

Shilpa Joshi was determined to be independent as soon as possible so she could create her own life and choose her husband. She began her career with a national airline carrier and took on many roles to learn and grow. After she had her child, she couldn't work the weird hours and switched to banking.

Shilpa was incredibly successful during the two decades she spent in banking. She continued to get promoted, take on senior management roles, and ultimately became the president of a prominent bank in India.

As Shilpa navigated her career, she didn't get much coaching or mentoring, so her skills in leadership, conflict management, stakeholder management, and dealing with critical, high-pressure situations were self-taught.

"People see your journey and the outcome and think it was easy for you. They have no idea how scary it can be sometimes. It didn't matter how great the culture and my coworkers were, I fought my inner critic every single day."

Whenever Shilpa changed roles, she felt she had to prove herself again. "You can't share your vulnerability or weaknesses because people will second-guess your capabilities. Sometimes being a leader doesn't give you the space to be human. My inner critic walks with me all the time. She's not always raging but is always there. If I got a win, the second-guessing and self-doubt would kick in. Every time you leave your comfort zone, your inner critic will be the first one waiting for you."

Shilpa believes her inner critic serves to keep her safe, but at the same time, she strives for growth, and that conflict is always present.

In 2020, with the advent of COVID-19, Shilpa faced an entirely new challenge. She needed to look after multiple teams, manage the new work-from-home situation, support team members who were struggling to catch up, keep the regulators informed, and maintain the workflow. All of this while dealing with her family, personal health, and financial challenges during this uncertain time.

"It was one of the most difficult leadership challenges ever. Getting through it made me stronger and made me realize what I can do despite the challenges. We stayed together as a team and are all the better for it."

Shilpa focuses on clarity, consistency, and correction when her inner critic visits her. When it starts to raise its ugly head, Shilpa looks for clarity, asking herself, "Why is this happening? What do I need to work on?"

Once Shilpa has clarity, she takes courageous action. Shilpa knows only action can drive out fear. Nothing else. From her bold action, she continues to learn and correct. She has an experimental mindset and doesn't consider failure the enemy. She knows it's part of success and essential for growth. This approach has strengthened her resilience and influence.

Despite all this success, Shilpa still felt something was missing. She felt like she had done all she could in banking and was ready to do something more meaningful. Her inner critic showed up again.

"You work for a great company, have a big job, fancy title, chauffeur-driven car, and everyone thinks you are successful. And when you're unhappy, it feels like you don't have a reason to complain."

Shilpa has gained a lot of experience controlling her inner critic and didn't let it stop her from starting her coaching practice. "I felt compelled to help others transform their careers and become better leaders. It's time for the next generation to step up and make their mark." Through her company, Impact Valley, Shilpa is helping new leaders make their way.

Using Second-Guessing as an Asset

Second-guessing isn't a good thing—or is it? It can either slow you down and make you question every decision you've ever made, or it can inform you about what went well and what didn't and lead to continuous improvement. Which would you prefer?

You look into the past when you get stuck in a second-guessing loop. You may be thinking, *I should have. Was that right? What do others think?* This thought process can be beneficial when you use its powers for good and not evil.

If you let your second-guessing run out of control, you'll stop trusting yourself and your instincts. It may be triggered by a fear of committing, which can cause you to give up ownership of a decision, leading to lower self-confidence and self-esteem.

How do you transform second-guessing from a paralyzing inferiority complex to an empowering tool that moves you forward? You treat it like a project and do a post-mortem. When a major project is complete, you get the team around the table and discuss the good, the bad, and the ugly. There are no tears (at least there shouldn't be), no handwringing, and no self-loathing. It's just a factual recap of how things played out.

The team has something to celebrate, lessons to apply next time, a few new ideas, and a few missteps that must be corrected. Do the same thing. Reflect on these elements when your second-guessing starts to spin out of control.

Be objective, test and challenge your negative thoughts, and come away with things you want to start, stop, and continue doing. You want to start doing something new, stop doing something that isn't working, and continue doing the things that work well.

"A mind troubled by doubt cannot focus on the course to victory."

— Arthur Golden

How does a high school British literature teacher in Texas become a counter-terrorism adviser working with senior White House officials? It's a story I was excited to discover when talking to John Schoew, CEO of Storied Future Ventures. With John's impressive background, you would never guess his primary motivation for success was deeply rooted in the fearsome four.

John attended graduate school at The Georgetown School for Foreign Service, where he studied national security, foreign policy, international business, and diplomacy. While he was there, he covered congressional hearings and wrote reports for leaders in the UN. He also met a lot of cool people during his time in Georgetown.

John cut his teeth on strategy and management consulting working at Monitor—a company founded by Michael Porter—the godfather of strategy at Harvard Business School. He met and worked for Richard Clark, the head of counterterrorism at the White House under the Clinton and Bush administrations. He and Clark opened an office in Abu Dhabi, working with its crown prince and other national security and intelligence agencies and companies in the region advising on cybersecurity and counterterrorism.

John then pivoted and became a partner at a boutique management consulting firm focused on cybersecurity and national security in the Middle East and for big pharma. They sold the firm to Accenture, where John was a managing director advising on cybersecurity in the healthcare, life sciences, and government sectors.

How did John make so many successful pivots? The imposter syndrome and second-guessing fueled John's ambition. He grew up in a small town in West Virginia, and his dad never made much money.

Every time John did something, it was a new situation for him. "I was always coming into new situations, environments, economic situations, and locations. I always felt like I was on the outside looking in."

John needed external motivation to grow. "I wouldn't stretch myself as far as I could on my own. I just didn't have it in me. I was too afraid to mess up. Putting myself in situations I knew would stretch me and pull me along gave me more confidence and the skills to achieve more."

John's survival trigger propelled him into a fantastic career. The fearsome four always lurking in the background caused him to build the skills to learn quickly and successfully adapt to new situations. He traded on his intellectual horsepower instead of being a perfect fit for a job.

John has a fascinating analogy about career growth. He starts with an image of two gears on an analog watch. One larger and one smaller. "We're on a certain orbit, a certain trajectory. And there are moments when the smaller gear we're on interfaces with a much larger gear. Often the large gear is out of reach because it's too far. Every so often, the big gear comes into contact with where you are on the small gear. At that moment, the step between those gears is relatively small. It's about timing and recognizing the opportunity as one of those moments."

John advises his clients, "Don't be afraid to be in situations when you're over skis. Build a great team, hire people who can be mentors, make them part of your network, and learn from them. Embrace an experimental mindset and continuously learn. Binary outcomes won't position you for the success you aim for."

Shortening the Imposter Syndrome Cycle

How long will it take before they find out you're a fraud? If your inner voice asks this, my friend, you have a massive case of imposter syndrome. The imposter syndrome is the most persistent member of the fearsome four if you are ambitious and take risks.

When you are in growth mode, you lack the knowledge others expect you to have, triggering all kinds of swirls in your head.

Imposter syndrome is how you process others' perceptions. You may find yourself thinking, *I'm a fraud. I don't belong here. Everyone will find out.* While this syndrome is primarily associated with women, I am here to tell you all men have it too. They just don't talk about their feelings, so the only ones who find out are their coaches and advisers, who are sworn to secrecy.

The more you do things you've never done, the more often this little beauty will show up to make you suffer. What are you supposed to do if you can't get rid of it?

Create your plan to shorten the cycle. When you know what triggers you, you can head it off, turn a death spiral into a speed bump, and get on with your day. When your imposter syndrome kicks in, listen to your inner voice and put your thoughts into one of two categories, emotional responses, and skill gaps.

For your emotional triggers, go back to the work you did for your inner critic and use those techniques to work through your emotional responses. Focus on closing your skill gaps. Get into high gear, learn what you need to, admit what you don't know, and come up to speed as fast as possible.

"Too many of us are not living our dreams
because we are living our fears."

— Les Brown

This process worked for me throughout my career. My imposter syndrome would fire up every time I started a new job. It was usually a promotion, and I felt like I was in way over my head. My inner voice would say things like, "I'm too young. I don't deserve this job. Everyone will know I'm a fraud."

This hit home hardest for me in a moment later in my career. I was in financial services and was put on a new team to solve a massive problem during the 2008 financial crisis. The stakes were high. I was surrounded by attorneys, regulatory experts, and high-powered business leaders. I felt like a fish out of water every single day.

I remember being in one senior leader's office where we were literally screaming at each other. I was stressed and terrified, but I stood my ground. Then, in the middle of our argument, his admin put through a call and he put it on speaker so I could hear the conversation.

My jaw dropped and I froze when the person on the other end spoke. It was a presidential candidate. The first debate had been the previous night, and the conversation started like, "Hey, dude, how'd I do last night?" (I'm paraphrasing here.) The conversation continued for about twenty minutes.

What the hell? I'm sitting here arguing with this man, and he is advising someone who could be our next president! It was surreal. I tried not to look like it affected me and failed miserably. I'm sure it was clear I was dumbfounded and a bit awestruck.

He hung up, we finished our argument (I lost), and I marched straight into my boss' office. I closed her door and started ranting, pacing, and dropping F-bombs as I recounted the story. I asked her, "Why am I even here? I am so out of my depth, and I feel like a total loser."

She let me rant for a bit, and when I started to calm down a little, she started to laugh. She asked me if I was finished. That cleared my head, and I started to laugh too. She said, "You are here because you aren't like the others. You were not part of the problem. You see things differently and aren't afraid to challenge. You are here because you get shit done."

It took me a while to honestly believe that, but over the next few months, I did start to see evidence of what she was talking about.

Reframing Low Self-Confidence Moments

Does your confidence come and go? It's a strange feeling to go through phases of your life when your confidence is sky high, and then at other times, your self-confidence takes a nosedive. When you have an accidental career, you are used to things moving along steadily and feeling like you've got everything under control.

When things start to go off track, your self-confidence goes on an extended vacation, and some days you don't know if or when it's coming back. You don't have these moments often and may lack experience in rebounding.

You start comparing yourself to others when you feel stuck in a low self-confidence moment. You may be thinking, *I can't do XYZ. I'm not enough.*

When you lack confidence, you are tired, withdrawn, indecisive, and put up with a lot more crap than you usually would. It often seems like you are drowning in a sea of worry and fear. But there is a way out.

Know the feeling is temporary, and you have the tools to rebound. You haven't always been like this, so go back to your rockstar moments and reflect on how awesome things have been in the past. Focus on doing things that energize you with people who energize you, and don't be afraid to ask for help.

I went through a period where my confidence was very low. I made a few big mistakes and brutally punished myself for them. My boss and I were very close, so he asked me what was wrong. I told him how I felt. "I just need a win." That day we spun up a small project in my wheelhouse, I rallied the team, and we got a quick win after a few months. This win went a long way to helping me get my mojo back.

If you say, "I can't," change it to "How can I?" Find a path forward; it's always there, and when you open yourself up to the possibilities and remove the roadblocks of negativity, you'll get out of your slump in no time.

"Nothing is impossible. The word itself says 'I'm possible!'"

— Audrey Hepburn

Walter Dusseldorp felt the calling to be an entrepreneur early in his career. Twenty years later, he finally made his dream come true. The whole time, the fearsome four were lurking in the background.

Although Walter's calling to be an entrepreneur was delayed, his path prepared him for his ultimate purpose. A native of the Netherlands, he moved to the US when he was eighteen with big dreams of becoming a doctor.

While those plans didn't work out, his passion for the healthcare industry remained constant. Starting as a paramedic, he shifted to following his passion for improving the healthcare system. He had aspirations of making it to the top. "As a CEO, I can help create my vision of healthcare that significantly impacts the patient experience."

Walter leveraged his MBA to learn and dig into every nook and cranny of the hospital's inner workings. He became an expert by understanding the business' foundation, organizational structure, financials, operating capital, and operational elements.

Walter missed being closer to the patients and moved to a more extensive healthcare system, where he was able to lead nurses and physicians. "This job was everything I loved. I could work with the medical providers and show them a better way. Now I had a team of almost 2,000 people and couldn't do everything myself. I made the transition from doing to leading and learned how to delegate and how to love the people I led."

It was time to make a pivot into the for-profit world. Walter led the Eastern Region of a leading lab and diagnostics company. When he arrived, the group was in disarray. He was leading eighty supervisors, helping them run their locations, fixing the operations, and being responsible for everything that happened. The scale and complexity challenged Walter beyond what he could have imagined.

Walter loved the work and hated how public companies operated. Every year, companies over-promised their earnings to their shareholders. Then, in the fourth quarter, Walter had to lay off people who were making forty-thousand dollars a year. That was something he couldn't come to terms with. In 2021, with significant layoffs at his company and elsewhere, Walter was offered a buyout. He took it.

It was time to realize his entrepreneurial dream. Walter started the Dutch Mentor, a leadership development program for clinical leaders to help them lead teams with vision and strong leadership fundamentals.

Walter would have started his entrepreneurial career a decade earlier if he had possessed more confidence and higher risk tolerance. "I knew I had the skills, knowledge, and attributes to succeed with what I'm doing today. But because of my lack of confidence in being a successful entrepreneur and being risk-averse, I waited."

Walter advises people who dread Mondays to increase their self-awareness and get in touch with their *why*. "Connect to the four Ps—passion, purpose, people, and the process. If you don't feel connected to these things, it's time to move on and set yourself up for success."

Summary

Your inner critic reflects your self-image. Second-guessing is when you look backward. The imposter syndrome focuses on others' perceptions. Low self-confidence is when you are comparing yourself to others.

Are monsters or dust bunnies hiding under your bed? It's time to take a look and find out. The fearsome four represent the different aspects of your inner voice, and you need to treat them differently. When you get stuck, follow these steps:

- Pay attention to your thinking.
- Find the fact/fiction balance.
- Get an outsider's opinion.
- Eliminate the haters.
- Find your center.

Knowing your triggers and building specific plans to shorten the cycle when one of the fearsome four shows up and starts to wreak havoc on your inner Zen is essential.

- If your inner critic comes calling, document what you're saying to yourself. Discard the things you know are BS and reframe your emotional responses.
- Use second-guessing to your advantage by learning and adapting instead of letting it slow you down.
- The imposter syndrome will be present every time you're in growth mode. Try to shorten the cycle by reframing your emotional responses and closing any skill gaps you have.
- When those low self-confidence moments creep in, change your dialogue from "I can't" to "How can I?" There is always a path forward.

Brain Candy – Important Questions for You to Chew On

Grab your journal and get started on your ABCs for growth.

Assess:

- What is your inner critic saying to you?

- Are you using your second-guessing powers for good or evil?

- How often do you feel like a fraud?

- What causes your low self-confidence moments?

Baseline:

- How much of the inner critic replay loop is total BS, and how much represents things you believe to be true?

- What circumstances cause the fearsome four to show up most often?

- How can you identify your triggers and shorten the cycle?

Conquer:

- How can your past successes help guide the way to an abundant future?

- Are you using the post-mortem process to use everything you've learned to fortify your leadership capabilities?

- Where can you reframe the dialogue from "I can't" to "How can I?"?

Part II: Align—Transforming Insights into Action

I hope you have acquired new perspectives in Part II of this book as we discussed the power of aligning and prioritizing to your vision. When you put yourself first and take the small steps you need, everything comes into focus and you step into your next big thing.

If you have been journaling your ABCs as you thought about all that brain candy, I'm sure you've had a flood of realizations come to light. Remember, "Vision without action is merely a dream."

It's time to transform your insights into action. Head over to the *Escaping the Career Trap Transformation Guide* and continue your journey toward creating a thriving career. Visit our website at: EscapingTheCareerTrap.com/Guide.

When you get there, you will find tools and a roadmap to:

- Design your personalized career success blueprint to identify what you want and how to align with your purpose.
- Create your vision and strategy and develop a roadmap to success with contingency plans.
- Learn how to identify and play to your strengths so you enjoy your work more and produce better business results.
- Tame the fearsome four and shorten the cycle when your inner critic, second-guessing, imposter syndrome, and low self-confidence moments show up to ruin your momentum.

PART III:
DISRUPT

BREAKING ALL
THE RULES

Everyone deserves to love Mondays.

Chapter 10

TREATING YOUR CAREER LIKE A BUSINESS

"When your work speaks for itself, don't interrupt."

— Henry J. Kaiser

Congratulations! You've just been promoted to the CEO of You, Inc. It's time to start treating your career like a business.

It is a misconception to think if you treat your career like a business, you are less loyal to the company you work at and its mission. Perhaps you fear that you might miss out on building great relationships with coworkers and team members.

Worrying about missing out is the wrong way to think about it. Some of my closest business relationships have been with my consultants, and I can guarantee as a coach, I am more dedicated to my clients' success than some of their employees are.

You can take a business mindset, become the CEO of your career, and still love the company and the people you work with—no compromises required.

How often have you been given more responsibility without a title or compensation change? If it hasn't happened to you, I'm sure you've seen it happen to others.

You have the honor bestowed on you to do more work, have more responsibility and accountability, and get nothing in return. Instead of negotiating or saying no, you are happy with the "recognition."

If you were a business and your client said they needed you to do 20 percent more work, that's called scope creep. You would issue a new statement of work for more money. You may be surprised at how successful you can be when you say, "Yes, and I'll be happy to help after we renegotiate our terms."

How often have you heard, "If you do the work today, I'll make it up to you at bonus time or the beginning of the year"? When I hear this, the *Popeye* comic strip comes to mind where Wimpy's standard line was, "I'll gladly pay you Tuesday for a hamburger today." You smile, thank your boss for the opportunity, and hope they don't get fired or develop amnesia between now and then.

If you were a company and your customer said, "We'll pay your invoices eight months after you've done the work," you would say, "Hell no." Yet when you have an employee mindset, you say yes to these situations almost every time.

Businesses pay and do as little as required. It's not about what is fair, what you're worth, or what you deserve. It's an economic decision. The lens they look through is always, "What's the best I can get for the least money?" It's how they work with their vendors and suppliers— and they do that to you too. It's how they stay in business. It's not personal.

But if they treat your employment like a business transaction, you should too.

Perhaps you're afraid it will get you fired or slow your career growth. Quite the contrary. Ambitious people negotiate better terms all the time, and they are taken more seriously. When I started saying no to being taken advantage of and advocating for myself, I started getting recognized and paid what I was worth.

Let me show you how to step into your new role as the CEO of YOU, Inc.

Setting a Bulletproof Strategy

Do you have a purposeful plan, or are you winging it, hoping something good happens? Every company needs a solid strategy to be successful. Remember that five-hour road trip you took a few chapters back? As the CEO of your career, you're driving.

Consider the elements of a good business strategy and apply them to your career. A bulletproof strategy has:

- Goals and objectives
- Compelling products or services
- Positioning for growth
- Customer segmentation
- Revenue and profit projections

Do you have all that for your career?

You've spent a lot of time thinking about your goals and objectives in Parts I and II, so you should be most of the way there.

What exceptional services does You, Inc. offer? Taking that business mindset, you want to provide a service in high demand and short supply. This makes your company highly sought after, and you can charge more because few others can do what you do.

As you think about your services, how are you positioned for growth? Align your services with market needs, solve big problems, and/or create ambitious opportunities for your ideal customer.

Who is your ideal customer (employer)? What segments are healthy and positioned for continued growth and maturity? Successful companies need raving fans; you'll want customers who love you, come back, and give you referrals.

What are your revenue projections, and what is your path to a continuous increase? How aggressive will you be in top-line growth?

As the CEO of You, Inc., these are the questions you need to answer to succeed. When you take this business mindset approach, don't spend too much time lamenting lost opportunities. Get excited about all the fantastic things that are about to happen.

> "Ability may get you to the top, but it takes
> character to keep you there."
>
> — John Wooden

Phil has mastered creating his vision and adapting to the roadblocks that are part of his journey. He realizes success is not linear, and an unexpected journey can be more enriching than taking your original path.

Phil started as a consultant for a company founded by one of his college professors. The first ten years he was on autopilot. He was challenged, learned a lot, and did some exciting work.

Because of his easy start, Phil didn't think much about his career's direction. All that changed when the founders announced they were returning to academia. It was time for Phil to figure out his next move.

Leaving the only job Phil had ever known coincided with the birth of his first son. Phil chose to step away from work temporarily to support his wife's career, raise their son, and do the introspective work he needed to do to find a new career direction. "I spent a lot of time thinking about what I did and didn't like in my prior role. I researched job descriptions and LinkedIn posts from people who had jobs I thought I might want. I concluded that I wanted to be a chief of staff at a tech company."

Wanting something and getting it are two different things, especially with an eighteen-month gap on your resume. The standard methods people used to get jobs didn't work for Phil. Getting ghosted was part of his daily life, and it began to wear on him. "Hiring is not a meritocracy. It's not equitable or fair. I was doing it wrong. I wasn't networking properly or doing the right things to land the role I wanted."

Phil had his vision and strategy nailed down. The execution part was lacking, and he set out to fix it like any good CEO would. As he was resetting his course to become chief of staff, an unexpected opportunity came his way, and he jumped at the chance.

Phil became the interim executive director of a homeless shelter he had volunteered at since college. They were being walloped by the events of 2020. "I had the opportunity to make a difference at an organization I deeply cared about. I wanted to be known as the person who runs toward crisis and transformation as I created my brand for a chief of staff opportunity."

Phil never considered himself a good fit for the non-profit world long term. "There are peacetime presidents and wartime presidents. I enjoyed the challenge of navigating a crisis, but I think, ultimately, it would have been difficult for me to be there long term." He found his successor, made the transition, and, as timing would have it, welcomed his second son into the world.

Things looked like Groundhog Day for Phil, but this time, it was different. It was 2021. The tech industry was booming, and Phil's networking seeds began to sprout. He had several opportunities to choose from, which posed a different challenge.

"I had two chief of staff opportunities that were the same financially: a mid-sized company and a startup that had just received their Series B funding. It was a tough decision." Because Phil had a strong vision and strategy, he was confident about the answer and went with the startup.

"I made the right choice. I got exactly what I was hoping for out of it. We've had some significant challenges, and I've learned a lot. It's never a straight line with startups." Today, Phil is serving as the head of finance for the same organization and broadening his skills again.

Phil's ability to adapt and align with his vision led him to exactly where he wanted to be. What's the next stop for Phil? He and his family have moved to Barcelona and Phil is rocking his current role.

Developing an Authentic Brand

What are the first three words that come to mind when people hear your name? If you're not sure, ask. All the best companies have iconic brands that go well beyond their logo. Apple, Adidas, Veuve Clicquot, and Pixar are just a few examples of brands that conjure up a desirable image to consumers. They are more than their logo. You expect a particular experience, quality, and image when you see them.

You, Inc. needs a brand people are drawn to, that aligns with the values and needs of your customers (aka your employer), and one you can demonstrate every day through working with your team, peers, and colleagues.

As companies build their brands, they build loyalty, trust, and relatability. They build their brand purposefully and carefully craft the image they portray. They decide if they are a savvy, fun, rugged, high-end, or prestigious brand. Everything they do aligns with their brand and their reputation.

Your interactions build your brand daily. What brand does You, Inc. have? Is it what you want? Is your brand thriving?

You can prosper quickly when you have something everyone wants and it's in limited supply. If you haven't given much thought to your brand, or perhaps you also have a giant case of "I-don't-give-a-shit-itis" as I did, and it needs some work, you can get back on track.

Always start with what lights you up. Your brand needs to get you excited. Once you're jazzed about You, Inc., others will be too. Don't try to fit into your environment—build an authentic brand, and they will come. What do you want to be known for? How do you want people to think about you when they hear your name?

You, Inc. should be known for fixing big problems, creating exciting opportunities, and inspiring raving fans. Fortunately, you can kill three birds with one stone. When you fix big problems, you make the pain go away. When the pain is gone, companies can leverage new opportunities. When people are reaping the rewards of opportunities, they become raving fans.

> *"Your personal brand is what people say about you when you are not in the room."*
>
> — Chris Ducker

I became a renowned transformational expert during my career. Whenever a crisis hit, the metaphorical building was burning, and everyone was running out the door, my team and I were running in. It was my favorite thing to do. As an adrenaline junkie who likes to take risks, high-stakes work makes me feel alive. The leaders I hired over the years loved it too.

We worked hard, laughed a lot, and argued like we were family. We had epic wins, stepped on more than our fair share of political landmines along the way, and the business was better because of our work.

The stress was always high, and the team needed to have fun, so I usually had an upbeat and snarky way of dealing with high-pressure situations. Occasionally, a newcomer would mistake my fun and bubbly personality for weakness. That would only happen once, and then they would find out how unfun I can be when someone underestimates or disrespects me and my team.

I never gave any thought to my brand. I did what came naturally, tried to do what was right for the company, and hoped my bold actions wouldn't get me or my team fired. The majority of the managers on my team over the years gave me the same feedback. They said they'd learned a lot, worked their tails off, and had a ton of fun doing it.

One night, my managers and I were at a local pub blowing off some steam. We all had too much "truth serum" in the form of vodka and tequila. One of the managers, Chris, called over the table, shouting in the noisy bar, "Do you know what we call you?" I was curious and drunk enough to keep the conversation going. "We call you the velvet hammer!" The table erupted with laughter.

It was the first time I'd heard this, and I wasn't sure if I should take it as an insult or a compliment. Fortunately, I didn't have to ask for an explanation. Brad took over. "When we need a kick in the ass or a smack upside the head, you hit us hard, but it never hurts. You do it with kindness." Hearing that made me so happy. As a Wall Street girl, I think that was the sweetest thing anyone has ever said to me.

I didn't build my brand with purpose. Living my purpose built my brand. Over the decades, the teams I worked with created my narrative and built my brand for me. I got lucky. I would never leave my brand to chance now that I know better. Would I have chosen the velvet hammer as my logo? You bet I would.

Creating a Buzz Around Your Message

Are you sending the right message? Companies need strong marketing. Without it, your ideal customers have no idea what you're about. You rob them of the chance to get excited about what you have to offer. And worst of all, they can't find you. If people can't find you, they can't buy. If they aren't excited about you, they won't buy. And a business with no customers won't be around for long.

The same thing applies to your career. As the CEO of You, Inc., you need to get your messaging straight within the company and externally within your industry or area of expertise. You need to get people excited about you and the results you can deliver.

Your external brand is as important as your internal one. Don't get so caught up in doing the work that you forget you should always be looking for your next customer (opportunity).

Whether it's the next hot project at your company or an exciting opportunity with a new firm, you should be one phone call away from your next big thing. A strong marketing message will help you get there.

Replicate what successful companies do to increase brand awareness and create excitement. Share your thought leadership and attend conferences to promote your brand. Compete for business awards, be visible on social media, and become actively involved in public speaking. Ask your managers and coworkers for testimonials, and showcase your best work.

Creating your internal marketing plan uses many of the same

techniques and is a lot easier because people already know you. Find opportunities to present your thought leadership, perhaps at an affinity group meeting or a town hall. Position the work your team is doing so it is recognized as some of the best in the company. Foster meaningful relationships with people outside your group or division. Ask those who love your work to advocate for you, particularly regarding promotions and bonuses.

And as the CEO of You, Inc., consistently market your capabilities, thought leadership, and the results you deliver. If you don't do it, no one else will.

Can the right people find you and get excited about what you have to offer? You, Inc. needs a strong sales team. As the CEO, this should be your top priority. Without a strong sales team, it doesn't matter how good your services are. Who are your salespeople? Who are your advocates? Who is excited and creating a buzz about you?

Thinking of your colleagues as an extension of your sales team may be a brand-new way of thinking about your career. You need internal and external salespeople. Who do you need in your corner to create that buzz? Look for people who are eager and excited about what you do, to the point where they can't help but become your most extraordinary sponsors and advocates.

The more people in your corner, the faster you will grow and the longer you will be successful. One of the easiest ways to build your sales team is to be an advocate and sponsor for others. If you are out there singing the praises of others and helping them grow, they will be more than happy to return the favor.

"If you want to achieve greatness, stop asking for permission."

— Eddie Colla

I'm a huge fan of Lori Crever, author of *Protégé Power: A Roadmap to Mentorship.* She's a Renaissance woman—an international banking leader, actress, poet, professional comedy improvisor, and leadership trainer. Her story and point of view are something we can all learn from. Lori is genuinely buzzworthy.

Lori is a small-town girl from Minnesota who dreamed of being an actress. After college, she set off to New York City to pursue theater and television opportunities. Six-and-a-half years later, Lori was headed back to Minnesota with a few paid acting gigs under her belt, excellent waitress skills, a beautiful baby, and the remnants of a brief marriage.

Lori needed a reboot once she got home. After hitting the reset button, she started what would become a twenty-year career in international banking. She spent a lot of time trying to hide her interest in the arts and blend in with the serious bankers she was working with.

Despite her best efforts, Lori did a shitty job blending in. Her bosses knew it, and they loved it. She continued to get feedback encouraging her to be her natural self. "Hiding your essence is sort of like having a cowlick. No matter how hard you try, there's just not enough hair gel in the world to keep it tamped down." Lori started following their advice and wore the vibrant colors she loved. She used humor to keep everyone on task and, over time, let her true theatrical nature shine.

Lori was clever about creating her brand and her message. As a unicorn, you have to show up differently. She spent the first eighteen months getting up to speed. She was seen as trustworthy, credible, and reliable. Once she established her baseline, she felt it was time to let her personality shine.

Lori knew her strength in speech writing, coaching leaders on managing an audience, and leading with humor, while staying within the corporate environment's guardrails was her brand. She hosted an internal video series and became the in-house Oprah. Everyone across her division of 40,000 knew her and enjoyed her playfulness and reliably authentic nature.

Lori started amping up her value by taking on what she calls unmanned battle stations. She would find missed opportunities and pitch her bosses a fix, taking ownership of the issue. From that point on, a large percentage of her job was opportunities she created that lit her up and delivered big for the company.

This was when Lori truly started to understand her branding message. "If you want the Lori Crever interview, communications plan, and innovation, then the only way to get it is through me." Lori consistently used her theater skills and her knowledge of the humanities as her superpower.

Creating a message is one thing—becoming buzzworthy requires extra effort. Lori created allies by saying great things about people when they weren't in the room. She advocated for her peers and endorsed them for opportunities they would be better at than she would. She took time to build trust with her coworkers. Once she started managing a team, it became even easier to spread the love and help everyone access opportunities.

"Your network is like a structure," Lori says. "Whoever you're helping to elevate will create more career sturdiness for both of you. Why wouldn't you pursue that?"

Use some of Lori's lessons to leverage your uniqueness to stand out from the crowd. Create a buzz around your brand by engendering trust and delivering high value to the organization.

Summary

When you choose to become the CEO of your career, you can no longer have an employee mindset. Start to look at every situation differently, make better decisions, and advocate for yourself.

No one said being a CEO was easy. You, Inc. is your baby. The time and effort it takes to treat your career like a business is worth it.

Create a purposeful brand both internally and externally. Control the narrative and take action to create a brand you can be proud of. Don't give away your power by letting others do it for you.

Create your marketing plans and become the go-to person in your company and industry. Make yourself buzzworthy and find sponsors and advocates excited about you. Create deeper relationships and be an advocate for others whose work you admire.

Treating your career like a business and stepping into the role of CEO is an entirely different way to navigate your career. You'll have to take a different approach if you want different results. Take small actions each day and you'll see your career move in the direction you feel is best for you.

Brain Candy – Important Questions for You to Chew On

Grab your journal and get started on your ABCs for growth.

Assess:

- What do people say about you when you're not in the room?
- Are you buzzworthy?
- Do you have a purposeful brand and marketing message?

Baseline:

- Where are your internal opportunities to build deeper relationships within the organization?
- How can you become more buzzworthy?

- Whom can you advocate for and then enjoy the reciprocity that comes with it?

Conquer:

- What services will you offer that are in high demand and short supply?

- Where are the opportunities to create an epic brand for You, Inc.?

- How will you get people to feel excited about you?

Chapter 11

BECOMING A SKILL-
STACKING NINJA

*"No one can discover you until you do. Exploit your talents, skills,
and strengths and make the world sit up and take notice."*

— Rob Liano

Great CEOs are aware of all available resources. They put the right
people on the field, at the right time and in the right position. The
ability to call upon needed resources depending on what's happening
is essential to success.

The resources and skills you need are the ones you've been building
over the past few decades. The problem starts when you forget what
you've done or marginalize your capabilities.

Leading You, Inc. into a future of abundance will require every skill
you've ever acquired. This requires you to change your mindset and
take on a completely different approach in leveraging your experience
and expertise.

I'll show you how to become a skill-stacking ninja and thrive.

Treating Your Skills as an Asset

What's your account balance in the skill bank? If I gave you two minutes to write down every skill you have, how many do you think you'd come up with? Would it take the full two minutes, or would you run out of ideas before time was up?

You don't typically keep an inventory of everything you've ever done throughout your career. You gain a skill, move up the ladder, gradually move away from that skill, and forget about it as you add new ones. As you move into senior leadership roles, you have less hands-on work, and when it comes time to pivot, you feel you don't have the resources to deliver.

At every career phase, you need to call upon skills past and present to thrive. When you lose sight of your full complement of experiences, you play smaller, and no CEO wants to do that.

Your skills are the assets you use to buy your next promotion, project, or new job. You know how much money you have in your bank or investment accounts. Your skills are as valuable as your monetary assets. Treat them as such.

The mindset shift is incredible. You routinely discount your skills and accomplishments because:

- You didn't do the work—your team did.
- You're not an expert.
- It's been a long time.

Would you throw away the interest or dividends paid on your savings or investment accounts? If you treated your money like your skills, you would come to these conclusions:

- You didn't process the interest payments so they shouldn't count.
- You aren't the financial expert—your advisor chose your investments, so say goodbye to your dividend payments.
- That savings account you opened fifteen years ago is way too old to accept interest payments anymore.

Sounds ridiculous, right?

To grow, you need to do things you've never done before. When you lack experience, you cannot lack expertise. Even though you're stepping into uncharted territory, you're never starting from scratch. Recall and leverage everything you have done so you can use your expertise to grow and gain new experiences.

Your skills are a precious commodity, and you should be looking under every sofa cushion, under the seat of your car, and in the pockets of your jeans to find them all. When your skills inventory is complete, and you become a skill-stacking ninja, it will allow you to compete and win over people with more experience but less expertise than you.

"The question isn't who is going to let me;
it's who will stop me."

— Ayn Rand

Simone is now an expert at using her natural talents and skills to pivot into a new role of her choosing, but it wasn't always that way.

Simone is creative and has had a varied career using her love for creativity and design as her foundation. She started working for record labels and entertainment companies to be around the creativity she loved.

Her next stop was in video communications, sales, and marketing. She spent way too long in that industry. Simone was bored, underpaid, and didn't know where to turn. She came from a blue-collar family and didn't have a role model for working in the corporate world.

"It was hard to find resources who could guide me. Today we have TikTok, Instagram, YouTube, and information is much easier to access. Growing up, information wasn't easily accessible, and I didn't have access to people who could help. I had to put myself out there to get the information I needed."

Serendipity stepped in, and Simone enrolled in CWC's career strategy program. She later said about it, "It changed my life. Tammy's story was a lot like mine, and her journey in corporate America helped me see my path forward. I saw where I missed opportunities and needed to start leveraging my transferable skills."

Simone had some amazing realizations. "Skill stacking was critical for me. I have talents and interests, but I need to combine my creativity and business mindset to create a new career path. What does that look like?"

The work led Simone to a product design role at a leading music streaming service. It felt like a significant pivot for her, but once she harnessed the value of all the skills she had been building up to that point, she had an epiphany. "I've been doing this for years, and I can't believe they're giving people six figures for this type of stuff. Wow! I've been missing out."

Simone got caught up in the tech layoffs of 2022. Without warning, she found herself out of the job she loved. She immediately put her ninja skill-stacking techniques to work to pivot into a product design role at a global investment bank. She is bringing an outside perspective to help them rethink how they do things. Simone is learning and growing, and she has seen another significant increase in compensation. No matter what life throws at Simone, she has mastered ninja skill-stacking and will always land on her feet.

Pinpointing Your Leadership Strengths

Are you a leadership powerhouse? Leadership is helping people align with the right priorities and taking action to get stuff done. If only it were that simple, right? It's easy to know what leadership is (and isn't). Getting good at it is hard and requires discipline, focus, and practice.

Are you leaving leadership opportunities on the table? You don't have to manage someone or have the title to lead. Leading by influence is substantially more complicated than leading through a hierarchy. People don't have to listen to you; they can tell you to shove it. When you control someone's livelihood, they treat you and your ideas differently.

Battle-tested leaders are worth their weight in gold because there are so few good leaders. If you are one of them, you should be living in career abundance. If you're not, becoming really good at this is worth the time and effort. Leaders are made, not born.

As you take on new challenges and risks to grow your career, you'll need all the leadership skills you can muster. You will be playing big and can't do it all by yourself. Bringing out the best in your team and motivating them to run into that burning building with you takes skill and practice.

Spend time inventorying your leadership skills and write them down. If you don't have at least thirty on your list, you're not being thorough enough. If you're stuck or short on ideas, look back at old resumes, search the top 100 leadership skills, and take credit for what you can, or look up job descriptions for the role you have now or the one you want. You can find plenty of ways to refresh your memory on all your extraordinary leadership skills. Once you have your list, keep it current so you don't have to go through this again next time you're ready to change gears.

"Leadership is unlocking people's potential to become better."

— Bill Bradley

Teresa Quinlan is an emotional intelligence coach who helps leaders show up differently for their teams and organizations. Spending two decades in leadership roles driving innovation during hyper-growth periods and ramping down when times get tough has taught her a thing or two about how to repurpose your leadership skills to improve and grow continually.

A lifelong athlete, Teresa took a job at one of the largest fitness companies in Canada as a temporary place to land. She never expected to spend the next twenty-two years there.

Teresa spent the first three years learning every position in the fitness club, moving up into leadership roles, and transferring to bigger clubs. Then corporate headquarters put her in a new training department.

Excited about the opportunity, Teresa spent the next fifteen years bringing innovative ideas to life. "I would identify a need, pitch the idea, and then offer to lead the work." Eventually, she led the department and grew it from a four-person team to forty.

Teresa thrived in an environment where she could connect strategy and business initiatives and help people realize their full potential. She didn't need an official job description to lead new work and drive significant organizational changes. She also knows the other end of the spectrum. She needed to shrink her department from forty to fourteen when the business faced a downturn.

Teresa had to systematically rip apart her baby and still meet the organization's needs. "The work had to be picked up somewhere else. This was when I learned how to get people onboard and deliver tough news with empathy and kindness."

Her leadership style served her and her coworkers well during good times and bad. The effort she had put into growth enabled her to be the leader people chose to follow and opened new opportunities for her.

The one thing Teresa didn't master was advocating for herself. As she continued to gain responsibilities, the title and money never came. After three broken promises, she realized her boss would never do the right thing.

"I started to feel less engaged at work and took these broken promises personally. It was the lack of respect for my work that hurt the most. When I thought about staying, it tasted like poison, and that was the signal I needed to make a change."

Teresa thought about going to a different company but was worried it would be the same shit with a different signature on the paycheck. She thought about the work that brought her the most joy and fulfillment. "Teaching emotional intelligence, coaching, and leading workshops are things I love and am good at." And that's how her coaching business was born.

By helping others harness their full leadership capabilities, Teresa has achieved her true purpose. She learned to be decisive in determining what is meaningful to her. She realized if you aim for things that don't align with who you are, fulfillment will never come.

Teresa guards her time as a precious commodity she cannot take for granted. She warns not to waste time chasing things that don't bring you fulfillment or settle for second best because it feels safe and comfortable. "I've gotten much better about saying no to things and focusing on the quality of the interactions in my life."

Teresa's biggest leadership lesson: If you want to go fast, go alone. If you want to go far, go together.

Amplifying Your Transferable Skills

Will your skills really transfer? Examples of transferable skills easily applied to every industry include strategy, project or program management, financial management, governance, and/or sales. Soft skills like problem-solving, analytical reasoning, critical thinking, adaptability, communication, teamwork, and creativity also fall into this category.

Why are transferable skills so critical? You can't be a rookie when you do something new. If you discount your transferable skills (which are highly valued across all businesses), you're discounting your value.

These skills are often the difference between the success or failure of mission-critical business initiatives. Very rarely are the technical merits of a project the root cause of failure. The lack of these transferable and soft skills will slow you down.

Write down all your transferable skills, and if you come up short again, go back and use the strategies we discussed in the leadership section. Keep looking if you don't have at least forty.

"Learning how to learn is life's most important skill."

— Tony Buzan

Stephen Morris is a CWC coach who used his transferable skills to make one of the most dramatic successful pivots I've seen. He spent his career in the US Army and rose to the rank of sergeant in the Rangers, leading sniper teams when on deployment. When Stephen wasn't blowing things up, he immersed himself in leadership training. That's where he fell in love with learning about leadership.

Stephen's uncle gave him a Bible when he enlisted. This wasn't an ordinary Bible. It was a King James version that John Maxwell had edited. The author referenced leadership on every page, creating leadership lessons from each story. Stephen took it with him everywhere. "Even if you take religion completely out of it, you have amazing leadership stories."

Stephen's mantra, "Action breeds clarity," came from when he was forced to jump out of an airplane. Stephen is terrified of heights and seriously considered quitting a career he loved to avoid having to jump. When jump day came, he put himself in a position to be the first, taking a rip-the-bandage-off approach.

Everyone stood up, clipped in, and started to do the shuffle-jog to the back of the plane. As Stephen got ready to jump, he froze and caused a forty-person pile-up on the plane.

One big shove and Stephen's bloodcurdling screams could be heard on the ground. After a few seconds of freaking out, he had to put his fear aside and let his training kick in to take the proper steps to hit his mark and try not to break anything. This is an extreme example of action bringing clarity.

Stephen was shot in three places while on a mission and barely survived. His injuries kept him from returning to the field, and he finished his military career creating training models. He loved what he was doing, but then one day, his career was over.

The Army was sending Stephen home. He was furious. "I had given everything to the Army, and I felt betrayed. Sitting here today, I know they did the right thing. I was damaged goods and a liability. I'm not mad about it anymore."

Stephen's transition to civilian life was challenging. He couldn't understand how little people cared about their jobs. He had a massive ego and thought he was better than everyone else. "I was a jerk to everyone I encountered. When you think you're better than someone, people can tell. It doesn't matter how nice you are to them."

Stephen struggled with losing the respect he had as a Ranger sergeant. "I felt like the skills I'd earned over the past sixteen years didn't count, and I worked my ass off to get there. It was tough, and no one cared. I knew I could never be as good of an employee as I was a soldier, so I had to start my own business. Starting my company, Renowned Leadership, was the only way I saw of achieving that level of badassery I had in the military."

Today, Stephen works with corporate leaders and former military leaders transitioning into the corporate world. He has cracked the code in translating military and civilian leadership and culture.

Being shot three times and nearly dying gives Stephen a perspective most of us don't have. "If you hate your job and it is the bane of your existence, you wake up daily with dread, and yet somehow muster the power to go to work, stop it. Just fire your employer and find something you love. If it means you lose your material possessions, you don't need any of that stuff to be happy. All you need is a fulfilling purpose; you won't get that hating your life."

Repurposing Your Industry-Specific Knowledge

Can you leverage your industry-specific skills elsewhere? You've built an illustrious career, becoming an expert in something. You understand all the acronyms, jargon, and unique interdependencies. There's only one problem—you have fallen out of love with your industry. The days that used to energize you now drain you, and it's time for a change. Now what do you do?

Leadership and transferable skills can help you pivot and take on more responsibility. A common misconception is that the industry-specific skills you've built are pretty much thrown away. These skills don't have to be; if you position them correctly, they can be used as one of your greatest strengths.

Instead of dismissing your experience, use it as a competitive advantage. When you show your ideal new employer how you can repurpose what you know, learn what you need to know, and revitalize how they get work done, people will pay attention.

You can repurpose your niche industry knowledge by de-industryizing (I know that's not an actual word, but it is today) your skills. You do this by getting to the primary function of your niche skills. Once all the fancy words are removed, what do you actually do?

If you are involved in regulatory compliance in the pharmaceutical industry, you can work in regulatory compliance in any industry. If you can sell highly complex technical equipment, you can sell any product. If you are an expert in a particular project or program management method, you can do the same work and adapt to any method.

Everything you have done can be repurposed, provided you take the right approach.

You already know the structure of these business frameworks; snapping into a new one becomes second nature. You only need a few weeks with the decoder ring to learn the jargon and gain context. The learning curve gets faster with more practice diversifying your work experiences.

Not having ten to fifteen years of experience in a particular industry can be used to your advantage. Coming in with a fresh perspective will allow you to see opportunities and new ways of doing things others can't see. You are a hero when you can take the playbook from a different industry and help your current organization work faster, smarter, and less expensively.

Many senior-level people I coach worry about needing more hands-on experience or credentials when making these changes. Keep this in mind—the higher you are in an organization, the less hands-on personal experience you need. Your job is to lead, remove roadblocks, and best use your resources to get stuff done. It's not to become an expert on the latest widget or to gain certification in an area you have no experience in.

"Every skill you acquire doubles your odds of success."

— Scott Adams

Kasey is a former client who oversaw an extensive program management team for a US pharmaceutical company. Her primary territory was Asia. After fifteen years working in big pharma, she was sick of it. She was always on a plane, and working both US and Asia-Pacific hours, she was missing time with her family, and her new boss was a jerk. It was demoralizing work for her.

Kasey wanted to do something more meaningful and feel what she did mattered. She needed her work to align with her sense of purpose. She longed for the moment when she could cut down on the travel and enjoy her family again.

Kasey felt trapped until she cleverly leveraged her niche skills and honed her vital leadership and transferrable skills. She pivoted to become a government liaison executive for a renewable energy startup.

How did Kasey go from a program executive in the pharmaceutical industry to a government liaison executive for a renewable energy startup and get paid 20 percent more in the process?

Kasey's superpowers were project management and negotiation (transferable skills). She had a decade of experience leading revenue-generating businesses (leadership skills) in highly regulated environments (niche skills).

This company hired Kasey over many other finalists with more relevant experience because they needed her project management expertise. The startup was growing fast. Organizing how work got done and increasing transparency and accountability were high on the CEO's wish list.

Kasey was a master negotiator, and the company needed those skills to negotiate with suppliers, resellers, regulators, and new customers because they were paying too much, charging too little, and taking too long to get things through each state's regulatory process.

Kasey has always been responsible for revenue. While it isn't her primary role in her new job, she takes a revenue-first approach to all her decision-making. The CEO needed someone who had a commercial mindset as they built the business.

The time Kasey spent in pharma wasn't a waste. She knew how to navigate the US and foreign regulatory systems. Before they said anything, she immediately identified where this renewable energy company was struggling. She figured out their path forward because she had a fresh perspective and deep experience in a related area.

Most importantly, this opportunity fed into Kasey's sense of purpose. It gave her a sense of doing something good for the world—and she wouldn't have to travel. The company was in hyper-growth mode, and her sage wisdom was precisely what the CEO needed.

Kasey inventoried her skills, pulled out the ones she loved using the most, and used them to showcase her unique abilities. She used them to land a highly competitive executive job doing something she'd never done before.

During our wrap-up conversation, Kasey said, "I really thought I was stuck and doomed to stay in the pharmaceutical industry. I never dreamed I had all the skills to pivot into something I love."

You already have everything you need. How will you harness it to create a better future for yourself?

Summary

Mastering the art of skill stacking can be a game-changer once you've made the mindset shift and realize your skills are the currency you use to buy your next big opportunity. They aren't things to be dismissed, discounted, or forgotten. You worked hard for everything you've experienced. It's time to put the skills you've worked so hard to obtain to work for you.

Inventory your skills and treat them with the same care as you do your bank and investment accounts. Look in every nook and cranny to find every leadership, transferable, and niche skill you have ever had. Then stack-rank them, and identify the ones you love using most.

With a clear image of your skills and priorities, it's time to take a more proactive approach to using those skills as often as possible. You won't get to spend most of your time doing the things you love until you start taking control and being more purposeful about what you do and who you're doing it for.

Brain Candy – Important Questions for You to Chew On

Grab your journal and get started on your ABCs for growth.

Assess:

- How many skills have you forgotten about?
- Have you been playing small when you shouldn't be?
- Are you ready to take credit for all of your skills?

Baseline:

- In which skills do you feel like a powerhouse, and what gaps do you need to fill?
- When you think of your next big opportunity, which skills will be most important?
- When you break down your niche skills to their essential elements, what are the basic skills?

Conquer:

- Which mindset changes do you need to make about how you treat your skills?
- Which skills in your wheelhouse do few people have, and how can you use this to your advantage?

Everyone deserves to love Mondays.

Chapter 12

FINDING YOUR IT FACTOR

"The one thing that you have that nobody else has is you. Your voice, your mind, your story, your vision."

— Neil Gaiman

Do you know what an *IT Factor* is? Have you experienced it? You need three things, and when they are at their peak, you have capitalized on your *IT Factor*.

The first element of your *IT Factor* is your purpose—the ideal work that lights you up. You gained clarity on your purpose earlier, so you are already one-third of the way there.

The second element is your expertise. You combine your unique skills, perspectives, and experiences to find a role that energizes you. Notice I didn't say your most marketable skills, where you had the most experience, or where you could make the most money. Follow the energy, and the rest will come along with it.

The third element is the market demand. Find opportunities where your passion and expertise are in high demand and short supply.

If what you have to offer is in high demand and everyone else has it too, that doesn't make you unique. If no one needs what you have to offer, then you can't leverage your awesomeness.

When you are in an environment that lights you up, doing work that energizes you, in an organization that desperately needs everything you have to offer, you have leveraged your *IT Factor*. Then you are thriving, making a significant difference, and growing your career.

Everyone has an *IT Factor*. Let's find yours.

Uncovering Your Superpowers

What is your superpower? We touched briefly on playing to your strengths earlier. Now we will dig into it more so you can make the most out of your awesomeness.

You may be making a mistake when figuring out your greatest strengths and looking at things through the wrong lens. You may be thinking about things in a commercial context:

- What will earn you the most money?
- What will get you promoted faster?
- What are you most experienced at?

When you ask those questions, you put the cart before the horse and set yourself up to fail.

The other rabbit hole you may go down is thinking about what you're good at. This strategy seems entirely logical, yet it's partially wrong. Just because you're good at something doesn't mean you like it. It doesn't make it one of your superpowers.

Of all the things I'm good at, only three things feed my energy: coaching our clients, strategizing with our coaches, and delivering keynote speeches and talks for our clients. I can do these things all day and end the day more energized than when I started.

Other elements of running the business are important, and I'm good at them, but after a few hours, I'm either bored or mentally exhausted and want to move on to something else. Consider finding your energy-based superpowers as you read this epic story.

> *"Style is knowing who you are, what you*
> *want to say, and not giving a damn."*
>
> — Gore Vidal

Brad felt the magnetic pull of the entrepreneurial spirit while he was in college. His dream was to launch a tech startup. Instead of going the corporate route, he dove into an early-stage tech company for about two years and learned how things worked.

When he was ready to venture out on his own, he created a productivity chatbot integrated into a popular workplace messaging platform to help software developers. It was an intelligent "do not disturb" bot.

After about a year, Brad didn't have the revenue needed to qualify for seed funding and had to call it quits. Brad learned he had a lot to learn about being a successful entrepreneur.

In his quest for knowledge and experience, Brad worked for various startups in the pre-product market fit. It was intense. "I wore many hats across product integrations, sales, partnerships, and operations. I had a lot of experiences but still wasn't in a place where I felt I knew enough to start a successful company."

Brad's next step was to look for a company with a successful product where he could understand what success in the marketplace felt like and grow and learn from that experience.

He ended up working for one of the world's most exciting startups. They were in late-stage funding and rapidly scaling a new product. "I had the opportunity to work for a startup within a more mature company. It was the ideal environment for me."

Brad could leverage his superpowers and immerse himself in work that energized him. The buzz and excitement, the hard work, and the wins and losses all fed into what he loved the most. It was a great paycheck and a daily adrenaline rush—what could be better?

As the organization grew, more opportunities became available, and Brad continued to let his entrepreneurial spirit lead the way. He had an opportunity either to work in an established region doing work that was exciting for him or an opportunity to join a new team that was spinning up because of the company's hyper-growth. Again, Brad chose a new adventure.

"When I feel like I'm not learning as fast and my career trajectory is leveling off, it's time to change. Growth is more important than the title, and I have made a lot of lateral moves, have plenty of battle scars, and will always choose a greenfield opportunity."

Brad is good at many things, but that doesn't mean he loves doing them. He refused to quit until he found an organization where he could feel the excitement and grow. Once he arrived, he didn't put his career on cruise control. Brad continually sought new opportunities within the company to feed his energy and leverage his superpowers.

Quantifying Your Value in Terms That Matter

How easy is it for you to quantify your value? If I asked you to put a number on it, could you? I guarantee you your employer can. Who do you want to control your value's narrative?

Quantifying value can be tricky depending on where you are within an organization. If you produce revenue or have a front office gig, it's easy. Your contributions are out there for all the world to see in the revenue you bring in.

Suppose you are in the middle office dealing with customers after the sale and coordinating with the rest of the organization. In that case, quantifying your value is more complicated. You point to things like organic growth, customer retention, and the operational things you do behind the scenes.

If you are in the back office and far removed from the customer, quantifying your value is much more challenging. Not only is your job not sexy (sorry—operations, audit, and risk), but they don't easily translate into monetary value. You'll have more work to do, but you, too, can put a dollar sign on your contribution.

Your value needs to align with the most important things to the company. If you are off chasing new business and the company is all about organic growth, then your successes will be less than fruitful for you. Do you know what the top three priorities of the company are? Do you understand the role you play in achieving them?

If you don't have these answers, find them, and don't stop until you do. You can't win if you don't know where the finish line is. If you can't connect what you do to what the company values, start looking for a new job where you can.

Value can be quantified in three ways for those not generating revenue: time, cost, and quality. Determine your influence on as many of these as you can. From there, it's easy to monetize your value.

How can you reduce the time it takes to do something? What are your volumes, how much time do you save, what are the direct labor costs, and what will be the increased revenue, if applicable? Annualize these factors and you've got your number.

Where can you reduce the cost of producing something? It could be reducing operational costs, renegotiating supplier pricing, or moving work to a lower-cost location. To the extent possible, you need to quantify how much cost you've subtracted from the processes you're involved in.

Are there quality improvement opportunities? Improved quality is the squishiest of the three, but you can still draw the connection. Can you attribute improved quality to customer retention, reduced rework, or fewer product returns?

In all three scenarios, make sure you are using data sources the company relies on. There's nothing worse than quantifying your value just to have your number challenged because you got your data from a wonky source. Use your systems of record and the data used across the enterprise to produce metrics and management dashboards.

In addition to quantifying your value in terms of time, cost, and quality, evaluate your contributions using the value pyramid. This three-level framework consists of intrinsic value, impact, and innovation.

At the base of the pyramid is your intrinsic value. These are the things an organization assumes everyone has, yet most people don't. Think about things like common sense, good communication skills, and teamwork.

Your impact is in the middle of the pyramid. You can measure these things using time, cost, and quality parameters. Approximately 70 percent of your impact value comes from things you can count and 30 percent from things you can't. Emotional intelligence, collaboration, and inspirational leadership are highly valued, but you can't trade exclusively on these things.

The tip of the pyramid is innovation. It covers the needle-moving activities that make your company better. Are you just taking up space, or are you actively involved in trying to improve the organization? The time, cost, and quality lens also comes in handy here. What improvements and innovative ideas have you delivered? How are things better?

Understanding your quantifiable value is the lifeblood of a long, successful career. Very few non-revenue producers focus on this to the degree they should. Take the time to understand the organization and where you fit, assess your three value tiers, and help everyone appreciate your value. (We'll cover getting good at self-promotion in Chapter 14: Conquering Your Self-Promotion Demons.)

"Strive not to be a success, but rather to be of value."

— Albert Einstein

Maureen Metcalf is the CEO of Innovative Leadership, an executive advisory firm advancing leadership and developing future-ready leaders and organizations. The company she built is solving some of the most complex leadership challenges companies face. And it all started with her getting fired.

Maureen was on the fast track with Anderson Consulting working in the utilities industry. She was one of the only females on the team and one of the youngest leaders on track to become a partner. Life couldn't have been better for her. Then the Enron scandal hit, and the entire industry collapsed. No one could make their numbers, and the team was let go.

"Here I am, up for partner one day and unemployed the next." It was a traumatic experience that Maureen wasn't prepared for. She was devastated. Having the rug pulled out from under her forced her to do a lot of introspection.

As part of her severance, Maureen had coaching resources to help her think through things. She was tired and burnt out after spending her career in management consulting. Maureen used this time to give herself a reset.

"I learned a ton and have no regrets about that time. But I was left with a burning question: Where do I fit in the world? I thought I had a direction, and it was removed from me. I didn't even know where to start."

These questions led Maureen to start her own business and start teaching in an MBA program. Her identity and brand had been tied to her employer's reputation rather than her capabilities. It was time to change that.

Maureen started by identifying what she stood for, who she was, what she wanted for her life and career, and how to get there. Her passion and superpowers had always been in strategy, executive advisory services, change management, business process reengineering, and doing whatever it took to transform companies. Her research showed only 30 percent of corporate transformation efforts succeed. She had found her *IT Factor* and value proposition.

Maureen went on to build a thriving business that solved her customers' most urgent needs. She shared her thought leadership through networking, speaking, publishing several books, teaching, and producing an incredibly successful podcast.

Maureen's road to finding her *IT Factor*, creating a thriving business, refining her brand, and perfecting the value she delivered to the marketplace wasn't easy. When I asked Maureen what she wished she had known earlier, she said, "I thought I was average. I didn't realize I had talents where I was exceptional. I wish I knew where I excelled earlier."

Now her value, contributions, and professional success will be her legacy. She wanted to change the world significantly; today, Maureen and her teams do it daily.

Successfully Positioning Your *IT Factor*

You have your purpose and work that energizes you, and now you can quantify your value. The last thing you need to do is identify the areas where this powerful combination is in high demand and short supply.

Markets shift, economies change, and companies come and go, but one thing remains consistent—the self-serving nature of humans. When you realize that every well-intentioned human is driven by WIIFM (What's in it for me?) first, and then everything else second, it becomes much easier to be in high demand all the time.

Start by working to understand what an individual wants and needs personally. Then begin to understand the outcomes they need to deliver based on the company's direction. Finally, position your powerful combination of passion and expertise as the bridge between the two.

When executives have personal desires, need to deliver significant results to the company, and see you as the connection between the two, you will always be in high demand.

Your demand is largely based on the value you deliver rather than the work it takes to get there. People care far less about how the sausage is made. What your boss and the company care about is how your contributions help them succeed.

Getting people to recognize you for your *IT Factor* and to seek you out requires you to position yourself properly. You do this with a powerful transformation statement.

A transformation statement is the "so what" to what you do. It conveys your unique capabilities by showcasing how you help others succeed.

Your transformation statement should flow like this: "My passion for *[blank]* enables me to *[your impact statement]* **SO** *[remarkable outcome for others]*."

Here are a few examples from past clients.

"My passion for *sales transformation* enables me to *disrupt the sales status-quo* **SO** *every chief revenue officer can deliver massive increases in top-line growth*."

"My passion for *driving a holistic customer experience* enables me to *see our company through our clients' eyes* **SO** *we wow our clients at every opportunity and crush the competition*."

"My passion for *optimizing operations* enables me to *cut out all the nonessential work* **SO** *everything we do is faster, smarter, cheaper, and better than ever*."

Have you noticed none of these transformation statements resembled your three-page resume, advanced degrees, and thirteen industry certifications? It's not about you but how you use your awesomeness to help others succeed.

Each transformation statement uses the words "so" as a binding agent to connect what you do with the outcomes you deliver. People will immediately see the WIIFM.

> *"Brand yourself for the career you want,*
> *not the job you have."*
>
> — Dan Schawbel

Finding my *IT Factor* worked like magic for me throughout my career. I was able to land roles I had no business having because I understood human nature and could be the bridge that delivered what my bosses personally wanted to what they needed to deliver for the company.

And I used the same bridge every time. You don't need to recreate the wheel. That's the beauty of your *IT Factor*—once you find it, you get to use it repeatedly.

My bosses were often faced with fixing a giant mess or starting new efforts that could fail. What they wanted personally was to avoid getting crushed by herculean tasks and spending countless hours doing damage control with angry stakeholders. They wanted to be seen as leaders who could tackle the big stuff so they would get promoted (without getting their hands dirty, of course).

The company needed these big scary things to get done as quickly, inexpensively, and perfectly as possible without pissing off our clients, regulators, or shareholders by landing on the front page of the *Wall Street Journal*.

As a transformation expert, I had a few things going for me. My passion was achieving the impossible; my superpower was to create an innovative strategy and move it off the PowerPoint deck and into the world. I was also a masterful collaborator, risk manager, and negotiator. That was my *IT Factor*.

Hundreds of people were more qualified than I was, so why was I sought out to do the work? Because I served as the bridge. I took the time to learn what my boss wanted and needed to meet their personal goals and learn what the company was expecting. Then I was ready to put my ass on the line to be the bridge from point A to point B.

What kind of bridge will you build?

Summary

Finding your *IT Factor* is worth the time and effort because once you find it, you have it for a very long time. The value you deliver, the fun you have doing it, and the resilience it offers enable you to thrive no matter what life throws at you.

Instead of focusing on the work you most often do, what you're best at, or the things you feel are most marketable, switch your focus to the work that gives you the most energy. What work can you do for twelve hours a day and still not feel tired? Find opportunities to do more of that work and delegate the work that drains you.

Quantify the value you deliver in monetary terms—you need to figure that out right away. Connect your value to time, cost, and quality outcomes, and use data trusted across the enterprise. Make sure you understand your value pyramid and others do too. Control the narrative of the value you deliver.

Become the bridge between what your boss wants and what the company needs. You will always have ample opportunities to contribute and grow when you lead with what's in it for them and use your *IT Factor* to get it for them. Create your transformation statement and incorporate it into your brand and mindset. You'll show up differently, and your colleagues will see the difference.

Brain Candy – Important Questions for You to Chew On

Grab your journal and get started on your ABCs for growth.

Assess:

- What work energizes you?
- Do you know what your *IT Factor* should be?
- What will your transformation statement say?

Baseline:

- How often do you get to do energizing work in your current role?
- What do you think your quantifiable value is?
- What personal wins can your purpose, superpowers, and value deliver to your boss?

Conquer:

- How will you incorporate doing more of what energizes you into your daily routines?
- How can you eliminate work that doesn't energize you?
- What opportunities do you have to innovate?
- How well do you know your boss' personal goals, and how can you help them get there?

Everyone deserves to love Mondays.

Chapter 13

STRENGTHENING YOUR POWER BASE

"There is no passion to be found playing small—in settling for a life that is less than the one you are capable of living."

— Nelson Mandela

Most people would rather get a root canal than be forced to network. The idea of networking strikes fear in the hearts of even the bravest. Very few like doing it, and even fewer incorporate it into their professional routines.

Do any of these excuses sound familiar?

- I don't know what to say.
- I haven't spoken to them in forever.
- They're too senior.
- I don't have time.
- It feels awkward.
- What if they don't respond?

Your age, profession, industry, leadership level, location, or identity as an introvert or extrovert do not matter. You can network in a natural way. Everyone needs a strong community, and your long-term success depends on it.

How strong is your power base? Are you one phone call away from getting great advice, a new job, or an introduction?

When you build a strong network, you'll have more influence and opportunities, make more money, become more interesting, and have more fun. You're good at building relationships in your personal life. Yet you fall flat when building your professional network and strengthening your power base.

It's time to change that.

Elevating Your Mindset

Do you know the difference between your network and your power base? A network is a collection of people you have met along the way. Your power base is a subset of your network. These people can and will help you grow.

You need to grow and nurture both. Most people who focus on growing their community focus on growing their network because it's easier. You need to have a solid power base and be a trusted source for others.

Many people have images of being corralled into a hotel meeting room with hundreds of strangers. Everyone is looking tense and awkward. You don't want to make the first move and pretend to look busy responding to email on your phone. This version of networking is not much fun.

What if you knew for every meaningful relationship you built with someone in that room, you would receive one thousand dollars per year for the next ten years? I bet you'd put down your phone, get your smile on, and start shaking hands and kissing babies.

If you could quantify the value of your network, you'd make the time to grow it more frequently. Porter Gale, an internationally known public speaker, networker, and entrepreneur, said, "Your network is your net worth." I have found this to be completely accurate.

Jack Flynn, researcher and writer for online recruiter Zippia, published some interesting statistics in a blog post titled "25+ Important Networking Statistics [2023]: The Power of Connections in the Workplace." He found 79 percent of Americans believe networking plays a vital role in their career progression, yet only 48 percent keep in touch with their network. It's kind of like eating your veggies. You know they're good for you, but you don't eat as many as you should.

When someone reaches out to you for help, you're the first to roll up your sleeves and pitch in. Yet being on the other side of that conversation feels uncomfortable. Despite all the excuses, one underlying concern weighs heavily. Asking for something makes you feel vulnerable.

What if you changed how you thought about this? What if you took a service approach to your networking conversations? How about instead of feeling like you were looking for a handout, you were there to offer help? Focus on making meaningful connections, getting work done, and creating opportunities to help others.

Building your power base is all about what you can do for others and how you can help others grow and get what they want. Doing so creates opportunities for meaningful collaboration and deepening relationships before you need them. If you don't fire up your network until you need something, that could be why it feels slimy and uncomfortable.

You already have a fantastic network you're probably discounting because you haven't contacted them in years. Don't throw away these valuable resources. These people have known you the longest and haven't contacted you either. No one is good at this, and someone has to make the first move.

To embrace a networking mindset, be curious, enjoy discovering how things are connected, demonstrate excellent listening and relationship-building skills, and have a strong bias for action. These are things you do every day. Now, direct these skills to grow your network.

"Networking is an investment in your business. It takes time and when done correctly, can yield great results for years to come."

— Diane Helbig

Charlie spent most of his career working in regulatory compliance on the investment banking side of the house for a few large banks. He was a senior leader and was ready to make a move.

At that point in his career, Charlie knew the only way to get a job at his level was through his network. There was just one problem—Charlie did a crappy job keeping up with his network, and it had been years since he'd spoken to anyone outside his organization.

Financial services in New York seems like a big world, but once you're in the industry, you see how small it is. It's like everyone is in a giant shoe box with a bunch of compartments, and every two or three years, someone puts the lid on the box and shakes it. The same people end up in new companies.

Charlie's situation is common. Who has time to network? Working twelve-hour days, having a personal life, and dealing with life's curveballs can send you into a self-shame spiral because of all the networking you should have done.

That's where Charlie was. When he looked at his network, he felt ashamed and embarrassed. He didn't want to reach out because it had been so long, and he felt he needed to start over and build new relationships.

Why would you throw away decades of long-standing relationships and start over? These connections understand your capabilities better than anyone. If you are afraid they won't remember you or didn't like you as much as you thought they did, stop quitting before you start. You'll never know until you reach out—and discover your fears are misguided.

Begrudgingly, Charlie started reaching out to his connections. Most were senior leaders at all the big banks in New York. The responses and willingness to help humbled him.

Charlie still hated having to ask for a favor during the first conversation. But he won't make that mistake again. He put all his connections into a CRM and reaches out to them quarterly to help make connections and keep in touch with his community. He spends about thirty minutes each week keeping up the momentum.

When you make maintaining your network a lifestyle priority and not a project when your back is against the wall, you'll have a more robust network and much less stress.

Creating High-Value Relationships

We often focus on how many people we know, but that's backward. We should think about how many people know, like, and trust us. When I led sales teams, my sales reps would come into my office excitedly and say, "I know the CIO" or some other important person. I burst their bubble when I was unimpressed and replied with, "Great. Do they know you?" If the people we know can't pick us out of a crowd of one, knowing them doesn't do us any good.

The whole point is to have meaningful relationships and connections with people. It is not to gather as many names as possible, hoping someday you'll find the time to reach out and have a good conversation.

Have you fallen into the vanity metrics trap? Your number of connections on LinkedIn could give you a false sense of security. If you have 5,000 connections, I bet you feel pretty good about that. How many of these connections know you? How many have you met in real life? Which ones have you worked with directly?

Moving beyond our click-and-forget world is imperative for a thriving power base and network. Someone sends you a connection request, you accept it, and nothing else happens. This is meaningless and won't help unless you make a personal connection.

Are you creating a purposeful network? During your career, you meet lots of people. As you progress, you hang on to the good ones, get rid of the jerks, and move on with your life.

Be more purposeful about who is in your network and diversify your power base. If you stay in your lane, you limit your options. Every client who has come to me for help with a career change needed significantly more diversity in their network. This gap was slowing them down.

No one thinks, *Hey, I might want to be a rocket scientist one day; I should start getting to know some of them ten years before I need to.* It seems impractical—until you need it. You will need to expand your power base at some point, so you may as well get started now.

Diversity isn't just for companies. Proactively diversify your community. You'll need a wide range of people from different industries, geographical locations, levels of leadership, educational backgrounds, and generations. (Yes, Gen Zers can help you.)

When you are connected with a broad group of people, you become more interesting because you're exposed to new things. You broaden your perspective and have more opportunities for collaborating in new and exciting ways.

Do you have rockstar sponsors? If you don't have at least three-dozen people who are super-connectors, you have more work to do. Your goal is always to be one phone call away from whatever you need.

If you are playing small with your networking, most of your connections are with people at your level and below. You need as many as possible who are one or two levels above you.

Achieving this rockstar power base takes time. Play the long game. These are people you've gone into battle with. They have seen your work, partnered with you on important initiatives, and gone to bat for you during talent planning and promotion cycles.

When you play big and take on meaningful projects, you have greater exposure to people who are more senior than you. You're showcasing your leadership and delivery capabilities while building a memorable brand. Don't waste your opportunity to work with senior executives. Continue building the relationship long after your time working together is over.

> *"Networking is not about just connecting people. It's about connecting people with people, people with ideas, and people with opportunities."*
>
> — Michele Jennae

Tom had to learn the importance of a solid power base the hard way. Armed with an economics degree, he started working for a rating agency and then moved on to work for a large hedge fund.

This hedge fund was ultra-aggressive. "When you work there," Tom said, "you were either a winner or got kicked in the hoo-has; there was nothing in between." Tom won a lot but eventually got bounced and was out the door. He jumped around to a few small shops and continued to learn along the way.

A few people Tom met through the hedge fund asked him to join a company they were starting. Tom felt this was a great new beginning. "I can make a career out of this situation because I was hired as a grownup. I'm being brought in as a senior person who will be able to do a lot of exciting things."

Tom created a division that bought portfolios of failing mortgages, rehabilitated them, and issued new loans. He ran the company for four years, and it grew from two to 200 employees in seventeen states, with licenses all over the country.

The business was thriving. Unfortunately, the hedge fund guys who sat on the board of directors started having their own financial problems. They ended up ousting senior management and taking over so they could collect huge paychecks.

Tom was powerless to stop this nefarious activity because he was kept at arm's-length from the primary financial backers. "My biggest failure was not being integrated with the big investors who had the most to gain or lose in the success of the company I was running. I mostly interfaced with the board, and they interfaced with the investors. As a result, I had a giant brick wall between me and the only path forward to save the company."

Tom did not survive the culling, and the fund was out of business shortly thereafter. The hedge fund managers continue collecting paychecks from the floundering mortgage company over a decade later. A solid power base could have prevented Tom's company from being hijacked by bad actors and saved hundreds of jobs.

He had to start from scratch with a new venture. It was an ego-bruising experience for him. He hated being in the spotlight, so he didn't build the relationships he should have in his previous role. Tom wouldn't make that mistake twice.

Tom founded a financial training and education company that required him to meet new people, build strong relationships, and get in front of thirty strangers each week to educate them and continue building his network. He had to master this or his company would fail.

Tom learned from his most significant career mistake and has become more confident at building relationships and putting himself out there. His hard work has paid off, and his confidence fuels his thriving career.

You have more than yourself to think about when you are a leader, and a solid power base sets you and your team up for success. Elevating your brand and expanding your power base go hand-in-hand. Return to your previous experiences, dust off your relationships with senior leaders, and use that as a starting point to strengthen your power base.

Building Lifelong Habits

Can you spare thirty minutes a week? Limit your doom scrolling and use the time to network. You'll soon have a vibrant network that enriches your career.

You need three things to become a master networker: a strategy that works for you, a plan you can execute, and tactics based on your authentic style that make networking fun.

If you want to get the most out of your thirty minutes a week of networking, take the time to create your strategy so you don't have to waste precious time thinking about what to do next. You can just go into execution mode and get a ton of outreach done quickly.

Follow these three steps when creating your strategy:
- Prepare
- Assess
- Execute

As you prepare, realign with your brand, and set SMART (specific, measurable, attainable, relevant, time-bound) goals. Find an accountability partner, create your two-minute intro, inventory what you can offer, and collect a few fun stories if needed.

Next, assess what you need, who you can leverage, what relationships you need to strengthen, and what gaps you need to close.

Plan your execution by identifying the fastest way to get what you want. Block time and create tasks to streamline your work. Create your conversation plan by setting your goal, preparing your pitch, preparing for outreach, and developing your follow-up strategy.

Another part of planning is understanding and working with your authentic networking style. If it feels uncomfortable, you won't do it. Here are a few things you want to consider as you create your plan:

- Are you an introvert or an extrovert?
- Are you a giver or comfortable asking for what you need?
- Is your style formal or casual?
- Do you like to focus on strategy or tactics?

- Do you create ideas or aggregate ideas from others?
- Do you prefer to ask questions or share your knowledge?

All these styles work, so use what you have and remember consistency wins every time.

Avoid making common networking mistakes and set yourself apart by being uniquely you. Make conversations about the other person, add value, be grateful, stay optimistic, and be a connector. Never sound desperate, push too hard, make it all about you, show frustration, or ask for something during the first conversation.

Where will you find your people? How do you expand and diversify your network? Try the "Factor of Ten" approach. The first step is to reengage with people you know, including former employers, colleagues who have moved on, professional associations, affinity groups, college alumni, philanthropic groups, community and spiritual groups, and anywhere else you spend time.

Identify the ten best people from your network sources to reach out to first. During your conversation, ask each to introduce you to someone in their network. Be specific. Ask for people who are at a leadership level you need and structure the interaction so you'll have an opportunity to do something small together. This is a great start to forming a more meaningful relationship.

Continue to deepen your relationship with your ten new contacts for three months. At the end of three months, ask them for a targeted network referral and do the same thing again. By the end of the year, you'll have forty meaningful contacts. When you do this year after year, your relationships will blossom and your power base will emerge.

"We think, mistakenly, that success is the result of the amount of time we put in at work, instead of the quality of time we put in."

— Arianna Huffington

I was a crappy networker until I got fired for the second time. I spent my career enjoying the people I worked with, but when we went our separate ways, I didn't keep in touch. I was too busy and was making shiny new friends in my new role.

A decade after being fired the first time, I found myself on the outside looking in. Only this time, I was more senior, the economy wasn't growing, and my network was stale. I hated feeling so disconnected from the people I'd done great work with. I was embarrassed to reach out after so long to ask for help. But I did it, and it worked. I landed a great job reasonably quickly, but I swore I wouldn't put myself in that position again.

I reached out to my power base first and started to reengage. I spearheaded a research project with one executive, mentored someone else's successor, and helped find a candidate for a previous manager. Reconnecting was nice; reengaging was valuable. It reignited a cycle of collaboration that had been left dormant for years.

Using the "Factor of Ten" approach, I deepened my existing relationships and took advantage of opportunities to diversify my network in an entirely new way.

Rebuilding my relationships has allowed me to guest lecture at Cornell University. I now engage with an advocacy group working for pay and promotion parity for underrepresented people in the financial services sector. I'm also asked to speak at various companies' Women in Leadership affinity groups. Through that work, I have met other well-connected mentors and we have been happy to help each other grow our network and strengthen our power base.

If you don't ask, the answer will always be no. Find your courage, reach out, and have fun while you do it.

Summary

Expanding, nurturing, and deepening your professional relationships will improve your growth opportunities, increase income, and help you have more fun. If networking feels awkward, shift to a service-based mindset and focus on helping others grow. You'll get what you need in return. Expand your power base and be a reliable source for others.

Don't have a false sense of security because of the number of connections you have on LinkedIn. The only relationships that count are the ones where you and the other person have done meaningful work together.

Proactively diversify your network and play bigger when curating your power base. Expand upon work you've done together, and find continuing ways to collaborate.

Networking shouldn't be a project; it needs to be incorporated into your lifestyle. Small efforts made consistently will produce excellent results. If you wait until you need something to reach out, it's too late. Create your strategy and implementation plan so you can begin your outreach and leverage your natural style.

Brain Candy – Important Questions for You to Chew On

Grab your journal and get started on your ABCs for growth.

Assess:

- What is the biggest thing holding you back from growing and nurturing your network?
- Do enough people know you?
- What is your natural networking style?

Baseline:

- How strong is your power base?
- How much time can you dedicate to making your network a priority?
- Where do you think your gaps are?

Conquer:

- What can you start doing today to create a rockstar power base?
- How will you approach implementing the "Factor of Ten" strategy?
- How will you diversify your network and expand your knowledge?

Chapter 14

CONQUERING YOUR SELF-PROMOTION DEMONS

"Leaders are not modest, and more importantly, the extensive social science research on self-promotion shows that these qualities and behaviors are useful for getting hired, achieving promotions, keeping one's job, and obtaining a higher salary."

— John Pfeffer

Now that you are reinvigorated and excited about reconnecting with old colleagues and meeting new ones, dust off your ability to talk about how awesome you are without sounding like a colossal jerk. Self-promotion is hard for almost everyone. It doesn't matter what experience you have, tooting your own horn feels weird.

Bad things happen when you don't self-promote. People either don't know you, or they aren't excited about what you can do. You become invisible, the cool projects go to someone else, and you lose out on the opportunity to grow.

Without self-promotion, your team suffers because they aren't getting the recognition they deserve, and you could end up working for an empty suit who isn't nearly as talented as you.

Let's explore the right way to self-promote.

Mastering Jerkless Self-Promotion

Do you hate taking credit for the work you lead? If you don't take credit for your work, someone else will. It's a total BS move and happens way too often.

You may tell yourself it's okay, but what about your team? They busted their tails and ended up feeling defeated because you're uncomfortable about bragging a little? That isn't the leader you want to be.

There are ways to raise awareness for your team with humility and gratitude. Grace has not gone out of style. Focus on the outcome. What have you done for the business? Share what you've learned from obstacles your team overcame to reach the goal so others can participate.

Acknowledge all the business partners and stakeholders who helped along the way. No one wins alone. This is your time to share the love and become a connector. The acknowledgment you need is automatically included if you can bring two people together through your successes. Embrace a service mindset as you make these connections.

Become known for something important and create a compelling dialogue tightly connected to the organization's top priorities. Everyone will pay attention when you talk about things people are compensated for.

Align yourself with great promoters. Some people have the gift of generating excitement over things they're enthusiastic about. Find those people and get them excited about you and your team. I always do that when I experience a product or service I love. I can't wait to tell everyone about it. The same applies in a corporate setting.

Be sensitive to timing and what's going on around you. If your company just had a massive layoff, it's probably not the best time to show off your team's victory in streamlining processes.

With so many options for self-promoting with style and grace, everyone can benefit when you do it right, and then the awkward feelings will be a thing of the past.

> "The image that concerns most people is the
> reflection they see in other people's minds."
>
> — Edward De Bono

Emily Soloby is the CEO of Juno Jones Shoes, a podcast host for *Hazard Girls*, and a trucking and logistics company co-owner. You would never guess Emily hated self-promotion and would do everything she could to stay behind the scenes. But her career had other plans for her.

A passionate advocate for women, Emily started her career as a domestic violence victim attorney. She fought tirelessly for women who had been victimized and their families. Emily found the work equally rewarding and emotionally draining. It was time for a career change when she hit an emotional brick wall.

Emily went back to school for broadcasting and communications with the intent of sharing women's stories and helping them. She met her husband, and they decided to buy out a family trucking business. They dedicated the next ten years to growing their business.

Emily noticed there was a problem with women's protective clothing. Everything was designed for men, and women had few options for clothing and footwear that fit correctly. "I began to speak with other women, and the excitement and encouragement was there. They said, 'You have to do this; we need options.'"

Fun fact: Emily used to make shoes as a hobby, and she turned her passion for supporting women, her love for shoes, and a market need into a thriving business. She was back in the business of following her passion and helping women.

But Emily couldn't hide anymore. She had a mission to fulfill and women to serve. She couldn't do that hiding in her office.

Emily is very private and shied away from posting anything personal on social media. "When it came time to let people know about Juno Jones shoes, I discovered people were hungry to know more about me. They wanted to know why I was doing this, who I was, more about my personality and family. The whole thing was a huge struggle for me."

She took her first leap into self-promotion by writing a blog post about her story, how she met her husband, and how they decided to enter the trucking industry. She also shared stories about her family and posted a family photo. "I couldn't believe I did it. I was terrified after posting it because I'd never shared anything publicly."

The overwhelming interest and support gave Emily the confidence to continue sharing through email newsletters and other social outlets.

Emily found a way to naturally self-promote through humility and being authentic. She's the first to recognize others' contributions when she's in the spotlight. "When you share the good work of others, hopefully, people will know your heart is in the right place."

Finding Your Sweet Spot

Do you know what your authentic self-promotion style is? If you don't self-promote on the regular, you probably don't.

Self-promotion can boost your confidence, crush your inner critic, and improve others' well-being. There can, however, be some downsides that may be lingering in the back of your mind.

When you put yourself out there, you open yourself up to criticism from the haters. You might start to feel pressure to knock it out of the park all the time or tie your sense of self-worth to others' opinions.

You can avoid these situations by following these self-promotion guidelines:

- Be truthful—this is not the time to embellish your successes.
- Provide a balanced view—share the wins and losses of your journey equally.

- Never steal credit for someone else's work—for obvious reasons.
- Keep it brief—people are busy.
- Connect everything to your audience's WIIFM.
- Continually seek feedback and welcome new points of view.

Your self-promotion sweet spot will be at the intersection of your leadership brand and your organization's culture. Carefully consider your approach and be purposeful with your strategy.

When you have work to showcase, you can share your ideas or highlight the ideas of others. You can self-promote alone or partner with someone else. Do you prefer to teach or learn? Is it more comfortable to take credit or give it? Does the corporate culture align with asking for help or offering help to others? Would you prefer to ask for connections or make the connections yourself?

You can self-promote in several ways. The best methods are the ones that will be most effective in the organization and authentic for you.

"Butterflies can't see their wings. They can't see how truly beautiful they are, but everyone else can. People are like that as well."

— Naya Rivera

Kate Milne founded Cardea Health Consulting and has been passionate about improving health through research, lifestyle, and nutrition for decades. While her career has taken a winding path, she has always focused on her passion for health and well-being.

She began her career on a clinical team working with people with long-term and difficult-to-treat psychological and chronic illnesses. She would do home visits, administer treatments, and help clients manage their daily needs while working around their limitations. Supporting clients individually was emotionally draining for Kate, so she took her first crack at entrepreneurship.

Kate is an ultra-long-distance runner. While traveling for work on the clinical team, she wanted to go run, but it wasn't always safe for a woman to run alone. That inspired her to start her first company— the world's first guided-running tour company. It was a fun business for her and the team until 9/11 happened and destroyed tourism. She quickly pivoted to corporate running groups, and the company thrived.

After the birth of her children, Kate wanted to focus on helping people on a much bigger scale. She went back to school and earned two master's degrees. Then she went into research and medical studies.

Kate has been working on extensive population health studies for governments, corporations, and cities to help people get healthy and stay healthy as they age. "What I'm selling isn't sexy. There's no magic pill, but even the smallest changes can have astounding impact."

Kate took a conservative approach to getting new clients by relying on word of mouth and responding to publicly available proposal requests. It limited her ability to branch out and serve a broader community. "If I could go back, I would have put my time and energy into learning sales and getting more comfortable putting myself out there. A lot of women struggle with self-promotion."

Kate struggled to find her self-promotion sweet spot because the question of worthiness was lingering in the back of her mind. Someone always has more experience or better qualifications than you, and it's easy to fall into overanalyzing and getting sucked into the perfection trap.

"I wish I hadn't focused so much on improving myself and constantly trying to bring something more to the table. I should have outsourced more and stayed focused on my superpowers."

Kate broke free from the things holding her back by aligning with her purpose. She asked herself, "Why am I doing this? Why is this important?" When your convictions outweigh your doubts, you can be bold in advocating for yourself and will find your self-promotion sweet spot. "What you provide to the world is so important and embracing that it gets you through those crazy times when the world falls apart."

Kate's business continues to thrive, and she is working on projects she's passionate about. "If you are miserable and doing something that's eating away at you, take the risk. Life is so short. I still believe we are meant to get up and live the shit out of life every day."

Kate has learned to take risks and self-promote. It wasn't comfortable at first, but decades of experience have taught her one lesson—when you jump, the net will appear.

Strategically Leveraging Setbacks

Did you know setbacks can get you promoted? I didn't until it happened to me.

You are so concerned with being perfect, limiting the number of slip-ups you and your team make, and protecting the dirty laundry from getting out and into enemy hands (aka your work frenemy) that you never thought a highly visible mistake could be a good thing.

I was leading a transformation project and we were overhauling the entire business process for one of our larger divisions. This group had a lot of problems. It took forever to onboard customers, it had failed countless audits, and it was blowing through money like crazy.

Big, slow, and expensive. There was plenty to fix, and our mandate was to fix all of it. By the time we were done, the initiative would save millions of dollars in operating expenses and increase revenue by getting our clients on the platform faster. This was high profile so the board watched us closely (no pressure).

The team was moving fast. Change was happening everywhere. The operations team knew staff reductions were inevitable and tempers ran high. We were running our playbook as planned. I had a strong team who knew what they were doing. Outside the usual bumps and bruises of any big project, things were going as well as could be expected.

Until my phone rang one day at 5 a.m. One of the technology changes we had implemented had failed. Transactions weren't processed, customer data was lost, compliance violations were flagged, and operations managers (who hated us anyway) were on the warpath. When I got to the office, I had a full-scale shitstorm on my hands. It took three weeks to clean up the mess, which was all our fault.

One week into the triage, I had to deliver my standing report to the board. I knew I would get my ass handed to me; it was just a question of how much flesh would be left when I got out. I prepped with my boss and his. I assumed full responsibility and was as prepared as I could be.

The room was dead silent when I walked in. This was completely unusual. This board was highly engaged, and they were typically wrapping up the previous conversation when I walked in.

I took my seat, and before my brain could stop my mouth, I said, "I totally fucked things up here." I had never dropped an F-bomb in a board meeting before, and even I was surprised to hear it come out of my mouth. I saw one board member smirk. I didn't dare look at the others.

I walked them through the screwup, remediation plan, damage assessment, and lessons learned. They had many questions, provided great insights to consider, and then I debriefed them on how the program was progressing, just like any other monthly report.

I didn't get my ass handed to me, and I didn't get fired. I left and felt like I had dodged a bullet; however, I was convinced my brand and reputation were irreparably damaged.

About three hours later, I got a call from the CEO's admin asking me to come back upstairs—the Board Chair wanted to meet with me again. My heart sank. I hadn't dodged the bullet; I had only received a very short stay of execution. I ended my meeting and went upstairs to meet my fate. I deserved it. This was a huge mistake and someone had to pay.

I put my game face on and tried to read his expression to understand what was coming. He was stoic and said, "We had some time to discuss what you said this morning. You took on a massive project critical to this company's viability. We knew mistakes were inevitable. This one was bigger than we expected, but we were incredibly impressed by you taking full accountability and immediately putting a triage team in place to get us back on track."

As he paused, I tried to understand how this statement would lead to him firing me. The chair continued, "We don't expect perfection; we expect correction, and your leadership has been exemplary. Keep up the great work (said with a grin on his face), and try not to fuck up as severely next time, please."

Apparently, I had started a new trend of dropping F-bombs in board meetings. I thanked him for the feedback and was gracious. I gave my team all the credit for the triage and even said a few nice words about the operations teams who had been making my life a living hell. I got out of there as fast as I could.

I'm not a crier, but I went into the bathroom and bawled my eyes out. Maybe it was the pressure release of not being fired or the utter shock of being commended for recovering from my colossal failure, but the emotions were flying.

A few months later, I was promoted to lead the global strategy team. This was a new role the board had created just for me. The company needed to move fast in various areas and feel confident mistakes would be corrected quickly and efficiently.

*"It's not what you achieve; it's what you overcome.
That's what defines your career."*

— Carlton Fisk

When you play big and fly close to the sun, everyone will see your successes and your screwups. It's not about being perfect; it's about being effective. When you can showcase your ability to deal with adversity, the right people will also see all the great things you have accomplished.

Summary

Self-promotion is a necessary evil and doesn't have to suck. You owe it to your team and yourself to create awareness about your great work and the value you add.

Find your authentic style and self-promote with grace and gratitude. Connect your accomplishments with the things the company values, and do it in a way that is authentic to your leadership brand.

Follow the self-promotion rules to avoid becoming an egotistical jerk and giving the haters a field day. Dole out the credit so everyone feels the love.

Share your lessons from obstacles your team overcame to reach the goal so others can participate in the win. And stop being so concerned with being perfect.

Sometimes your biggest screwups and how you course-correct highlight all the great work you and your team have been doing.

Brain Candy – Important Questions for You to Chew On

Grab your journal and get started on your ABCs for growth.

Assess:

- Are you feeling more confident in your ability to self-promote?
- What's your natural style?
- Will you leverage all your opportunities to self-promote?

Baseline:

- How does the company culture affect your strategy?
- Which tactics have you seen others use successfully?
- Are you playing too safe?

Conquer:

- Where can you put self-promotion into practice a little at a time?
- How can you leverage important teaching moments?
- Who can you partner with the next time your team has a win?
- How can you parlay mistakes into positive outcomes?
- How often do you give your team the credit they deserve publicly?

Part III: Disrupt—Transforming Insights into Action

I hope you have acquired new perspectives in Part III of this book as we discussed the power of disrupting and breaking all the rules. When you treat your career like a business, your perspectives shift and you start making better decisions for you and your career.

If you have been journaling your ABCs as you thought about all that brain candy, I'm sure you've had a flood of realizations come to light. Remember, "Vision without action is merely a dream."

It's time to transform your insights into action. Head over to the *Escaping the Career Trap Transformation Guide* and continue your journey toward creating a thriving career. Visit our website at: EscapingTheCareerTrap.com/Guide.

When you get there, you will find tools and a roadmap to:

- Treat your career like a business and make better decisions for yourself.
- Become a skill-stacking ninja and leverage every asset you have ever acquired.
- Find your *IT Factor* and leverage your edge to compete and succeed.
- Strengthen your power base.
- Master the art of self-promotion.

PART IV:
THRIVE

BECOMING THE CEO OF YOUR CAREER

Everyone deserves to love Mondays.

Chapter 15

LEADING YOUR WAY

"All of the great leaders have had one characteristic in common: it was the willingness to confront unequivocally the major anxiety of their people in their time."

— John Kenneth Galbraith

Once you've got your career in good stead, it's time to help others get there too. Having the freedom to lead your teams authentically is becoming increasingly difficult for many leaders.

Your company's decisions are pissing off your team. Who isn't bitter and resentful about trading in their PJs for a one-hour daily commute? The confines of the HR legal structure make it feel like the hoops you need to jump through have been purpose-built to make your life difficult. Decades-long declines in employee engagement challenge even the most compassionate leaders.

Teams are stressed and burnt out. Companies are struggling. Leaders are left in the middle trying to hold everything together. Strong leaders are becoming increasingly crucial and scarce.

The data is alarming. An article by Kristin Kizer, "35+ Powerful Leadership Statistics [2023]: Things All Aspiring Leaders Should Know," highlights troubling statistics. The article states:

- 77 percent of organizations report they are currently experiencing a leadership gap.
- 48 percent of employees view their company's leadership as "high quality."
- 79 percent of employees will quit due to lack of appreciation.
- 69 percent of employees say they would work harder if they felt their efforts were recognized.

Over three-quarters of US-based companies know their leadership is lacking, and they are doing little to nothing to solve the root cause of the problem. If 69 percent of your team started working harder tomorrow, what would that do to the bottom line? All you need to do is give them meaningful work, say thank you, and recognize their contributions more often. How hard is that?

This woeful leadership gap has a well-known bottom-line effect, and it continues to be ignored. Over half of US employees continue to feel disengaged, yet companies with high employee engagement are 22 percent more profitable.

Companies neglecting to create an environment where good leaders and their teams can thrive is not just shortsighted—it's fiscally irresponsible. I'm willing to bet we'd finally see an improvement if you tied employee engagement results to executive compensation.

These trends have been consistent for a long time. The likelihood of a turnaround is small. But in the chaos, there is opportunity. This is your time to shine and make the most of the turmoil we find ourselves in by becoming an epic leader.

It's time to become the leader people choose to follow.

Honing Your Purposeful Leadership Style

Do you focus on strengthening your leadership skills and your leadership style? Many leaders don't purposefully develop their leadership style. They focus on strengthening their leadership skills and becoming adept at thinking strategically, motivating teams, setting goals, building teams, and such. But how much time do they spend improving and modifying their leadership style?

Leadership skills get all the attention, but your leadership style makes the biggest impact. You are more effective when you are purposeful about your tone and how you lead. Strong leaders master the ability to flex and adapt based on current conditions.

You have a natural leadership style. You may be the coach, the pace-setter, the servant, or a transformational or bureaucratic leader. You tend to stay in the style that feels most natural to you. The best leaders, however, can read the room and adjust their style to fit the moment.

Start adapting your style to the situation and your teams will respond favorably. If your natural style is servant leadership, that may be fine for your daily routines, but sometimes you must show up differently. Dial up the bureaucracy when dealing with a political landmine. If you launch a significant change initiative, call upon your visionary and transformational styles to excite everyone. Sometimes you need to be the coach or the pacesetter, or you can choose to chill and take a relaxed approach to give the team a much-needed break.

One size does not fit all in terms of leadership styles. Be more purposeful in how you show up. Build your situational leadership style to adapt to what's happening around you and give your teams what they need to succeed in each moment.

> *"The single greatest 'people skill' is a highly developed and authentic interest in the other person."*
>
> — Bob Burg

Paula never wanted to lead people. She had avoided such opportunities and was happy being an individual contributor. Unfortunately, her ambition got the better of her, and a few of her bosses had to burst her bubble. The only way to grow was to lead people.

Paula's expertise was in program and project management. These skills gave her experience in multiple business lines and a wide range of functional knowledge. Paula was always learning something new.

She and her husband moved to a new country and had their first child. After returning from maternity leave, Paula had several jobs to choose from. A role managing people was the least stressful and required the least travel, so Paula tried it.

Things didn't go well. "I absolutely hated it. Managing an operational team with all the process formality and metrics we had to meet, the routines and repetitiveness of it all made me miserable." Paula's function was essential to the company, but her role didn't allow her to use her greatest assets.

After sticking it out for a while, Paula decided not to return after the birth of her second child. She took time to be with her family, recharge, and reassess her career options. She was happiest being an individual contributor, but her ambition continued to tap her on the shoulder.

When Paula was ready to return to the game, she got recruited for a position she never expected. On paper, she didn't look like a fit at all. Once she understood the role, she saw how her diverse functional knowledge and program management skills were precisely what the organization needed.

This time Paula got to build her team. The roles were highly skilled and she led more strategically, which energized her. Even though she loved the work, being a strong leader still felt unnatural to her. "Initially, it felt strange. I missed getting into the weeds of a project and doing things myself. After two-and-a-half years in this role, I've moved so far away from the details, it would take me a week to assemble a project plan I used to do in a day."

Slowly and begrudgingly, Paula was honing her unique leadership style. It's good she did because no one saw what was coming next. Her boss quit and all hell broke loose.

"Our leader was the glue holding us together. When she was gone, everything fell to pieces." Usually when an executive role opens up, everyone is vying for the position. Not this time. No one wanted the group she was in. It was like a massive game of hot potato. To make matters worse, the company was in the midst of a massive transformation, business was slipping, the stock price was falling, and the executives were having a fit.

With all this uncertainty, most of Paula's peers were in panic mode. With no leader and no prospects for a new one, the environment was changing fast. Paula's peers stopped trusting each other and retreated into their silos. Confusion and speculation quickly replaced strategy and execution.

Paula knew what she had to do. She utilized her coaching and transformational leadership styles to protect her team from the chaos. "My biggest role was to keep my team calm during these changes. I protected my team from all the chaos and gave them meaningful work with hard deadlines to focus on instead of feeding into the panic. It was probably the best thing I've ever done as a manager. I kept steady and stable while everything else was chaotic around them."

The uncertainty didn't last forever. A new leader was appointed and a clear strategy was set.

How each leader dealt with the uncertainty determined their role in building the future. The panicked leaders were no longer there, and those who remained focused saw an increased scope and responsibilities. Paula's approach served her and the team well. She now leads a bigger team and is critical in designing the company's future.

It's a good thing Paula's previous managers had encouraged her to develop various leadership styles. The world needs more leaders like Paula.

Building Bidirectional Trust

Do your colleagues trust you? Do you trust them? It's safe to assume your coworkers, team members, and colleagues won't trust you until you've earned it. Start from that baseline assumption and work to create an environment of trust.

When you start from the premise that everyone trusts each other and you sing "Kumbaya" around the water cooler, it gives you a false sense of security. It makes you lazy, and then you take shortcuts when doing the vital work of trust-building.

I coach a team of executives and their leadership teams. I know them individually and they're all great people, but it's bizarre when they start talking about interacting with each other. When they need to collaborate and I gently steer them in each other's direction, they become uncertain about who they can trust.

Trust is bidirectional. With all the competing priorities and hidden agendas, it's easy to see how things can be tricky. Without trust, things quickly fall off the rails. Productivity declines, team morale drops, your team disengages, your top talent quits, and you wonder how things got so bad.

The first step to building bidirectional trust is being trustworthy. Are you sending signals that you can be trusted or warning signs for people to approach cautiously? Are you keeping your promises? Do your words and your actions match? Do you communicate transparently, eliminate surprises, treat people fairly, and resolve conflicts quickly and openly? If you don't, there's a good chance people don't trust you.

How can you tell if your colleagues don't trust you? The first sign of trouble is when no one relies on you for support. If you are not empowered to make decisions, you are the last to hear important information, or no one is willing to give you direct feedback or bad news, the team doesn't trust you yet.

Everyone needs to go through the know, like, and trust cycle. You can't take shortcuts to get there, but you can speed up the process. Create opportunities for collaboration and set shared success goals. When team members collaborate for the common good, they build trust faster.

Orchestrate opportunities for your team to get to know each other personally. I've seen archenemies become best buddies because of a mutual admiration for Harlequin Great Danes. You can't make this shit up.

Avoid setting competing priorities. If your team's success criteria conflict, you create unnecessary drama. This happens more often than you might think. At the first sign of friction, verify what each person is accountable for. Nine times out of ten, you are both following directives from the same leader and being sent in opposite directions.

The most extensive mindset shift everyone needs to make is to always assume good intent. It's easy to vilify someone who disagrees with you or who appears to be undermining your every move. While a fair number of jerks are out there, they are in the minority—most people aren't trying to screw with you for sport.

When you assume good intent, it forces you to try to see things from a different perspective. Have the conversations you need to iron out any misunderstandings and conflicting priorities.

Creating an environment that fosters trust at the individual and team levels requires focus and high emotional intelligence. Take the time to get everyone onboard and keep everyone there. You will accomplish amazing things together.

"Trust is like love. Both parties have to feel it before it really exists."

— Simon Sinek

I got a rude awakening from one of my favorite managers. Dan had been a client, then recruited me to work for him. Over the years, we accomplished some incredible things. I thrived under his coaching and guidance. At the time, I was on the road to self-destruction and never saw it coming.

My family had recently moved from New York City to Charlotte, North Carolina. It was a massive adjustment for me. I grew up in a fast-paced culture where people told you exactly what they thought and threw in a few expletives for added color.

It felt like I was transported to a different planet. The pace was slower. People smiled and asked how your day was. If they disagreed with you, you'd never know unless you understood the true meaning of "Bless your heart."

I was leading a project that was moving at a glacial pace. I was frustrated, the teams were frustrated, and there was no end in sight. I complained to Dan, "I miss New York. Up there, I felt like I was swimming with sharks and it was fun. I feel like I'm in a pool of minnows here."

Dan smirked and let loose one of his infamous analogies. He said, "You're not swimming with minnows. You are swimming with dolphins, and a pod of dolphins can kill a shark very quickly." My eyes widened, and in an instant, I understood what he meant. I was the shark—the dolphins were circling me! He continued, "You're an outsider and the team doesn't trust you."

That shook me to the core. I may be many things, but being untrustworthy was never one of them. I didn't understand why no one trusted me.

Dan left me to figure it out on my own. Over the next few weeks, I started to pay attention to how business was done instead of plowing forward with my New York ways. I watched, listened to conversations, and paid particular attention to what wasn't being said. I bought a wooden dolphin statue and kept it in my office as a reminder of Dan's story.

Over time, I learned how to adjust my style to fit in with the new culture. I learned how to be nicer. I made an extra effort to show I genuinely cared about how everyone was doing and learned about their families, hobbies, and interests. I learned moving slower made things progress faster. I made it my mission to earn trust in this new environment. I also learned what "Bless your heart" really meant and used it like a local when needed.

Communicating Powerfully

Are you a good communicator? The best leaders are masterful communicators. They can inspire and evoke emotions that compel people to act. Author and presidential speechwriter James Humes said, "The art of communication is the language of leadership." I completely agree.

Talking is easy. Communicating takes a lot of work. When you get it right, everyone around you is on the same page and will achieve great results. When you get it wrong, your teams bang into each other and are hindered by misunderstandings, rework, and confusion.

How do you become a masterful communicator? You connect everything to the "why." Managers and leaders are often excellent at telling people what to do, how to do it, and when to do it. Very few take the time to help everyone understand why what they are doing is important.

Research shows most employees need a sense of purpose and connection to what they do for a living. Explaining why something is important, why a priority changed, and why what they do matters is essential to helping each individual make the connection.

You need to be a powerful communicator if you want to make a meaningful connection with your team. The golden rule says to treat people how you would like to be treated. Have you heard of the platinum rule? The platinum rule says to treat people how they want to be treated. It's a subtle nuance that makes a big difference.

I prefer when people are straightforward and leave nothing to the imagination. If I spoke to people the way I prefer to be spoken to (the golden rule), I would make a few of them cry, and I would put off and offend most.

The golden rule needs to be revised, especially when considering culture, personality, geography, education, and socio-economic backgrounds. These dynamics inform how a person communicates and absorbs information.

People prefer communicating in their own way. As a leader, you need to meet people where they are. It's about reaching them on their terms.

Have you ever been in a meeting where it seemed like everyone understood each other and agreed to an outcome, and then a few hours later, you talked to someone or saw an email that was so far off-base you started to wonder if you were even in the same meeting? Doesn't that drive you bonkers?

Assuming yes means agreement is a mistake many leaders make. Yes often means understanding. So, you hear yes and happily move on with your day assuming everyone is on the same page—until you realize they're not and you have to start all over again.

Another communication breakdown stems from the need for more awareness of and adjustment to different communication styles.

The communication styles are analytical, functional, intuitive, and personal.

- Analytical communicators are logical, dependable, numerically driven, and can make unbiased decisions.

- Functional communicators are inquisitive, process-driven, and execution-focused.

- Intuitive communicators are creative, prefer things at the macro level, and need to know how things fit in the overall strategy.

- Personal communicators feel connected to the team, are diplomatic, and are transparent with their ideas.

When you only use your preferred communication style, you leave people with the other three styles out in the cold. Adjust your style to meet your audience and to improve understanding.

> *"If you just communicate, you can get by. But if you communicate skillfully, you can work miracles."*
>
> — Jim Rohn

For example, I remember being frustrated when it felt like my team, manager, and stakeholders didn't "get it." I would devise a big idea to fix a problem and start to talk about it because I was excited. As an intuitive communicator, I was not prepared to meet the communication needs of the entire team.

My boss was an analytical communicator and wanted to dive into the data. I didn't have the data yet—it was just a big idea I wanted to share.

My leaders who were functional communicators would dive into the rabbit hole, wondering how we would pull off my big idea. Of course, I had no clue because I hadn't thought that far ahead yet.

The personal communicators on my team wanted to understand the employee impact and how we would engage them, and again, I didn't have the answers they needed.

They weren't trying to be difficult. They genuinely needed to see things through a lens they understood naturally. Once I learned how to meet them where they were, excitement grew and we could work more cohesively.

To be fair, when a communicator of the other three types came to me with their big ideas, I probably drove them crazy by asking how it fit into the big picture. We all need what we need.

The best leaders also listen more than they speak. Your team needs to be heard and to feel understood.

Are you just listening or are you trying to understand? For a long time, I sucked at understanding people because I filtered all the information I was getting through my personal lens.

If I heard someone lost their job, I would say I was sorry because I'd been fired twice and knew how they felt. No, I didn't. I had no idea how the person felt. They could have been thrilled because they were ready to quit and got a giant severance package. I didn't ask, so I didn't know.

Presuming empathy degrades your ability to help people feel understood. If you want to know how someone feels, ask them. Listen intently without judgment, confirm understanding, and validate their feelings with humility.

Communication is powerful when you get it right. You can build a cohesive team, achieve goals faster, and become an inspiration to those around you. When you use the platinum rule, don't assume yes means agreement; and when you start with the why and seek to understand, you will have mastered the language of leadership.

Cultivating High-Performing Teams

Do you feel like your job is too easy? You would if you had high-performing teams. I felt like I won the lottery whenever I had a rockstar team. We collaborated on setting our direction, my leaders would get their teams into action, and all I did was remove roadblocks and clear the path for them to run as fast as possible. It was truly a thing of beauty.

If you are overwhelmed or burnt out, most of your problems can be solved by upgrading your team's capabilities. What's the point of having leaders if everything ends up on your desk anyway?

Before you can put all your energy into upgrading your team, you need to do some spring cleaning on your leadership habits and confirm you're not part of the problem.

Are you holding on to poor performers for too long? When you have dead weight, it affects the rest of the team's morale. Do what is required to meet the HR requirements and eliminate toxic, poorly performing team members. Even without replacing them, your team will be more productive.

How much time are you freeing up for your team to think and get work done? If you allow an environment where their days are full of back-to-back meetings, you are crushing their spirit. Lighten the load and give them time to think and work.

Are you keeping things strictly professional and avoiding getting to know your team personally? Are you hesitant to share information about your personal life? Keeping everyone at arm's length creates a disconnection and slows trust building. AI hasn't taken over the world (yet). You lead humans; you are human; act like it.

High-performing teams need a shared vision so they are empowered to grow and fail forward, trust and respect each other, be results-oriented, and have a safe place to hold one another accountable.

This is best achieved when you create a family feel. People need to feel connected. It increases everyone's commitment when they feel unique and part of the family. The "we win and lose together" family vibe also comes in handy when someone makes a mistake. You defend them publicly and take the fallout, if there is any. When you return "home," you give them some tough love and private coaching.

Have fun. Days in the office can be so serious, and there's no reason for it. Laugh, lighten things up, keep things in perspective, and have a good time. There's nothing in the employee handbook against that.

Give your team a break. High-performing teams work hard. They don't do it because they have to—they do it because they want to. It's your job to be the adult in the room and replace their toys for some forced R&R. I've had to go so far as to cut off a manager's access to our systems on the weekends because she wouldn't unplug. Keep an eye on the hours your teams are putting in and force them to take breaks often.

> *"Talent wins games, but teamwork and*
> *intelligence win championships."*
>
> — Michael Jordan

Hailing from a large family of academics and journalists, Miriam Gilbert bucked the trend and decided on a business career. Fresh out of university, she started to work with one of the big five consulting firms.

Involved in restructuring teams and overseeing various business functions during mergers and acquisitions, Miriam worked in transportation, banking, and financial markets. She mastered how large companies operated and how to get things done in highly complex and political environments.

Then it was time for Miriam to leave the sausage factory and broaden her horizons. She was part of the strategic leadership team for a 1.2 billion-dollar insurance startup and a billion-dollar transportation project in Scotland. She was involved in saving a bankrupt company running the London Underground after it had gone public. Miriam ultimately became the CFO of a consulting firm.

Miriam has seen it all regarding size, scale, complexity, and political volatility. As a senior leader on these teams, she had to have high-performing teams or it would have been the death of her career.

Miriam frequently had three types of team members on her projects: full-time employees, contractors, and vendors. While everyone rallied around the same goals, each had their agenda. Getting these three constituents to align and perform at their peak was always a challenge.

Miriam is a huge proponent of having each team member play to their strengths. "Unless it's disruptive, telling an adult to work on their weaknesses is a bit patronizing and a waste of time. If they concentrate on their strengths, and I do my job right by balancing out the team, everyone is pulling in the same direction."

Creating trust within the team was a huge priority for Miriam. She encouraged the teams to interact on a more personal level. They would hit the pub after work, and she would encourage information sharing to help the team bond.

Miriam built trust by advocating for her team members when they needed something that didn't align with the company rules. One of her top performers needed a flexible work arrangement to deal with a personal situation at home. Remote work was unheard of then, but Miriam got the necessary approvals. That leader went on to deliver fantastic work on some of Miriam's most challenging projects.

Miriam's ultimate goal was for her teams to be self-sufficient after she was gone. In most cases, they did not name a successor when she left. She views that as a great compliment because it demonstrates her ability to bring people up in their careers and help them reach their potential.

Wherever Miriam worked, she left a legacy of high-performing teams, but it was time to chart a new path and start her consultancy. Coincidencity is a boutique consulting firm helping leaders build high-performing teams and grow their businesses. Today, Miriam gets her joy and energy by helping her clients leave legacies of being great leaders.

Putting the pieces in place to create high-performing teams is worth the effort. You have more fun, you help your team members and the company move forward, and everyone grows. Creating a family dynamic and ensuring everyone is having fun is essential. Laugh often and criticize sparingly.

Summary

You can disrupt the system and lead authentically. You don't have to be like everyone else, and it's best for your career if you leverage your uniqueness. The data shows most companies have a massive leadership gap and an equal level of disinterest in solving the problem. Your leadership capabilities can make all the difference.

Spend just as much time honing your leadership style as your leadership skills. You will create great followership by being purposeful about adapting your leadership style to the moment and being the leader your team needs.

Without trust, you have nothing. Trust can't be a one-way street. Bidirectional trust needs to be your top priority if you plan to succeed. Start with being trustworthy and show your team how to do it.

Communication is power. Speak to people how they want to be spoken to. Start with the *why* so you can connect everything to a purpose, and don't assume empathy. Seek to understand, not just listen.

High-performing teams make your job easier and everyone has more fun. You'll be thrilled with the results when you put the pieces in place and let your team run. If you discover you're part of the problem, correct your actions as needed. Create a family feel, have fun, and give your teams the breaks they need to be fresh and energized.

Brain Candy – Important Questions for You to Chew On

Grab your journal and get started on your ABCs for growth.

Assess:

- How many different leadership styles come naturally to you?
- What is your natural communication style?
- How can you create a family atmosphere and have fun every day?

Baseline:

- How can you help your team trust each other sooner?
- How can you level up your communication style?
- Do you have the right players in the right positions?

Conquer:

- Where are the best opportunities to foster collaboration and personal connections?
- Do you start with the why and use it as your guide when you need to adapt and redirect?
- Can the team embrace a "we all win or lose together" mindset?

Everyone deserves to love Mondays.

Chapter 16

THRIVING DURING TIMES OF CHAOS

"A great leader's courage to fulfill his vision comes from passion, not position."

— John Maxwell

What type of leader are you? Are you exceptional at changing the business, or do your strengths lie in running the business? Both leadership approaches are critical yet require very different skills. Rarely can a leader do both equally well, and it is even rarer to find a leader who enjoys changing and running the business equally. Understanding your leadership focus is essential as you master the ability to thrive in chaos.

Those who can guide through times of uncertainty are highly prized. During difficult times, the factors you consider, the approaches you take, and the business results you deliver depend on whether you're a "change the business" or "operate the business" kind of leader.

Our crises *du jour*: hyperinflation, cryptocurrency volatility, the threat of recession, geopolitical instability, environmental disasters, the metaverse, AI taking over the world, Chat GPT displacing knowledge workers, tech layoffs, companies calling everyone back to the office despite the resounding preference for hybrid or remote work—the list goes on and on.

It makes sense to play it safe. However, if that's your strategy, it's no surprise you feel stuck. When you think about it, when haven't we been in uncertain times? Yet each season of chaos feels different.

Have you become good at adapting to the current craziness? Or have you perfected the ability to fly below the radar and survive? Earlier, you learned to take control of how you change. You know the perils of giving away your power and the bounty of taking personal responsibility.

Often when things get scary, people freeze up and play it safe. Uncertainty, risk, and fear hold most people back. We need leadership at a time when leadership is at its most scarce. When others are hiding under their desks, it is the best time for you to surge.

In times of crisis, there is always opportunity. Every economy has its winners and losers. You have the tools—now put them to work.

Focusing on What's Really Important

Can you sift through the clutter and focus on what's most important? Crises and chaos are best friends. They unleash this frenetic energy you can almost see buzzing in the air. If you pay attention, you will see your colleagues running around like they've just chugged a case of Red Bull. Everyone is busy…busy…busy. They're stressed out, exhausted, and burnt out. Yet nothing of importance gets done.

The best leaders rise above the fray and rally their teams to focus on what's most important. Each day has a million priorities, and when things get complicated, the ability to focus and prioritize ruthlessly is indispensable.

How can we be one of these leaders? Most of us have adopted the magpie as our spirit animal. We are chasing shiny objects around as they glitter in the sun. I'm guilty of the same thing, especially when I'm stressed or want to avoid an unpleasant situation.

When things get hard, we focus on easy work. It makes us feel like we can accomplish something. These things are usually the least important and take precious time and focus away from what's needed most.

Here's a quick example of the magpie syndrome. One of our coaches was struggling to bring in new clients. She wasn't booking enough strategy calls. When I dug into where she was spending her time, I discovered she had spent four hours one day creating the graphics for her email signature. Wait…what? Granted, it was beautiful, but it won't bring in new clients.

Use times of chaos as an opportunity to differentiate yourself and bring your teams along with you—learn to thrive in chaos.

The best leaders focus on the things they can control. You can't dictate market conditions, control your competition, or fix geopolitical instability. You can maintain your customer relationships, product pricing, and operational efficiency.

Spend time understanding and adapting to the changing conditions around you instead of worrying about them. This level of strategic agility will help you thrive.

When things get complicated, the "nice to have" projects must be put on hold. This is the time to focus all your organization's resources on a few concrete goals. The rest will just have to wait. Understand the organization's top two or three priorities. Is it revenue, customer retention, efficiency, or accelerating new products to seize a unique opportunity? Everything you and your teams do should align with critical priorities.

> *"Men make history and not the other way around. In periods where there is no leadership, society stands still. Progress occurs when courageous, skillful leaders seize the opportunity to change things for the better."*
>
> — Harry S. Truman

Canceling work in progress isn't the most popular thing with your team because realizing their work isn't mission-critical triggers a scarcity mindset and they begin to fear they may lose everything. Overcommunicate why the change is happening, redirect their work, help them visualize their part in the shift, and give them a safe place to voice their concerns.

A client encountered a situation I hadn't experienced before. The CEO put a lot of work on hold so they could spend four months on a mission-critical initiative desperately needed to increase quality and profitability. They suspended all work that conflicted with the strategic direction, which resulted in about thirty team members having almost nothing to do.

It soon came to light that these team members were sneaking work through the approval process by adding it to work still in progress. It's like when politicians attach self-serving riders to significant legislation and hope no one notices. It worked for a few weeks until someone caught on. You can only imagine the storm that followed.

The team members weren't given a role in the strategic work. They were told to sit tight and await further instructions. Can anyone say unemployed?

Idle hands are the devil's workshop, and all this waiting turned into team-wide panic. Picture a herd of zebras running from a pride of lions that just rolled up and you'll get a sense of the fear-based stampede this team was in.

They might become unemployed anyway because of insubordination, but that's a story for a different day. What should have happened? The CEO should have overcommunicated to help the team understand what their world would look like once the strategic work was finished.

Even if things aren't finalized, transparency is vital. In the absence of data, people will assume the worst. Don't give them any more cause for alarm than they already have. The team needed to glimpse what their new future could look like to give them hope. Instead, they were staring into the abyss.

The team also needed a role in the strategic work. There's always more work to do than people to do it. The leader should have repurposed this team to make them feel like part of the solution instead of part of the problem. Meaningful work would have gone a long way in stabilizing morale and getting work done simultaneously.

Don't make the same mistake this company did. It may feel like you are slowing things down when you have to spend so much time communicating. When you slow down and think through your opportunities and the implications of your decision and communicate them effectively, you can anticipate problems and head them off.

Creating Urgency Instead of Panic

What's the difference between urgency and panic? There's a fine line between the two. Urgency is based on optimism and working toward a bright future. Panic is fear-based and works to prevent something terrible from happening. Which side of that thin line are you leading from?

Do your teams feel engaged, stable, unstoppable, and in control? Or do your teams feel ineffective, impulsive, and lacking in direction? You can be in the same situation and have two completely different outcomes based on the tone you set as their leader.

How do you stop the panic, get your team to align, and move with urgency instead? You do everything possible to stabilize their environment and provide a view of the future. The biggest reason people panic is because they fear the loss of their jobs, their control, or their routines. While you may not be able to prevent these outcomes, the more transparency you can provide about the steps the organization is taking, the easier it will be for your team to maintain a productive flow.

One thing teams forget during moments of chaos is that you're human too. They forget you face the same uncertainty, challenges, and potential for a grim future that they do. The team looks to you for guidance and reassurance. You may be just as freaked out as they are, but you have to put your team's needs ahead of your own.

You may inadvertently send your team messages that spark panic and undermine what you mean to say. You're only making matters worse if you constantly change their priorities, micromanage, communicate erratically, and keep secrets.

When you empower them to be part of the solution, you establish a sense of influence and control that your team can anchor to. They need to know the light at the end of the tunnel isn't a freight train as you direct them.

Lead with heart, collaborate with others, and know your team's pressure points. Be more available and visible to the entire organization. A crisis is no time to hide. Give your team and yourself the space to destress and recharge.

Control the narrative. Your team will fill in the blanks if you don't. When that happens, the doomsday scenario they paint will be far more catastrophic than the current reality.

If you don't know or can't divulge confidential information to your team, be as open and honest as you can. My leaders were much more comfortable when I said, "I know the answer but can't share it with you yet," or "We haven't figured it out yet and have a few options we're still considering." At least then they know the leadership team is aware and working on the things they're concerned about.

If you are in an unfortunate situation of knowing staff cuts are coming or you'll be losing a big chunk of work, and you are sworn to secrecy, there are tactics you can use to increase transparency and channel the stress.

Several times, I knew parts of my team would be eliminated, but I couldn't say anything. When someone from my team would ask me a straightforward question about their fate, I would confirm we were looking at cost-cutting options across the company. Then, I'd let them talk through the scenarios of what could happen. Nine times out of ten, they'd see the writing on the wall, and while I never confirmed it, I didn't say they were wrong either. Sometimes what you don't say speaks volumes.

When you can genuinely and honestly instill optimism and a vision for the future, do it with as much energy as possible. You have to work twice as hard to get your team to see the bright side of a situation when they are stressed. What you say will not be absorbed the first time, so you'll need to slow down, be repetitive, and give people time to process.

"One of the key qualities a leader must possess is the ability to detach from the chaos, mayhem, and emotions in a situation and make good, clear decisions based on what is actually happening."

— Jocko Willink

Dave was thrust into chaos and needed to act fast. He was an executive at a prominent hotel chain and led the crisis management team. He and his team had built a robust program recognized as one of the best crisis management programs in the industry. He would lecture at conferences and advise peers when asked.

Behind the scenes, the executive leadership team was a mess. One executive tried to oust the president so he could take over the top spot. In his coup attempt, he got the board members riled up. The dysfunctionality and leadership culture was toxic.

When COVID-19 started to unfold, everyone panicked. The world was ending, and Dave assembled the crisis management team. The executive team and top leaders were on the phone.

Dave recalls, "I remember thinking, *I've got the three top guys in the company. They ought to say something.* I kept pausing to let them speak and they wouldn't. I kept waiting for the president, and he just wouldn't say anything. So, I spoke from a place of true grit. Letting something fail wasn't in my nature and I wouldn't let this fail."

Dave shared a great analogy to describe what was happening around the leadership table. "It's like the president was driving a very expensive car and then suddenly this global crisis appears and he stops the car, leaves the key in the ignition, and walks away. Someone had to drive the car, so I hopped in and floored it. I peeled out, didn't stop at stop signs, and took corners too fast, but I ultimately got the car where it needed to be. Whether I keep my job or not, I will do what I feel is right."

Once Dave took the reins, he knew he had to act quickly. Seeing how the rest of the world responded, he knew there had to be a better way. He arranged for the hotel chain to be used as quarantine sites. Dave didn't ask for permission, and within a matter of days, the government started moving people in.

Industrywide, hotel occupancy was in the single digits during the crisis, and some of their competitors didn't make it. Dave's company never dropped below 44 percent, and their layoffs were minimal compared to the industry average. Dave and the team moved with purpose and didn't panic. They had an urgent need, and it required swift and decisive action.

Dave correlates this experience to a scene from *Forrest Gump* where Forrest and Captain Dan are in a shrimp boat during a hurricane. They chose to keep their boat out when everyone else docked theirs. Most of the docked boats were destroyed. Forrest and Captain Dan were the first to return to the water and caught the most shrimp. Dave states, "We decided early on to do everything possible to keep every hotel open. Fortunately, only a few closed, and we got up to 90 percent occupancy. We were keeping the business alive and supporting people in need."

Dave's ability to prevent panic, act urgently, and bring the team with him resulted in him being promoted to president. Strong leaders can bring companies and their teams through a crisis and make them more resilient. This was a defining moment for the company. Dave rallied the team to respond to a crisis, rebuilt the culture, and positioned the company for a bright future.

Taking the Right Risks at the Right Time

How much risk are you willing to take? Most organizations and people lose their risk appetite during times of chaos. They're not willing to play big anymore. There's a lot of second-guessing, hedging, and slowing things down.

Taking risks when everyone else is hedging is a prime opportunity to accelerate your career. It's also an opportunity to make a big difference in the organization and solidify your reputation. But you have to be strategic about when you choose your moment to surge.

Identify where your company is and is not willing to experiment. For example, if your business isn't earning the revenue they need, how much money and time are they willing to invest in trying something new? Knowing the answer could mean the difference between the corner office and the unemployment line.

Suppose your organization is unwilling to look at creative solutions to increase top-line growth. In that case, look at optimizing instead, finding ways to remove costs to increase profitability. If the organization is willing to be creative with bringing in more revenue, that is where you should focus your efforts.

How much risk are you willing to take personally? Taking on a highly visible project without guaranteeing success is risky. Which season is your career in? Are you positioned to try to hit a home run, or should you take a base-hit approach?

Sometimes you can be the hero by not doing anything at all. Simply challenge the initiatives already in progress that should have been stopped a long time ago. You need to ask, "Why are we still doing this?"

When you ask the same questions to different people and get different answers, it becomes painfully apparent no one is on the same page. In a crisis, everyone has to have laser-sharp focus on the objectives and the finish line. If you see a lot of time, effort, and money wasted on "roads to nowhere" projects, kill them. You'll be the hero for being brave enough to say stop because the entire team has probably been thinking the same thing for a lot longer than you have.

I lost count of how many times I saw millions of dollars wasted because no one dared to say stop. When the plan you started a year and a half ago is no longer relevant—almost everyone knows you should just cancel it.

The politics involved in squashing a big project can be tricky due to the complexity of changing course after committing time, money, and resources. If you have the opportunity and courage to do it, you can accelerate your career without lifting a finger.

Once you have identified your path forward, find things that could go wrong. Identifying risk is an excellent job for those on your team who are eternal pessimists. They're the first to tell you everything that could go wrong, so use them to your advantage.

And then, once you've identified all the things that could go wrong, figure out what you can do to detect and prevent the potential dangers from happening. You know it's a matter of when, not if, things will go sideways, so make sure you have a solid plan.

With your strategically aligned initiative set, goals established, and risks identified and planned for, create your bailout plan. You can go from failure to genius instantly when you create an exit strategy for high-risk projects before you begin. Communicate your bail-out plan with the organization so everyone is on the same page.

Chunk out your work in small pieces and deliver fast. During times of chaos, things change quickly, so don't get stuck in long delivery cycles that increase your likelihood of failure. Check in constantly on the progress of your micro-goals and modify the project as needed to verify things are working as intended. Give yourself time to observe what's happening and make the right decisions for you and your team.

"Opportunities don't happen. You create them."

— Chris Grosser

Denise built a rockstar team as she was helping her company grow. She took her team from eight to one hundred people in twenty countries. By the time the organization was ready to go public, the company had grown to 15,000 employees.

It's a rare luxury to build your team from scratch. As Denise grew her team to meet the company's growing demands, she hand-selected nearly everyone. The teams were loaded with talent. She examined how these hired guns worked together and created a dynamic culture of high-energy, ambitious experts.

The company was preparing to go public. Everyone was excited. Teams were working around the clock, the press was swarming, and the buzz around the company's future was electric.

Denise's team continued to conquer every challenge she threw at them, and as the company grew, she knew she had to make some tough decisions. "When you hire top talent, they want to grow, and there were so many things happening simultaneously, the opportunities for them to grow were everywhere."

There was just one problem—these opportunities to grow were in other parts of the company. Despite Denise's deep insecurity about making this next move, she knew it was right and began.

One by one, she met with stakeholders around the organization and negotiated the transfer of parts of her team. If she were selfish and kept them, they wouldn't have had the opportunities to grow. The company would have lost out on having talented people in the most essential parts of the business.

When all was said and done, Denise had negotiated the transfer of almost her entire department to other teams, leaving her with minimal staff. She brought her recommendations to the C-Suite and they supported her decision. They told her not to worry; there would be plenty of work for her.

Denise left the meeting happy for her team, yet feeling incredibly exposed professionally. She surrounded herself with top talent, and it made her a better leader. When they outgrew her group, she was selfless enough to do the right thing for them and the company, putting herself at risk.

As it turned out, the IPO (initial public offering) fell apart and the company went from skyrocketing to fame and fortune into a death spiral. Because Denise had given away her team, she could focus on whatever was blowing up. She was pulled from one catastrophe to the next, fixing everything as she went.

"I was able to jump in and start restructuring. I didn't wait to be told what to do. I just did what I knew had to be done to get things back under control." Ultimately, Denise ran several critical initiatives mandated by the CEO to help the company remain viable after the failed IPO.

She was a critical member of the leadership team that saved the company. There was no way anyone could have predicted this would happen, but she was ready for the challenge when it did. Doing the right thing is always the right thing to do.

Becoming the Leader People Choose to Follow

Times of change provide you with the opportunity to become the leader people choose to follow. When you consider the best leaders you've ever worked for, what do they have in common? What did they do (and not do) to rise above the rest?

Help your team maintain a positive outlook and remain connected to their purpose. Stay steady and stable even when things around you appear to be falling apart. Communicate often, listen even more, and always connect the "why" to any changes in direction or priorities. Remain humble and empathetic, and remind the team that everyone is going through these moments together.

It's vital to double down on building personal relationships. While you may have your hands full leading and keeping everything afloat, take a genuine interest in the people working for you. Check in to see how they're handling the uncertainty. Learn about their goals, hobbies, family situation, and things they are excited about. Connecting with team members personally goes a long way toward gaining the trust you need to lead.

Share your vision with everyone. As you tackle projects to create a better future, bring everyone along. Tell your story in pictures, draw connections to the work others do, solicit feedback, and describe the WIIFM to your team, peers, and stakeholders. When you create a vision people can get excited about and you give them a role to play, it gives them something positive to focus on. It takes their mind off the stress and worry and creates the urgency they need so people are working toward an optimistic future.

Empower the team, give them all the credit, and take the blame when things don't go as planned. Become the sounding board for new ideas, the roadblock remover when they hit resistance from other parts of the organization, and the cheerleader when they need a bit of motivation.

Have fun. You learned earlier that people who laugh more live longer. When chaos reigns, it's easy to get stuck in the gloom and doom. Levity and humor are excellent ways to lighten the mood and make everyone laugh as they move about their day.

When you become the leader people choose to follow, your influence goes far beyond your department. You'll start seeing your business partners and your stakeholders leaning on you and coming to you when they need help. This is the ultimate sign you're doing everything right as a leader, particularly during times of chaos.

"Become the kind of leader people would follow voluntarily; even if you had no title or position."

— Brian Tracy

The dot-com boom was in its heyday. Unlimited venture capital fueled the land of milk and honey and valuations grew at a breakneck pace. It had been glorious helping our clients build sexy new technology and prepare for Y2K.

If you were in the technology services industry, you ended 1999 with your hair on fire, exhausted, burnt out, and wealthy. Companies couldn't throw money at us fast enough. I led a professional services team, and we served most of the big banks. I tripled the size of our group, and we still couldn't keep up with the demand.

We had no idea how quickly this would all come to an end. The follow-on work from Y2K never materialized. In March 2000, the dot-com boom started showing signs of turning into a bust, and we were powerless to prevent the bubble from bursting.

Revenue dried up, clients lost budgets, and tech companies disappeared overnight. The markets were in a panic and our clients were getting laid off. We were screwed.

My competitors had started laying people off, and I was getting pressure from corporate headquarters to do the same. The team had become family, and the thought of a mass layoff was heartbreaking. Everyone had worked so hard.

You could sense the fear. Some people dug in and worked harder; most people gave up. My peers leading other parts of the business were spending less and less time in the office. Our vibrant, high-performing office felt more like a morgue.

I finally got the ultimatum from my boss. If business didn't pick up in thirty days, I had to fire half my team. My peers received the same mandate. I got a crazy idea, pulled my peers into a room, and shared my plan.

Everyone contributed to the strategy and the plan got better. We agreed to tell the entire office what was happening the next day. Informing the team went against the mandate from HR, but we concluded it didn't matter because if the plan didn't work, we'd all get fired anyway.

We got everyone together and confirmed their suspicions and worst fears. The room was heavy and quiet. I let the news settle in for a few minutes. Then we started to reveal the master plan. You could feel a little bit of energy coming back into the room. Questions started to fly, ideas were shared, and the faint glimmer of hope and optimism made its first appearance in months.

We managed to get 100 people to commit to attempting the impossible. Then it was time for the hard part. I had to return to my boss and negotiate a reduced sales number the team felt they could cover. It was grueling, and it took days to get the bar lowered.

We all worked seventy-hour weeks that month. My days were spent focusing the team on our goal, remaining optimistic, removing roadblocks, helping develop a plan B when something didn't work, keeping corporate at arm's length, being the shoulder to cry on, and keeping my peers motivated and on task.

We slowly made progress and everyone's energy and vitality returned. The team had a unified purpose. While the chances of succeeding were slim, they focused on a brighter future.

The team made fantastic progress and accomplished more than anyone thought possible. At the end of the month, we still came up short. My peers and I were devastated. The team was crushed. We had purposefully blocked out any idea of failure, but now it was staring us in the face.

I called my boss the next day and told him the whole story. After getting a bit of shit for breaking HR protocol, he commended our progress, saying it hadn't gone unnoticed. We were the only office in the company that grew month over month and by a wide margin.

We spent hours negotiating to keep my teams employed until we finally agreed on plans B, C, and D. I brought the details to my peers, who decided to assemble the team again.

Plan B—I bought us another month to get us where we needed to be financially and the team was thrilled. Plan C—if in thirty days we couldn't meet our numbers, everyone would have to take a 15 percent pay cut. Plan D—if we didn't reach the profitability we needed after the pay cuts, we would have to start cutting staff.

It wasn't the news everyone wanted to hear, but everyone was informed. Ultimately, the headwinds were strong and we eliminated two positions. Without this effort, fifty people would have lost their jobs with little hope of finding a new one soon.

The collective effort of the team saved forty-eight jobs when the tech bubble burst. It was a leadership challenge I didn't know I was ready for, and the things I learned remained with me throughout my career.

Summary

The opportunity to lead always exists, and people will follow regardless of what the organizational chart says. These are your moments to thrive. When chaos reigns and you are the steady head people can trust, you can make your mark on the world.

Pause non-mission-critical projects and redirect focus to efforts that will produce the results your company needs. Redirect them to the needle-moving work and get the important things done faster.

Create urgency, not panic. Teams will panic enough without you making things worse. Give the team an optimistic view of the future; if you can't do that, at least let them retain as much control over the outcome as you can so they can feel they are part of the solution.

Take the right risks at the right time. When everyone is hiding under their desks, hoping not to get fired, it is time to surge. Align your efforts to deliver the business results needed, hedge your bets with a bailout and robust risk-mitigation plan, and provide small wins often through pilots to achieve your micro-goals.

We are always in a state of flux, and crises happen often. Get ready to be the leader your team, peers, and company can count on. Humility, empathy, honesty, and courage are vital for solid leadership. Give the team room to become the hero and collaborate transparently and optimistically.

Brain Candy – Important Questions for You to Chew On

Grab your journal and get started on your ABCs for growth.

Assess:

- Do you know what your organization's top three priorities are?

- Do you empower or micromanage your team?

- Do you have the confidence to lead without the title?

Baseline:

- How closely aligned is the work you're doing to your company's top priorities?

- Are you meeting the emotional and work needs of your team?

- How will you recognize opportunities?

Conquer:

- What work can you defer or cancel to make room for priorities that matter more, and how are you going to bring your team along?

- How can you control the narrative?

- How can you show up big when others won't?

Chapter 17

HIJACKING THE RIGHT "THIRD-RAIL PROJECTS"

"Victory comes from finding opportunities in problems."

— Sun Tzu

Did you know the fastest way to accelerate your career is to reorganize yourself out of a job? I know that sounds crazy, and it may feel like you're committing career suicide, but it is true. When you want to fast-track your career and stop playing small, take on a big project and eliminate your own position. It's an excellent way to land a big promotion.

You accomplish this by taking on what I call "third-rail projects." These projects remind me of the New York City subway system. The tracks have three rails, and you die if you touch the third rail.

You've seen big and scary business problems. They are systemic, complicated, and a massive pain in the ass to fix. Everyone is suffering, yet no one is taking the lead to solve the problem. Others have tried and failed. Hopping into the melee practically guarantees failure, and everyone assumes if they touch them, their careers are over.

These are golden opportunities for leaders bold enough to take on the challenge. These projects are going to accelerate your career faster than anything else. If they were easy, they would have been done already. Any improvement is a significant victory.

When you take on one of these projects, you need to control the narrative and expectations constantly. Once you have that under control, you and your teams are well-positioned to win.

Another huge benefit of taking on these projects is they provide you with exposure to lots of people and they help build your brand. You'll find yourself presenting in leadership meetings two levels above where you usually play. You'll advise on the future during governance meetings and be a key strategic planning member.

Third-rail projects are transformative. Reorganizations are typically part of the solution. When you create the future state org chart and are brave enough to eliminate your "box," you'll become a trusted leader who can make the tough calls. As you design the future org chart, you'll have the opportunity to write your next chapter.

Are you ready to see if you have what it takes?

Finding the Right Opportunity

Which is the right third-rail project for you? You need to choose your opportunity wisely. There's a difference between career-limiting projects and career-accelerating ones. Career-limiting projects are highly visible problems that (for whatever reason) no one cares about enough to fix. Career-accelerating projects solve problems the most senior leaders in your organization need to fix.

When the right opportunities align with a significant business need and have the right executive sponsorship, people are willing to put in the sweat equity it takes to fix it.

Connect this work to eliminate a significant pain point within the organization or to maximize significant opportunity. It has to be cross-divisional and, ideally, global. You have to get out of your sandbox for this to work.

The bigger, the better. The more departments, countries, and functional interdependencies, the bigger the opportunity for you to win.

Solicit different points of view, understand the up and downstream impacts, and get the right team around the table; you need people who understand the nuances of how the different pieces work.

Become good at navigating different agendas, giving away most of the credit, and bringing people together to solve a critical problem they care about. Any degree of success in this environment is a major win.

Deliver quantifiable results quickly. If you can't count it, it doesn't count. It must improve something important to leaders at the top. If it doesn't meet these criteria, move on—you've got a career suicide project on your hands.

The right problem must involve your function and go broader. That way it makes sense for you to be involved, and you have enough domain knowledge and interdepartmental relationships to get off to a good start. When these conditions are met, it's your time to make a bold move.

*"This fork in the road happens over a hundred times
a day, and it's the choices that you make that will
determine the shape of your life."*

— Liz Murray

Gabby has the right frame of mind and is a pro at hijacking third-rail projects. "Regardless of what you hire me for, I'm going to create a job I want, which is always based on where I see the business opportunity."

Gabby's foundational background is in project and program management, which is a sweet spot for identifying the hard stuff no one wants to tackle. She works in financial services, where something is always broken.

Finding suitable projects isn't easy. While you may not be as excited as Gabby about taking on massively complex projects, much can be learned from her experiences and expertise.

When taking on a new role, Gabby digs into details and asks hard questions. She doesn't need to know how everything works, but she finds out why things work the way they do. When identifying projects to tackle, ask *why* instead of *what*. It's a game-changer. Here's another pro tip: If the answer people give you is "Because we've always done it this way," you're on the right track to finding your ideal project.

The next thing Gabby wants to learn is how her function interacts with everything around her. Who is dependent on her group? Who is she dependent on? What do stakeholders and business partners need and expect? Having a complete 360° view of your function and the interdependencies will save you a lot of heartburn later.

Too many leaders focus on superficial problems because they are easy to spot and fix. But they don't solve the problem. Gabby gets direction from her leader on what needs to be done. She inevitably returns, shares the real problem, and then becomes accountable for fixing it.

Managing the narrative means managing assertive personalities. Gabby had totally sucked at this for a long time. She would either withdraw or attack, depending on the situation. Neither was effective, and she worked hard to improve how she led through influence.

"I've learned to figure out their angle," Gabby says. "Why is this person pushing back on everything I'm saying? What are they driving for that I'm not seeing? Sometimes it's as simple as they don't want to do the work or fear the changes. Other times it's a gap I've missed. I've learned to slow down and listen."

Figuring out which project to take requires stakeholder engagement and willingness to be led. Stakeholders need to see an upside. You can only make that assessment if you build rapport and show them you're not the enemy. "Even when I think I know the answer or leadership has a firm idea of what direction to take, I include the teams heavily. Listening to their insights taught me that things are never that simple, and the prescribed solution is often wrong. I then have what I need to push back on the senior leadership team and do the right thing."

Making people feel included and heard is the only way to succeed. Even if they don't like what's happening, everyone wants and deserves a say in their future. Gabby recommends looking beyond what you're doing to see what's happening around you. Don't be afraid to ask questions. You may think you're asking a dumb question, but you are likely focused on the right things. Trust your instincts.

Finally, always assume good intent. "One of the things I struggled with was gaining consensus to do the right thing and fix a problem," Gabby says. "I couldn't figure out why no one would get onboard and thought they were just being difficult. They're really not. It's my job to determine where the blockage is coming from and help that person align on their terms."

Delivering third-rail projects is hard and worth it if you want to grow quickly. Choosing the right one is essential. Choose well to give yourself and your team the best chance to succeed.

Gaining Momentum and Support

Can you get the support you need? You need to get sponsorship once you've chosen your career-catapulting project. You will need an army of people to bring the project over the finish line. If no one is willing to lead it, how will you get anyone to work on it?

Put yourself in their shoes. Would you help out if you could be part of the solution to a problem without taking on any of the political risks? You'll have plenty of people behind you if you gain momentum and support the right way.

When seeking sponsorship and support, be humble, highly collaborative, genuine, and completely transparent. If your motives are questionable, you won't stand a chance. The collective organization will turn into a pod of dolphins and take you down in the blink of an eye.

You gain sponsorship by creating a win for everyone. Identify what each stakeholder wants personally and professionally and try to build the outcomes they need into the solution. If a team member is looking for a promotion, or to be recognized as a transformational leader, give them the spotlight to get what they want. If this person needs to improve the business performance their bonus is based on, include it in the scope of your work.

When they can see their lives getting better, and there is minimal risk to them, you will have new best friends lined up out the door and down the hall.

As you gain sponsorship, focus on strategic outcomes everyone can agree on. Most of the time, everyone will agree on the results you're going for. The disagreement comes when deciding how to get there.

Strategic elements that align everyone typically involve revenue, operating costs, customers, and risk. These are great topics to get a diverse group of people to agree on quickly.

The way to lose momentum is to be overcommitted on how things should be done. There will be time for that later. Keep things at the ten-thousand-foot level and avoid getting in the weeds too early. If you stack the decks properly, you won't be the smartest person in the room, so make sure you're gathering all the best ideas.

Focus less on how things get done and more about the outcomes the team can deliver. Identify one or two principles you won't compromise on and let everything else go to the experts. When you know your non-negotiables and let go of everything else, your team will move faster because you're less wedded to the details.

"To avoid criticism, do nothing, say nothing, and be nothing."

— Elbert Hubbard

Victor has dedicated his career to philanthropy and advocating for underserved communities. He oversees programs for a large philanthropic foundation and has become an expert at gaining momentum and support to fix highly complex problems in the community.

Victor's city had unusually high rates of lead poisoning. The problem affected impoverished children and pregnant mothers. While the solutions for this problem are well known, the path forward is complicated, so people had been spinning on the problem for decades.

At one point, there was a perfect storm of public outcry, political promises, and commercial pressure. Victor connected the remediation of the lead crisis to the goals of everyone whom he needed to be a part of the solution.

Fixing the lead poisoning issue would get everyone what they wanted. Victor looked at the situation from the grassroots all the way to the political elite. "How do we make this a win for everyone? Who has deep pockets? Who has power?"

Victor interviewed seventy people, including people from state and local government, community organizers, parents whose children had been poisoned, academics, and lawyers. He found a lot of good work happening, but it wasn't coordinated. The work was scattered without a unifying voice. The narrative was confusing. Lead was in the soil, water, and paint. The problem needed to be simplified.

"This was not a question of whether we were resilient enough to tackle the issue," says Victor. "It was a question of: Do we have political and community support? Do we care enough about this to align our values and investments to tackle it?"

With the weight of the foundation behind him, Victor assembled a diverse coalition of people who could help solve the problem. "I got a very powerful councilperson, the head of the building and housing department, the head of the public health department, a community organizer, a mom whose children had been lead poisoned, a housing expert, and an environmental justice advocate to agree to attend a conference with me. No one knew who else was invited. There was only one problem; they either didn't know or distrusted each other."

Victor understands change happens at the speed of trust. He brought this team together and took them out of their environment on two separate trips. First to a conference to learn, and secondly to a neighboring city that had solved the same problem. "Now that they trusted each other, they needed to see what was possible."

In the background, Victor and a few other foundations had commissioned a report on the effect of lead poisoning locally so everyone could understand the gravity of the situation. "This wasn't just a national issue—it was about what we did to our kids."

In January of the following year, Victor achieved a significant goal. The formerly reluctant mayor and council president were standing on the steps of city hall with forty people in the background announcing the launch of a coalition. Policy recommendations were made six months later and revealed at a major event.

"We hosted 600 people at a local conference about healthy housing and lead poisoning prevention. We brought in the doctor who blew the whistle on lead poisoning in Flint, Michigan. She gave an amazing keynote address. The city council had their final reading of the legislation at our conference, then voted on it a few weeks later. The law passed in July of that year."

Victor took a lingering problem that no one could solve and got sponsorship and support from unwilling and adversarial stakeholders who had capitulated over the problem for decades. Seeing the problem, simplifying the narrative and defining success, building trust, helping them see what was possible, and making the situation relevant to each stakeholder were Victor's keys to success, and his community is healthier because of his dedication and exemplary leadership skills.

Setting Expectations for Failure

How can you control the narrative? You're going to fail, and you're going to succeed. What will people say? The narrative depends on your positioning and the strength and advocacy of your sponsors.

Failure is part of success, as we covered in Chapter 7: Setting Your Vision and Strategy. Unfortunately, everyone doesn't know this, and plenty of people will be sitting on the sidelines waiting for you to screw up so they can say, "I told you so."

One thing you'll have going for you is executive sponsorship. You'll get some air cover from the senior leaders who want to see you succeed. If your project is critical to the business, it virtually guarantees the people who matter will be in your corner.

That being said, you can't fall all over yourself making too many mistakes. When that happens, your most powerful allies lose confidence in your ability and things can fall apart.

When you look at all the monsters under your bed and see everything that could go bump in the night, you can start building your prevention, detection, and mitigation plan. Once you've got a good plan, publicize it from the top of the organization down so everyone knows and can anticipate the problems they will encounter.

After you've scared the crap out of everyone, it is common for people to get stuck in the "We can't" mindset. Doubts flood in, old mistakes take on a new life, and fear grabs a seat at the head of the table. When people are pulling back, lean in and help them reframe. Turn the

"We can't" conversations into "How can we?" Instead of "We've never done this before," change their focus to "What if we did it this way?"

Your team will have moments of doubt. They will make mistakes and things will go wrong. The tone you set, the safety you provide, and the humanity you demonstrate will help your team get through the rough patches.

You control the narrative by moving the conversation from "We failed" to "This was an expected setback and we have a plan." Be transparent about the fact that you're not going to get 100 percent of this done, but you're going to get a lot of it done, which will make a massive difference for the company, your teams, and your career.

> *"Rejection is a common occurrence. Learning that early and often will help you build up the tolerance and resistance to keep going and keep trying."*
>
> — Kevin Feige

Heather had the opportunity to face fear head-on when she was asked to take on the company's most important project. She needed to lead the effort to reengineer the company's quote to cash system. The current system had been broken for years. Sales contracts, invoicing, and revenue recognition were all faulty, and the company was burning money by fixing everything manually.

This initiative was a beast. It was complex, expensive, and a political hot potato. Five leaders had tried to fix the problem before her, but they all failed and eventually lost their jobs. Unsurprisingly, Heather thought long and hard before agreeing to take it on.

She lined up her best people, hired the most innovative vendors, chose the best software, and negotiated a fixed-price contract. She is a master collaborator and the entire leadership team was with her every step of the way.

Things were hard for everyone on the team, but they were progressing, and Heather felt optimistic. Then it came time to start testing the new system—and everything fell off the rails. Nothing worked as intended, and the blame game started between her team and the vendor. This was the first of multiple iterations, so they started with the easy stuff, hoping to get a quick win.

It was a disaster. A year of work, millions of dollars in contracts, and the company's livelihood were at stake. The vendor went to the CEO and complained about Heather, saying she was the problem. They were so convincing that the CEO brought an unbiased third party in to evaluate the situation. He concluded Heather was right and the software company was just trying to cover their asses.

Every time they fixed one problem, another would pop up. It was like the team was playing a giant game of whack-a-mole. After months of delays and promises to get back on track, the project was still stuck.

Heather did the brave thing and recommended they kill the project. No one had done that before—her predecessors fought to keep things going until the bitter end. Her recommendations were met with mixed results. The CIO and CAO wanted to keep it going. They felt they had put too much time and money into the project and were too close to the finish line. The CEO and CFO wanted to kill it and stop hemorrhaging money and resources.

Heather was the tiebreaker. This was her baby, and she knew it wasn't right. No amount of money or effort would get it over the finish line. And even if they did, it would be like having to look after Frankenstein's monster for decades. When I asked her how she found the courage to kill the project, Heather said, "The anguish I saw on my team's faces trying to get testing done was all I needed to see. Everything was too hard; my team was exhausted trying to get this over the finish line. We had no confidence about this ever becoming a success."

Heather didn't end up like her predecessors. Her bravery improved her reputation with the executive team, showing them she was a leader who could make the tough calls.

Celebrating Your Wins

How often do you celebrate? These massive projects offer equal amounts of high visibility and high stress. Think differently about what you celebrate because traditional reward mechanisms aren't as effective as they used to be. Celebrating the team hitting a milestone or deadline lacks creativity and inspiration.

Celebrate things like learning from a mistake or someone coming up with a creative solution to a brain buster that has been stumping the team. Celebrate when someone challenges the status quo, negotiates a great outcome with a difficult stakeholder, or raises an issue no one else saw. Pay attention and make sure your managers do too. When you see something good happening, bring out the pom-poms.

Create a culture where everyone is empowered to grow and managers are expected to recognize and celebrate growth. Recognition should be used as a motivator. You can only motivate your teams once you know what motivates them as individuals. The peanut butter approach won't work. For example, if you publicly acknowledge an introvert in a large meeting with a lot of senior people, that will not motivate them; that's probably going to embarrass the crap out of them. If you have a highly ambitious extrovert and pat them on the back during your one-on-one, that will likely fall flat because they feed on public recognition.

Focus on the person you want to recognize and understand their motivation. Meet their needs and make sure they feel appreciated and valued.

Celebrate regularly in a variety of ways, whether one-on-one, at a team meeting, or through broader recognition. It could be a private message from the executive sponsor saying, "Hey, great job. I heard you were killing it," or a broader message to the department.

Recognize and celebrate the difficult things, not the unimaginative things. Do it in a way that motivates the individual and taps into what they need to feel valued. You will then find your teams will run through brick walls without being asked.

"No man will make a great leader who wants to do it all himself, or to get all the credit for doing it."

— Andrew Carnegie

I remember my HR partner's excitement when he revealed the new reward and recognition system the company had just put in place. It was a technology platform where you could recognize a colleague and they would get a badge for every recommendation. Then, once you accumulated enough badges, you could buy a gift for yourself.

I'm sure someone thought this was a good idea, but I couldn't stop laughing as he explained it to me.

It reminded me of when we were potty training our daughter. All the books said to use a sticker chart, so we put a chart up in the bathroom, and every time she went, she got to put a sticker on the chart. Then, when the chart was full, we'd buy her something at the toy store.

We did this for a week and had zero success. I was frustrated because she had no accidents at her babysitter's house. Finally, I asked her babysitter what she was doing. "I give her a marshmallow every time she uses the bathroom." The sitter was handing out marshmallows and I was giving her a damn sticker—no wonder it wasn't working.

Unfortunately, my HR partner didn't find my story as funny as I did. I walked him through what I thought would happen. Everyone would flood the system to get their prizes, and then no one would find it motivating, and it would sit unused. It took six months to kill the program.

Shortly after we killed it, I offered to sponsor a training program for our managers. This program teaches participants how to share credit, recognize team members in a way that motivates them personally, and connects purpose to what each person does.

Giving our leaders the skills they needed to recognize the outcomes we needed went a lot further toward increasing engagement than our stupid badge program.

Summary

Choosing the right third-rail project can accelerate your career faster than anything else. Make sure you've got the right executive sponsorship and it is complex, mission-critical, measurable, and that you can deliver quick wins iteratively.

Gain the right momentum and support by ensuring your stakeholders have a win, and meet their personal ambitions. Being humble, transparent, and collaborative will go a long way toward getting the right people on the team and getting them excited about creating meaningful change.

Prepare for failure and make sure everyone knows about it. Control the narrative and create a safe space for your team to fail forward. Communicate your contingency and bailout plans so there are no surprises.

Don't forget to celebrate. Things will get tense and your teams will get tired. Keep morale up, give everyone else all the credit, and take all the blame. Keep the narrative pragmatically optimistic. No one trusts a perpetual cheerleader, so temper your approach to match the organization's tone. Taking this bold step will set you up for long-term success.

Brain Candy – Important Questions for You to Chew On

Grab your journal and get started on your ABCs for growth.

Assess:

- What is your risk appetite during this season of your career?
- Who do you need in your corner?
- Can you control the narrative?

Baseline:

- What do your sponsors want and need to be successful?
- Who are the negative nellies on your team whom you can leverage for risk planning?
- Can your managers spot the right things to celebrate?

Conquer:

- How can you quantify your success?
- How can you get people who don't report to you inspired and excited to be a part of the solution?
- Are you brave enough to have a bailout plan?

Chapter 18

PAVING THE WAY FOR OTHERS

"Don't judge each day by the harvest you reap but by the seeds that you plant."

— Robert Louis Stevenson

Why do you care so much about what you do? Where do you find true joy and fulfillment throughout your career? The most epic moments in your career are about the people you've worked with. The work you do is fleeting. The impact you have on other people's lives and careers truly lasts.

When you pave the way for others, you create scalability, resilience, and a lasting influence beyond your time within a company. You know how to align your career, set your strategy, play to your strengths, and adjust your mindset. Now it's time to help others do it too.

Who will think of you as the leader they want to emulate? Who will move forward faster and have a thriving career because of the time they spent with you? What legacy will you leave?

Everyone can leave a legacy; let's create yours.

Accounting for Equity and Equality

Are you setting your team up to fail? Today, there is a heavy focus on diversity and inclusion. The system is finally forcing equality in roles from board seats to interns, creating more leadership opportunities, higher compensation, and focused startup funding.

Most leaders and organizations aren't accounting for the equity gap. John Taylor Cummings has a YouTube video that highlights this point better than anything I've seen. He's got a bunch of college students standing in a line, racing to win one hundred dollars.

Before John starts the race, he instructs the students to take two steps forward each time the statement he makes is true, and if the statements are false, the students are to stand still.

John starts calling out different scenarios. Take two steps forward if your parents are still married. If you had a father figure, access to tutors, and private education. If you never had to worry about your cell phone being shut off or having to help your parents pay the bills, or if you knew your college would be free even if you weren't an athlete.

After he made these statements, he made everyone in the front of the line look back. There was a massive gap between the students. He pointed out that the kids with a head start were lucky. It had nothing to do with any decisions they could have made; it was just how life worked out. If the students in front think they're winning the race fair and square, they are dead wrong. Yet everyone has to run their race. No matter where they start.

You promote diversity candidates and think your job is done. It's not enough. True equality is achieved by accounting for and closing the equity gap. As a leader, you must do more.

A colleague was called in to coach five African American women who had recently been promoted to very senior levels of leadership. These talented women were promoted into these roles partly in a response to advance the company's DEI (diversity, equity, and inclusion) commitment. They were struggling because they lacked the grooming, experience, or exposure to the same situations their peers had. The company knew more support was needed to close the equity gap so they sought to help these leaders succeed. Not all organizations are as perceptive.

"A diverse mix of voices leads to better discussions, decisions, and outcomes for everyone."

— Sundar Pichai

My client Tara was in the same boat. She had changed jobs and was promoted to a senior position in her new company. The leadership team was welcoming and very supportive. As she settled into her new role, Tara realized she needed to be equipped to hold her space at the leadership table with the others.

One day in a coaching session, Tara was talking through a situation where she needed to strongly oppose something and was uncomfortable dealing with the conflict. She said, "I don't know how to be the only black woman in the room." As a white female, I didn't know how to be the only black woman in the room either, so I contacted my African American friends and coaches to find out what that meant.

It boiled down to the fact that no one had come through the ranks like she had. She was missing the context for many of the discussions and was uncomfortable slowing the conversation down so she could catch up.

Tara worried about disagreeing, so she tried extra hard to avoid coming across as aggressive. She felt this deep sense of obligation to be hyper-successful so she could pave the way for the next generation.

Tara felt extra pressure when everyone else around the table was only worried about doing their jobs well. Tara got the support she needed on her own. But we need to do a better job accounting for the equity gap as we drive our equality measures forward.

Choosing Your Tribe Wisely

Who are you spending most of your time with? You want to grow and you want a rockstar team. Many leaders focus most of their time and effort on the low performers. Trying to get disengaged, uninspired, low performers to achieve adequacy takes a lot of work, and you don't get a return on your investment.

It may sound unfair, but become highly discerning with your mentorship. Select who you support and help grow based on their ambition, drive, and talent. When you spend time moving A players to A+, you create the next generation of leaders.

Once you've identified the people you're placing your bets on, the most important thing you can do is align work to their goals (not yours). Often our best performers want a different path than we want for them. Offer them the benefit of your perspective, honor their wishes, and help them grow in their chosen direction.

Thought leaders say you become the total of the five people you spend the most time with. Are you spending time with people who are well-positioned to help you improve your game?

Are you spending time with negative, uninspired, or small thinkers? Or are you spending your time with optimists who are ambitious and creative? Take stock and make sure the people you surround yourself with are the ones who will help you continually grow.

We've covered in previous chapters how to surround yourself with people who are smarter than you, who will be brutally honest, and who will help you see your blind spots.

Choosing whom to mentor and associate with brings that practice to the next level. With your business relationships in mind, whom will you mentor and where will you spend your time?

> *"Before you are a leader, success is all about growing yourself. When you become a leader, success is all about growing others."*
>
> — Jack Welch

I've had two moments in my career when the leadership team I was on was phenomenal. We were strong teams with fantastic chemistry. In both cases, everyone was intelligent, opinionated, ambitious—and we all had a bit of an ego.

We were a shining example of what a good team looks like and how it operates, and we got the hard stuff done. I've also been on teams where we collectively had the talent, yet the teams never gelled, and the results weren't quite as epic.

You can have two equally matched teams on paper, but one team is killing it and the other is killing each other. It comes down to three elements that must be present in every team member and continually reinforced by the leader: trust, transparency, and a transformational mindset.

My peers and I had big personalities and even bigger mandates. The executives were dynamic, leadership-first leaders who purpose-built their dream team. They were experts in their field, and their ability to inspire, rally, and mobilize the masses was a thing of beauty.

Bringing a bunch of high performers together requires a delicate balance. Tempers fly, egos get in the way, and agendas are ambitious. You can't simply set it and forget it. The leader needs a delicate hand on the rudder to maintain balance and momentum.

While working on these standout teams, we trusted each other implicitly. Among ourselves, we would disagree, test, and challenge. Externally, we were united and everyone stood up for each other. It felt like growing up and having a younger sibling. You can pick on them, but if anyone else tries, you'll punch them in the nose.

We also had no secrets or hidden agendas. Even though we all led different functions, we were interconnected and the dependencies were significant. No one was perfect; we were all moving fast and made mistakes regularly. When you screwed up, chances were good one of your peers suffered collateral damage. We would own our mistakes, call them out early, and work together to help fix them. No one had a "not my problem" mindset.

Everyone found excitement in transforming the business, our functions, and ourselves as leaders. With a collective experimental mindset, innovation was high, blame was low, and new ideas were brought to life.

When choosing a team, I learned to focus on aptitude and attitude equally. If talented people can't unite to form a high-performing team, it's a waste of talent. If they can, it's magic—you get the best and brightest working synergistically.

Inspiring a Culture of New Ideas

Do you inspire your team to think bigger or just tell them to? Motivational writer William Arthur Ward said, "The mediocre teacher tells, the good teacher explains, the superior teacher demonstrates, and the great teacher inspires."

Inspiring creativity greatly enhances your team's sense of self-worth and engagement. Most great ideas come from the team. Set the tone by giving everyone responsibility, accountability, and empowerment to continuously improve.

Opportunities to improve are everywhere, but teams aren't generally rewarded for innovating and trying; they are often punished for failing. Remove those roadblocks from your organization and give teams room to run. We've covered how failure and success are interconnected. Share that concept with your teams. And don't just say it—show them how it's done.

Creating a culture of intrapreneurship requires you to inspire your teams to think differently, protect them as they fail forward, and celebrate as they produce epic business results. No one wants to slog through their days dealing with the same BS day in and day out. Your team is in the best position to make their jobs better. They know where the bodies are buried and have the most to gain by improving their environment.

Empower them to improve their jobs and align their focus with the things that matter most within the organization. Position everyone for success. Your team will move mountains for you, and they will be excited about doing it.

To effectively create a culture of innovation, change how work gets done. Flatten your organization and ditch the hierarchy regarding thought leadership and sharing ideas. Manage your team based on outcomes, not tasks, and kill the micro-management. Give your team the freedom to deliver excellent outcomes their way with a mutually agreed upon deadline. Kill your KPIs (key performance indicators), OKRs (objectives and key results), and standard HR performance metrics. Instead, get to know your team more personally and motivate them.

"Without leaps of imagination or dreaming, we lose the excitement of possibilities. Dreaming, after all, is a form of planning."

— Gloria Steinem

Beth is a client experience executive in the manufacturing and logistics industry. These industries aren't the epicenter of innovation in the client experience space. They tend to stick with what they know.

Beth was a magnet for toxic work environments. As a single mom, she needed to focus on income first and career satisfaction second, and she worked for a few narrow-minded organizations for way longer than she should have.

Early in her career, Beth understood what working in a great corporate culture felt like. She saw how people could grow and learn together when they had great mentors. She also saw how things slowly morphed into a toxic environment.

She felt trapped by inertia and divisiveness, yet still had the passion to innovate. Customers are the lifeblood of every organization, and Beth was an expert at looking at their experiences holistically and putting together strategies to increase organic growth and win new customers.

In these dysfunctional work environments, Beth's attempts to effect change within the company were met with negative repercussions, so she focused inward on her team to inspire innovation and change.

Beth didn't let the corporate culture hold her or her teams back. Now that her daughter is grown, she finally put career satisfaction first and landed an executive position with an innovative logistics company that loves her spirit and the benefits it brings the company.

"I think it's important to be a great listener and to give people the platform and voice to share their ideas in a safe space. There are no stupid ideas. One idea will inspire someone to add to it, and the combination takes us to the coolest places we could never have gotten to alone."

As the leader, Beth sets the tone and leads by example. Beth also gets the whole team involved. She embraces a tone of gratitude and poses challenges to her team, giving them time to think about it, and then they come back and solve the problem collectively. That way, they don't feel chained to a desk, and they are molding the company's future.

Beth fostered an intrapreneurial mindset with all the teams she led. The people doing the work are often in the best position to see where the opportunities for greatness are. Giving them the latitude to dream big and a platform to flesh out their ideas and take action is the most significant level of empowerment a leader can give.

Leaving Your Legacy

What will your legacy be? What stamp will you put on the future, and how will you know your life and contributions matter? Most of us won't have buildings erected with our name on them or have statues carved in our honor. And at the current pace of change, your business contributions will likely be history before you retire.

All the craziness you've gone through has got to be worth more than a paycheck. You want to leave something better than how you found it and feel like your contributions mattered.

Your legacy won't be the vacation you worked through, the project you finished, or the business results you delivered. Your legacy will be the people you've inspired, the lives you've touched, and the lessons you've taught.

In Chapter 6: Creating Your Career Success Blueprint, you dug in and worked to understand your *Level 7 Why* and purpose, which is the foundation of your legacy. Imagine this is the last day of your life. Write your memoir in one sentence and then live your legacy daily.

What would your one sentence be? If you feel like all you've been doing is collecting a paycheck and shuffling through your career, it's time to take stock and make a few changes.

Start taking the risks you read about in Chapter 16: Thriving During Times of Chaos. Become a mentor, sponsor, and advocate for your high performers, spread your knowledge, and show others how to share what they've learned. Kindness, gratitude, generosity, and optimism are all gifts to leave behind.

Transition your focus from your success to helping others achieve their goals. Don't tell them the way; show them. Add value even when there's nothing in it for you. Live your personal vision, mission, and values daily. Share your story, be vulnerable, and be humble.

Your legacy will be the indelible mark you leave on those you've encountered.

> *"If you want to be a true professional,*
> *do something outside yourself."*
>
> — Ruth Bader Ginsburg

I was inspired to write this chapter as I texted with a long-standing client who said goodbye to a company she had been wholly devoted to for a long time. Two years ago, she knew her time at the firm was ending. She was employee 100 and had seen the company skyrocket to international stardom and fall just as fast. She watched CEOs and colleagues come and go and high-stakes drama play out in the headlines. She helped the company scale up during its hypergrowth period and shrink when the bottom fell out.

She was committed to leaving a legacy. She spent two years tirelessly preparing the organization for her departure. She was driven by a compulsion to leave the organization better than when she started and to set her team up to thrive in her absence.

It took her two years to get everything in order. She accomplished her mission and is charting an exciting new future. They had her going away party, and the number of people who attended touched her heart. The room was full of love and gratitude.

They shared stories of the lessons she had taught, the example she had set in leading with grace under pressure, and how her mentorship was her legacy. She posted her farewell on LinkedIn, and the number of people who have written in great detail about how she has touched their lives is overwhelming.

She left behind a powerful legacy, and while she'll be missed, the organization is prepared and significantly better because she was there.

Summary

Paving the way for others is the ultimate rush for a leader. The transformation from "me" to "we" is gradual, yet before you know it, you realize you've seen it all, done it all, and the only thing of genuine interest and value is to put your time and effort into helping others along their journey.

Diversity is better for everyone. We can't reach parity fast enough. Leaders who have the opportunity to make a difference yet haven't had the luxury of an equitable upbringing need more support. Nurturing talent and closing the equity gap is the only way to achieve self-sustaining equality.

Choose your tribe wisely. Those you mentor and those who influence you are incredibly important. Focus on your top talent and show them how to play to their strengths. And what about you? You become the total of the five people you spend the most time with. Are they helping or hurting your growth?

Inspiring innovation requires more than just lip service. Reset how you lead and how work gets done. Help your team embrace the intrapreneurial spirit. Flatten your organization, focus on outcome-based success, and make sure the team aligns with the company's priorities.

Write your one-sentence memoir. Embrace your service mindset and see where your legacy statement can take you.

Brain Candy – Important Questions for You to Chew On

Grab your journal and get started on your ABCs for growth.

Assess:

- Are you setting your DEI leaders up for success or failure?
- Are you providing the environment for your team to be successful, or are you making things harder for them?
- What will your legacy be?

Baseline:

- What can you do to create opportunities for equity within your team?
- Who's in your tribe?
- What can you do to inspire an intrapreneur mindset?

Conquer:

- Are you playing bigger or still playing small to fit in?
- How can you sidestep your current structure to allow creativity to flow?
- What knowledge are you sharing to help others thrive after you move on?

Chapter 19

LOVING MONDAYS
AGAIN

"The future depends on what you do today."

— Mahatma Gandhi

Are you ready to love Mondays again? With all the time you spend working and how significantly it affects every aspect of your life, it seems self-destructive not to have fun while you're there, doesn't it?

Throughout this book, you've learned strategies to reignite your career and regain control. You've read dozens of stories of leaders who have escaped the career trap and are thriving while doing things on their terms.

If they can do it, you can too by making a fundamental mindset shift and knowing deep in your gut that a fulfilling career is not a luxury item, nor is it reserved for the elite. Loving Mondays and having a thriving career are as essential as the air you breathe.

The day you refuse to settle and take action, you've escaped the career trap. You'll never get back the stolen moments consumed by getting stuck in the soul-crushing grind or being preoccupied with a job that doesn't serve you. But those can be the last moments you'll ever lose.

I hope you never lose another moment. I hope you create a fulfilling career and achieve whole-life success as only you can define it. Imagine waking up every day excited to do what lights you up. Imagine feeling the confidence and the pride that comes from fulfilling your purpose and making a positive difference.

You have everything you need to create a life where you live your legacy. Imagine a life lived vibrantly without the heavy cloak of stress, apathy, and regret tarnishing those precious moments. It's an investment worth making. You're worth it, and so are those you love.

Everyone deserves to love Mondays.

Embracing an Experimental Mindset

What does this button do? To have an experimental mindset, you need to take life less seriously. When you don't treat every decision as life or death, you feel less pressure and are more receptive to different ideas and outcomes. When the pressure is lowered, new doors open. When these doors open, will you be ready to walk through them?

A big part of loving Mondays is adapting, adjusting, and living in the moment. The illusion of permanence slows you down. Your decisions become shrouded in fear because you are so jacked up by the pressure to get it right you suffer from analysis paralysis.

Here's a pro tip: If you make the rules, you can change the rules. And if you don't like it, you have all the power, skills, resilience, and permission you need to change it. You are the boss of you.

Stop ruining all your opportunities for fun by making life harder on yourself than it needs to be. Your life and your career are not stationary. The playing field is constantly changing, and your goals will change as the seasonality of your career progresses.

What's important right now? Even if you get it perfect, it will only last for a while because life is too dynamic. Have fun. Take the pressure off, and try something new. You'll be surprised how addicting continuous growth using an experimental mindset can be.

> *"Do not be too timid and squeamish about your actions. All life is an experiment."*
>
> — Ralph Waldo Emerson

Bryce Balls is the cofounder of Career Collective, a recruitment firm for architects, engineers, and construction professionals. Her motto: No experience is wasted.

Bryce has spent her entire career jumping into new situations and figuring things out as she went. A friend from her MBA class was raving about recruitment, so she jumped in to try it. Her friend quit right after she started, so Bryce was on her own to figure things out.

She loved the connection aspect of recruiting. It took a lot of trial and error as she learned the ins and outs of the skills required for these specialized professions. As she mastered sales techniques to find new clients, she found that making her clients and candidates happy was what energized her.

When Bryce started a family, she was ready to leave corporate life and try her hand at converting her side hustle online store into a brick-and-mortar business. In over her skis yet again, Bryce learned as she went. This time, a recession had different plans for her, and her business went down in flames. "It was a huge failure, but I learned so much and honestly don't regret it."

While Bryce doesn't regret the experience, she's not immune to the downsides of failure. "It really messed with my mind, and I had to do a lot of work to reset my money story and gain clarity on my values so the fear of failure wouldn't hold me back."

Bryce had another opportunity to start a business. She learned from her mistakes. She knew how her tendency to make decisions quickly and take risks affected her decision-making, and she saw firsthand how those traits could both help and hurt her. "I moved into this next venture a bit more slowly this time. I have a family and two kids and am the breadwinner, so there's more at stake now."

Bryce and her business partner did a lot of research and prep work, lined up clients, and had a solid business plan. They looked at office space and technology platforms and did a lot of due diligence before they opened their doors. "I felt inspired, and my husband was very encouraging. He believed in me, and that helped me believe in myself."

Today, they are running a thriving recruitment business, and Bryce knows this is the best decision she could have made. As they grow their business, they still embrace an experimental mindset. The market is changing, the hiring landscape continues to evolve, and the business will continue to serve the community because of their innate adaptability.

Finding Your Joy

Do you know the difference between being joyful and being happy? Happiness is what you show outwardly. Joy is what you feel on the inside. I know a lot of people who are happy and not joyful. You may also fall into that category.

You go through life happy enough, but something is missing. Joy is a choice.

You hear that life is 10 percent what happens to you and 90 percent how you react. You have control over your joy. So why would you give that power away? A study in Norway followed 50,000 people for fifteen years. People with a sense of humor who laughed a lot lived an average of eight years longer.

Joy doesn't require perfection; it requires intentionality. You have all the tools you need to have a joyful life right now. Taking control of your career is a great start. After that, add a dash of gratitude, surround yourself with people who energize you, build your resiliency in containing the fearsome four, and have fun.

To feel joy, you need to be present in the moment. If you are running around continually distracted, it's time to break the cycle. Your phone and wearable devices are binging and vibrating nonstop. No one (including you) gets your full attention. With all these distractions, it's even harder to be present.

When you are joyful and living in the present, you become a magnet for great people, fun opportunities, and epic experiences. *New York Times* bestselling author, entrepreneur, and investor Dean Graziosi said, "Your focus is your expanse." I believe it. What you think about and where you apply your energy mentally, physically, and spiritually will magnify. So, where are you putting your energy?

"Find joy in everything you choose to do. Every job, relationship, home…it's your responsibility to love it, or change it."

— Chuck Palahniuk

I had an unusual experience after recently moving to Mexico City. We did a day hike up a volcano about an hour outside the city. Our guide was an anthropologist, and I was fascinated as I learned about the culture, flora and fauna, and the Aztec people and some of their customs.

My joy recharging station is nature. Let me play in the woods, scuba dive, or sit by any body of water and I am in my happy place. The more I'm outside, the happier I feel.

We were walking along a river when our guide told us about an old Aztec custom many Mexican people still practice. He told us to pick up a rock, close our eyes, and think about something that's stressing us out. We would call upon the Aztec goddess of water to remove the causes of stress in our lives.

Chanting to the spirits felt too "out there" for me, and I don't believe in this kind of thing, but I figured, "What the hell? I'm here and everyone else is going along with it, so it can't hurt."

At the time, I was worried about revenue. We had a bad month and the pipeline was building slower than we had forecast. So I put all my worries about the business, money, doubt, and negative energy into that poor little rock.

The guide told us to open our eyes, throw the rock in the stream, and recite this Aztec prayer calling on the goddess for help.

When I thought the ritual was over, the guide directed us to some giant trees nearby. Each tree was majestic and well over one hundred years old.

We weren't done asking Mother Nature for a little backup. Our guide told us to take that same worry and fear and hug the tree—the tree is strong and can shoulder all of our burdens. So there I was, hugging away and sending all my money worries into that big old tree.

Everyone else seemed to feel great after the activity. I felt ridiculous and started thinking we were getting punked, keeping an eye out for a video camera. Maybe I did it wrong.

Here's where things got weird. Three days later, two new deals came in. It's been a constant wave of new business ever since. Do I believe the rock and the tree did this? No, I don't. But I believe it changed my mindset. I believe acknowledging I was worried and releasing that stress put me in a place where I could take the actions I wasn't taking before.

Would I throw the stone and hug a tree again? You bet I would!

Reigniting Your Vitality

Are you always tired? Work, family, community, and maybe an ounce of personal time demand your attention. It's no wonder you're exhausted. You lose vitality when you don't recharge your batteries.

Everyone recharges differently. If you're an introvert, you may need a little time to recharge after a long week of being surrounded by people and leading from the front. If you're an extrovert, brunch, a round of golf with friends, or a long talk with one of your besties might be what you need to revitalize.

If you're stressed and preoccupied, tap back into your wellness practice. Whether it's meditation, walks in nature, yoga, or my favorite, bottomless mimosa brunches while dining al fresco and people-watching, do whatever it takes to get revitalized.

You monitor the charge on your cell phone battery throughout the day, and when it gets low, you plug it in. Yet you run yourself ragged, never checking in or recharging your batteries—then wonder why things feel more demanding than they should.

When you take time to unplug, you become more productive, make fewer mistakes, and feel more vibrant. I believe taking care of ourselves is a vital part of our approach to life.

Are you running on empty? Some common behaviors indicate you are draining your battery and not taking the time to recharge. How many of these mistakes are you making?

- Working on vacation.
- Checking email once more before bed.
- Logging in on Sunday afternoons to get a head start on the week.
- Wearing your tech device at all times.
- Having your phone within reach at all times.
- Keeping your phone on.
- Checking your phone when your eyes open each day.
- Allowing every day to fill up with back-to-back meetings.
- Filling every minute of the weekends with obligations and errands.
- Putting your priorities at the bottom of your to-do list each day.

Do any or all of these things feel familiar? I also get sucked into them and need to pull myself back and reset my habits consciously. Your energy and drive are not limitless. You are human, after all. (Don't worry; I won't tell anyone.)

If you live without vitality, you are living half a life. So how do you shift to a life full of vitality?

Change your mindset and embrace recharging and disconnecting as good things. If you run around thinking recharging isn't important, or a sign of weakness, you won't make it a priority. When you realize recharging is as essential as breathing or drinking water to stay alive, you give yourself the grace and strength to improve your life and enjoy it.

Make boundary-setting your new superpower. You learned earlier how saying no improves your career. That also applies to your life and the distractions preventing you from recharging.

Setting boundaries at work is the most important thing you can do. When you're done for the day, you're done. You don't work on vacation or log in on Sundays anymore. Everyone needs to know that. You've already learned how to break up with your addiction to being needed, so enjoy being disconnected and trust everything can wait.

Disconnect from technology. Give yourself thirty minutes in the morning before you look at a device. Take off your wearables when you get home. Leave your phone on silent so you're not distracted by constant notifications. And leave your phone in another room to avoid temptation. End your screen time at least an hour before you go to bed.

Start spending time doing things you enjoy as part of your wellness practice and put them on the top of your to-do list. Give yourself time on the weekend to do absolutely nothing—block time on your work calendar to think.

Getting caught up in our "always on" culture is too easy. Commit to breaking the cycle. It feels difficult at first, but once you've mastered it, you'll never return.

> *"There is a vitality, a life force, an energy, a quickening, that is translated through you into action, and because there is only one you in all time, this expression is unique."*
>
> — Martha Graham

A good friend of mine is a beautiful example of the benefits of regaining vitality. One time, we were working on a brutal multi-year project. From the start, this project was one step forward, two steps back, and the pace was relentless. We worked twelve-hour days, on weekends, and vacation. The team was huge and no one escaped the chaos or the stress. Our downtime was spent commiserating at the bar. Vodka and chicken wings are an incredible elixir.

Neither of us was in great shape, but I noticed my friend was gaining weight. She looked like crap and became increasingly short-tempered because she wasn't sleeping well. I let it go for a while. I'm not the epitome of fitness, so I felt I was in no position to judge.

During one of our vodka and wing therapy sessions, she went off on a tirade about how fed up she was with everything. Her boyfriend was ready to call it quits, none of her clothes fit, and her grandmother was convinced she was pregnant. She was stressed out, looked like shit, and hated everything and everyone. She was miserable.

I was well into the vodka portion of my night and mostly listened. At the end of her tirade, I said, "You have the power to change everything you just spent an hour bitching about. The person I know would spend a lot less time bitching and a lot more time fixing."

She told me to fuck off and stormed out of the bar, sticking me with the tab.

A few days later, she and I were out again, and she told me her ideas for getting her life back on track and wanted some help setting boundaries at work. We hatched a plan, and she executed it like a champ.

She came in at nine, was out by seven, and stopped working outside the office. She amped up her self-care routines, dropped the weight, got her sleep schedule back on track, and finally convinced her grandmother she wasn't pregnant.

Two months later, she was running a half marathon which led to more half marathons, then marathons, and now she is training for her second Ironwoman competition. She still works like crazy and thrives in fast-paced environments.

Now she realizes the toxicity of limiting life to work and how fast things can go off the rails. The training she needs to compete in Ironwoman competitions doesn't allow her to work like she used to. Her career, health, and life are in harmony.

Achieving Whole-Life Success

How do you define whole-life success? Various wheel-of-life frameworks help you assess and achieve alignment. The significant areas making up your life are career, money, health, fun, love, family, spirituality, and community. I know how important it is to look at your life holistically. I haven't always felt this way and needed to learn the hard way.

For most of my corporate career, I was compulsively focused on work. I spent 80 percent of my time and most of my emotional and intellectual focus on my career. I ate, drank, and breathed work. I was always on, working twelve-hour days, coming home for dinner, and having a little chill time with my daughter and husband before hitting the home office again at 10 p.m. for a few more hours before going to bed just to do the same thing the next day.

Being consumed by work wasn't a hardship for me. I loved every minute of it. I reconciled this behavior by telling myself I was doing it to support my family and create a better future for us. In hindsight, I was addicted to work and the sense of purpose my job gave me.

Everything else was good enough, so I didn't believe I needed to pay much attention. I put everything else on cruise control while I gave almost everything I had to my career. I did this for twenty years.

What happens when you ignore the other aspects of your life? For me, getting divorced was one outcome I hadn't expected. Here are some more perils you may not see coming. If you focus on your career at the expense of most other things, one day, your career will no longer serve you. You will need to find your joy and purpose elsewhere. This becomes a dark and scary place if you have not nurtured all the elements of your life.

The life of abundance that helped you thrive becomes a hollow shell of what used to be. It reminds me of that high school quarterback, now in his fifties, still clinging to his glory days as a high school jock.

I was slowly falling out of love with my corporate career. I wasn't feeling challenged anymore. The things I loved were starting to annoy me, and changing jobs felt like it would be the same shit with a different logo on my paycheck.

My marriage had fallen apart about five years prior, my daughter was learning to become an adult in college, and it was just me. I was totally alone.

I had let friendships go by the wayside and had no outside interests other than playing golf and traveling. My identity as a mom had changed, my health and wellness were at their worst, I wasn't in a relationship, and I was utterly disconnected from my community. I was driving on a dark road to Nowheresville, and it felt like a one-way trip. I worried my best years were behind me.

It took me a long time to turn that car around. I needed to rebuild friendships and create new ones. I struggled to decouple who I was from what I did for a living. I searched for new interests, found new hobbies, became active in my community, and built a wellness routine that energized me.

It was a lot of work, and doing it when my mindset wasn't at its best made it even harder. Had I been working on these things all along, this dark time wouldn't have felt so overwhelming.

I still struggle to align everything today, but the most important things are in place. My career has moved from 80 percent of my time to about 50 percent. The other half comprises love, family, friendships, experiences, culture, and wellness. Detoxing was hard, but worth doing.

You do not want your best years to be behind you. You want a future full of excitement, vitality, and joy. If you are overly focused on your career, you *can* end that cycle before it's too late. Start with one other aspect of your life and focus on that. And then continue moving through your wheel of life to find the abundance that comes with whole-life success.

"You only live once, but if you do it right, once is enough."

— Mae West

Summary

Taking an experimental mindset approach to your life will do wonders in helping you lighten up. Have fun, be willing to try new things, and learn from your mistakes. More opportunities will come your way when you are constantly testing and learning.

Joy is a choice. You have the ability right now to live a joyful life. Will you choose joy over discontent? Be present and recognize when you are just going through the motions. Surround yourself with people who energize you.

If you treated yourself as well as you do your cell phone, you would never run on empty and always live a vibrant life. Give yourself time to unplug, set boundaries that position you for success, and try to be present in each moment instead of being distracted by what's next.

A singular focus on your career will not bring long-term fulfillment. Take a holistic and balanced look at your life and clarify what success looks like for you right now. Focus on the essential aspects of your life and strive to achieve whole-life success.

Are you ready to step into abundance and start loving Mondays again?

You've learned many career and mindset strategies that set you up for the success you want and deserve. When you take an experimental mindset, choose joy, reignite your vitality, and focus on whole-life success, you'll experience the pure joy of escaping the career trap.

Brain Candy – Important Questions for You to Chew On

Grab your journal and get started on your ABCs for growth.

Assess:

- Are you ready to embrace an experimental mindset?
- What can you do to be more joyful?
- How would you define whole-life success?

Baseline:

- Are you taking things too seriously?
- Are you present in the moment, or do you have more work to do?
- Which behaviors will you stop doing, and which new habits will you put in their place?
- Where are you on your whole-life success journey?

Conquer:

- What are you most curious to learn as you embrace this new mindset?
- What are you focused on, and will it bring you abundance?
- Would you throw the stone and hug a tree?

- What's the most effective boundary you can establish at work?
- Which small actions can you take right now to grow?

Part IV: Thrive—Transforming Insights into Action

I hope you acquired new perspectives in Part IV of this book as we discussed how to thrive and become the CEO of your career. When you take control, step into your authentic leadership style, and pave the way for others, you have escaped the career trap.

If you have been journaling your ABCs as you thought about all that brain candy, I'm sure you've had a flood of realizations come to light. Remember, "Vision without action is merely a dream."

It's time to transform your insights into action. Head over to the *Escaping the Career Trap Transformation Guide* and continue your journey toward creating a thriving career. Visit our website at: EscapingTheCareerTrap.com/Guide.

When you get there, you will find tools and a roadmap to:

- Lead your way so you can watch your teams thrive due to your authenticity.
- Create a plan to thrive during times of chaos.
- Hijack third-rail projects to grow and accelerate your career.
- Deepen your ability to pave the way for others.
- Start loving every Monday again.

A Final Note

MY CHALLENGE TO YOU

What's next for you? What insights did you gain from chewing on all that brain candy and working through your transformation guide? Will you make the small changes that will move the needle, or will you slide back into your normal routine?

Most readers' good intentions will fade when they put down this book. If you find your enthusiasm waning as time passes, I encourage you to consider this: What is the cost of doing nothing? Where will your career and life be if nothing changes in three months…six months… or two years from now? Next, close your eyes and imagine a life where you've reached your goals and you are experiencing a life of abundance. How does it feel? Are you worth it? Hell yes, you are!

Comfort is the enemy, and hope is not a strategy. There is a better way, but only if you take action. All the stories in this book were about regular people just like you and me. They aren't smarter, richer, or more skilled than you, but they do have one thing in common: They took action. After reading this book, you have everything you need to regain your power and shape your future.

In this book, you learned how to successfully navigate a woefully broken system and break free from the soul-crushing grind. You now know how to debunk the five lies that have been holding you back, the power of playing to your strengths, and how to crush the fearsome four so you can thrive. You understand what it means to become the CEO of your career, how to lead during times of chaos, and how to pave the way for others in order to create your ultimate advantage. And most importantly, you've seen a path forward where you can transform your apathy into ambition and never hate Mondays again.

This is the moment when you decide which path you are going to take. Will you stay on the path you're on, or will you start a new journey toward having a thriving career that energizes you? When you apply the strategies, experiences, and techniques offered in this book, you can escape the career trap.

I'd love for you to reach out and tell me what you thought about this book. Feel free to email me at Support@CareerWinnersCircle.com to share your story and your goals so my team and I can help you. I'm offering you a complimentary, no-obligation strategy session with one of our incredible coaches, where you can experience the power of straight talk, deep discovery, and achieve real results. You can schedule your session through our website at CareerWinnersCircle.com

Thank you for taking this journey with me. I truly hope you have embraced new ideas, found inspiration, and established your strategy to achieve a higher level of success, joy, and prosperity. Cheers to a thriving career that energizes you. You've got this!

ABOUT THE AUTHOR

Tammy Alvarez is a former C-Suite corporate executive who believes at the heart of every successful business are leaders who inspire courage. As the CEO of the Career Winners Circle, she is an author, professional keynote speaker, inspirational coach, trainer, and epic storyteller with an unwavering commitment to advancing ambitious business leaders so they can grow their careers as far as their drive will take them, and continue to thrive once they get there.

During her twenty-year corporate career, Tammy became a renowned business transformation and turnaround expert on Wall Street. She held roles as a managing director at AIG, first senior vice president at Bank Leumi USA, chief operating officer at Genesis10, and senior vice president at Bank of America. Tammy has been a colloquium lecturer on various leadership topics at Cornell University and delivers epic keynote speeches for companies worldwide. She holds a degree in International Business Administration from American Intercontinental University.

Tammy has seen a lot of shenanigans during her time in corporate. It drives her nuts when her client's ambition and drive are squashed because they don't know how to successfully navigate their environments. Her spirited "Break All the Rules" approach blends decades of C-Suite experience with a pragmatic, results-based coaching style that helps business professionals create a big impact and love every Monday morning again.

ABOUT
CAREER WINNERS CIRCLE

Think all coaching companies are the same? Think again. CWC is all about supporting successful leaders who want more. When you work with our battle-tested coaches, you'll see the power of straight talk, deep discovery, and real results.

If you are an individual who is looking to revitalize your career strategy or to become the leader people choose to follow, we've got you covered.

As a business leader or entrepreneur, you can rely on CWC to help you develop stronger leaders, create high-performing teams, grow your business, improve your operations, and receive world class advisory services for the CEO and executives because your decisions are too important to go it alone.

The results our clients get are pretty awesome. Career strategy clients land a new role they've never done before within five months and earn on average 20 percent more. Businesses benefit from a five-times return on their investment in less than a year after working with CWC.

Here's how we do it:

- Our coaches have sat in your seat and know what it's like to be on the struggle bus or to have an opportunity too good to pass up.

- The CWC coaching methodology is steeped in pragmatism and real-life experiences so you move faster and make fewer mistakes.

- Tools and job aids (much like what you see in the *Escaping the Career Trap Transformation Guide*) help you organize your thoughts and execute on your decisions.

- A state-of-the-art coaching portal helps you stay on track and do the important work between your coaching sessions. Your coach is available at the press of a button.

- You have fun! Life is serious enough as it is. We bring joy, humor, enthusiasm, and energy to every experience you have with CWC.

We've got the model to fit your needs, whether you thrive from group training, need a peer sounding board, or want to capture the power of one-on-one coaching, our coaching and training programs will help you achieve more than you thought possible.

No one wins alone. Who's in your corner?

To learn more or to book your free strategy consultation,

visit **CareerWinnersCircle.com**

or email us at

Support@CareerWinnersCircle.com

ABOUT
TAMMY ALVAREZ
EXECUTIVE AND BUSINESS
COACHING

After reading this book, you won't be surprised to learn that working with Tammy is fun and about as real as it gets. Together, you and Tammy will get to the heart of what's been slowing you down, you will receive advice and strategies proven to work, and Tammy will challenge you to reach higher. Most importantly, you'll enjoy levels of success that may have been eluding you for years. We don't call it the Winners Circle for nothing.

Are you ready to deliver stronger business results and create an amazing culture all while accelerating your own career? The best leaders are constantly taking stock and improving.

Leadership and professional development should be fun.

If you're asking these questions, it's time to give Tammy a call:

- Should my capabilities and talents be utilized more comprehensively?

- Something's not working. How do I figure out what it is and fix it?

- How do I stay motivated and inspire my teams when we're all tired and burnt out?

- Why is it so hard to get everyone on the same page?
- Am I making the best use of our team's talent, budget, and time?
- How can I avoid playing office politics and still be effective?

Do you want to massively grow your business without killing yourself in the process?

You need to work with Tammy if:

- Despite all the changes you make, everything still lands on your desk.
- You spend more time firefighting than planning for strategic growth.
- Keeping yourself and your best people motivated and enthusiastic is hard.
- You don't have the right data to make good decisions quickly.
- The business is out of balance and you're spending too much time on the wrong things.
- The business is having a hard time scaling and you're not sure how to fix it.

To learn more or to book your free strategy consultation,

visit **CareerWinnersCircle.com**

or email us at

Support@CareerWinnersCircle.com

BOOK TAMMY ALVAREZ TO SPEAK AT YOUR NEXT EVENT

Tammy is an award-winning author, professional keynote speaker, inspirational coach, trainer, epic storyteller, and the CEO of Career Winners Circle. She is a change and transformation expert and a former Wall Street executive.

Tammy is the ideal speaker for leaders who have "heard it all." If it's time to break away from the norm, she's a speaker who instantly adds a ton of energy, humor, and inspiration to any room. Her content is delivered with a pragmatic "keeping it real" conversational tone and epic storytelling that delivers breakthrough moments for her audiences worldwide.

People who have the opportunity to participate in her virtual and in-person keynotes and workshops leave feeling challenged to think differently, compelled to take action, and inspired to change.

Whether your audience is ten or ten thousand in North America or abroad, Tammy Alvarez can deliver a customized message of inspiration for your meeting or conference. A sample of Tammy's previous keynote speeches include:

Career strategy and accountability

- Break free from the soul-crushing grind
- Five lies holding you back from a thriving career
- Becoming the CEO of your career

Build stronger leaders

- Leading courageously through uncertainty
- Five ways to become the leader people choose to follow
- Executive presence and how to get more of it

Engage and mobilize teams

- Moving teams from indifference to inspiration
- A new way to think about empowerment and accountability
- Overcoming fear and uncertainty for you and your teams

Innovate and grow your business

- Five steps to take the right risks at the right time
- Igniting innovation and intrapreneurship
- Foolproof methods to de-risk your decisions and move faster

Diversity and Inclusion

- Own Your Power! Strengthening women in leadership
- Diversity strategies that improve the bottom line
- Accounting for the equity gap

To see Tammy in action and book a call to talk about your event,
visit **CareerWinnersCircle.com/Keynote**

Made in the USA
Columbia, SC
24 March 2025

55646687R00215